Four thousand years of war, poverty . . . beauty and serenity. THIS IS CHINA—the great and ancient nation that has given to the world one of the richest cultures ever created by man. In what lies her strength?

The secret can be found, says Robert Payne in his brilliant introduction to *The White Pony*, in her poetry:

". . . a line of poetry, a single stroke of a brush on a sheet of silk, or perhaps some song sung by a girl in a rice field will tell us more than we have ever learned from books. . . .

"We have nearly always aimed high in our poetry; the Chinese deliberately aimed at the earth, away from the angelic hosts, and made something that is universal, because it is common to all men. There is a sense in which this is their greatest glory. They contrived to write poetry without dreaming, they saw clearly. . . . The land was impenitent. No gods could make it richer. With their own strength they made the landscape, and their poetry for all its quietness is the sign of their spiritual strength.

"And so it will go on, this poetry that is eternal, like the people, more lasting perhaps than ours. . . . We who are constantly changing, at the mercy of every influx of scientific ideas, may do well to ponder sometimes the poetry of these people who are as unchanging as the stars."

Other MENTOR Books of
Special Interest

A TREASURY OF ASIAN LITERATURE *edited with Introduction and Commentary by John D. Yohannan*
The literary classics of the Orient. An abundant collection of poetry, stories, and scriptures from Arabia and the Far East. (#MQ714—95¢)

A TREASURY OF MODERN ASIAN STORIES *edited by William Clifford and Daniel L. Milton*
The cream of contemporary fiction from India, Pakistan, Arabia, Israel, China, Persia, Malaya, Japan, and Korea. (#MD329—50¢)

THE GENIUS OF THE ORIENTAL THEATER *edited with Introduction by George L. Anderson*
A rich sampling of Indian drama, Japanese No plays, Kabuki, and Joruri, with a general introduction, as well as introductions to each type of drama, explaining its history and significance. (#MQ683—95¢)

MAO TSE-TUNG: An Anthology of His Writings *edited with Introduction by Anne Fremantle*
Communist China's leading political figure, revealed through his writings. With an introduction by the editor, well-known author and former editor for the United Nations. (#MT379—75¢)

Edited by Robert Payne

THE
WHITE
PONY

AN ANTHOLOGY OF CHINESE POETRY
FROM THE EARLIEST TIMES TO THE
PRESENT DAY, NEWLY TRANSLATED

A MENTOR BOOK

Published by THE NEW AMERICAN LIBRARY,
New York and Toronto
The New English Library Limited, London

For Rose and Jacqueline

Published as a MENTOR BOOK
By Arrangement with The John Day Company

SECOND PRINTING

MENTOR BOOKS are published *in the United States* **by**
The New American Library, Inc.,
1301 Avenue of the Americas, New York, New York 10019,
in Canada by The New American Library of Canada Limited,
295 King Street East, Toronto 2, Ontario,
in the United Kingdom by The New English Library Limited,
Barnard's Inn, Holborn, London, E.C. 1, England

PRINTED IN THE UNITED STATES OF AMERICA

CONTENTS

INTRODUCTION

We can understand a people best through their poetry, and the Chinese, who have written poetry since the beginning of time, have always regarded poetry as the finest flower of their culture. There were bronzes and paintings, porcelains and calligraphy, there were moral precepts and there were genii who lived in the high mountains, and all this was a part of their culture; but in poetry the culture achieves its most living expression. We see the beautifully carved characters on the page, and like the motionless but eternally moving waves of Korin's fiery screen, they move, they have force and volume, and they speak across the centuries, so that we can almost hear the authentic voices of people who sang nearly three thousand years ago. For all Chinese poetry is song, to be sung in a high-pitched voice by some dreaming scholar under the shade of bamboos. We cannot imitate those voices, for our language consists of interminable long words without the pitch and vibrancy of the Chinese monosyllables; but at least we can know what they thought and how they dreamed through the long nights of their long wars.

The Chinese until recently did not share our passions. Their greatest passion was for decorum and for some kind of understanding with heaven. Though they sang love songs, they did not exalt romantic love; and though they hated wars, they seem to have seen war in a spirit of fatal expectancy, as though they knew they would always recur. They were people with the strength and the virtue of moderation; they delighted in the smallest things of life, and took pains to remember the details of which life is made. And having no sense of their own impermanence, for they knew that they would remain in their grandsons, they were never affected with too great a sadness. Though there is sorrow continually in their poems, it is not the final sorrow of the Vergilian West, which looked forward to the end of the world in some catastrophe or a resurrection outside time. There is, in Chinese poetry, a sense of the permanence of the world so great that we remember it even when the poet breaks out in lamentations, even when he sees the bleached bones on the frontiers. They thought they possessed the world, but they knew at the same time that there were continual dangers from south, west, and north; and so much of their poetry is concerned with war that one might think there was never a time when the barbarians were not knocking at their gates. And perhaps this is true. During the Han dynasty, it was the barbarians who taught them new meters; and now once again it is the pale-faced barbarians from the West who are teaching them a new kind of song. We may regret that Chinese poetry is eternally changing, but like the Chinese earth itself, we know that it is eternally the same.

I remember a Chinese scholar who said: "If you wish to understand China at all, you must read her poetry and *The Dream of the Red Chamber*." It may be true. There are times when China can never be understood—there are permanent barriers that can never be forced—but there are other times when a line of poetry, a single stroke of a brush on a sheet of silk, or perhaps some song sung by a girl in a rice field will tell us more than we have ever learned from books. There is a delicacy in the Chinese language that we shall never hope to understand as long as we remember our thundering hexameters; and those who would despair of any understanding between West and East should remember that we have at least in the English lyric something comparable with theirs. They have made language finer than the softest silk; they have deliberately cultivated their sensibilities until the sound of a petal falling may be louder than the crash of kingdoms. They have exalted poetry into the place of the angels, and they have written more poetry than all the other nations of the earth put together.

And it is here that we are faced with difficulties. How can one choose amid so much excellence? In the T'ang dynasty at least 2,200 poets wrote 48,900 poems. These poems are preserved, but a million others are lost to us. Li Po took pleasure in writing poetry and then throwing the paper on a stream and watching it sail away into the distance, and of how many other poets may we regret that so little has been preserved? We shall never know more than a small fraction of the treasures that Chinese poets have written during the long pilgrimage of the Chinese race. Unless like Socrates meditating in the sunrise, we see the whole universe at our feet, the treasures of Chinese poetry will never be entirely revealed to us. Time is short: the poets responsible for the construction of the immense pyramid of Chinese letters were perhaps more conscious of this even than their readers. In deference to their labors and our own monumental ignorance, we must sometimes attempt to achieve the impossible. This book is therefore no more than an attempt to suggest the immensity that lies behind even the briefest exploration of Chinese poetry.

Nor is it, even in its suggestions, complete. There is nothing here from the Ming dynasty, and little enough from the Ch'ing. We have authority for omitting them—the best

Chinese scholars insist that there was little advance, and
what is worse, there was ceaseless repetition. Even the T'ang
dynasty poets regarded themselves as old men incessantly
repeating the poetic dogmas of the Hans; they wrote their songs
to tunes that had been handed down from a dynasty that perished four hundred years before; and they were content not
to be competitors. Yet, because they were new and saw with
fresh eyes, we remember them as more glorious than their
ancestors. It was in the time of T'ai Tsung that Chinese poetry
began to extend toward new frontiers; and perhaps there is
some lesson here, for it was a time of peace and great traffic
with a newly discovered world beyond the frontiers of China.
All races gathered together in the streets of Ch'ang-an. The
first Chinese philosophers ventured to India, the first Chris-
tians set up their temples in the Chinese capital. Toleration
produced genius. There was war and starvation and slaughter
to follow; but in those early years of the T'ang Empire, men
found the condition under which the best poetry is written—
a land at peace.

For four thousand recorded years the Chinese peasants
(who later became soldiers) have hated the arts of war. They
were a reasonable people encamped on the shores of a yellow
river. They began as huntsmen—their early war poems are
indistinguishable from their poetry of hunting, the enemy a
wolf or a wild boar or a dragon. In the supreme bewilderment
of the modern wars, they speak with the same voice that Confucius heard in his wanderings. The war poems of modern
China contain no bitterness. Behind the flame-throwers and
the poisoned gas, they see the villages of their childhood, the
rice flowing like a river, and the faces of the village boys flood-
ing the valley like an eternal springtime. This happened, they
say. All my family has been destroyed. The wells have been
poisoned. God alone knows who is responsible, but who can
destroy my memories of childhood? When the Japanese were
approaching Peking, Pien Chih-lin would write about them
with amused tolerance, without cynicism, imagining the whole
city as a kite that has broken loose from its moorings, the world
a child's plaything as it has always been. There are strength
and anger in Tien Ch'ien, but even when he is most angered,
there are moments of the most amazing tenderness. Chinese
poetry does not change with the times: you will see in the
very beginnings of her poetry, in the *Book of Songs,* the same
delighted awareness of the physical universe that you will see
today. Here is poetry, clear, concise, etched sharply on the
clear minds of the people and written in those characters that
more than any alphabet conspire to make the word read the
same as the thing seen, the emotion experienced, the thought
made luminous.

Here you will find poetry of every kind, from the wildest abandon of grief to the most tender exaltation of feeling. Sorrowing over the world, Tao Yuan-ming found beauty in the chysanthemum. With a still greater sorrow the last emperor of the T'ang dynasty finds consolation in the fall of the peach blossom. All goes, they say: the peach blossom follows the moving water, but in this terrible impermanence of things there is a sharply felt regret, but also a sense of illumination. Li Ho, the ghostly descendant of kings, finds an arrowhead in some abandoned battlefield, but his grief is forgotten when he is reminded that the arrowhead may still be used. And so it is with the other poets. Tu Fu calls on the heavens to witness that virtue has gone out of the world, but at the moment of his greatest grief he will remember with a kind of amused delight how someone wore a dress on which the embroidered mountains and seas were upside down. Ts'en Ts'an was himself a warrior, and his memories of the wars were of the texture of things—a squirrel's fur, the thickening of a horse's mane in the frost, the glint of armor, and the impact of the wind on the pennons in the van. The imagery is swift, the pen races the thought, the heart beats time, the invention never falters, but beneath and around all this there is an atmosphere of tender pity, a universal friendliness, of how mellow a wisdom, how golden a simplicity. At the moment when the general dips his brush in the ink, he notices that the ice melts in the inkwells. He notices, too, how the icicles in the horse's mane become strings of cash or five-petal flowers. His imagination is tumultuous and he is at home among hailstorms and endless journeys over the deserts of the northern frontiers. Almost alone among Chinese poets he rejoiced in the wars.

Not all Chinese war poets were warriors. Lu Lun was a scholar whose ancestors for four generations were connected with the court, and his four sons followed the same tradition. There is no evidence that he saw war at close quarters, yet the richness of his imagination is something quite unique in Chinese poetry. In "Dark Night, the Wild Geese Fly High" he composed that rare thing, an ode in honor of a Chinese victory. The ode is extremely short, but the strands of meaning are many: it is condensed, as all Chinese poetry is condensed, but though image after image is made to follow across the page in rapid succession, the poem possesses a hardness and sharpness of vision that is uncommon even in this dynasty, when men saw with precision things that were unseen before. Until the T'ang dynasty, there was little complexity in poetry: emotions were as clear-cut as the simple colors that adorn the *Book of Songs*. But now, as the Chinese empire grew larger and men of all nations flocked through her ports, it was inevitable that the minds of the Chinese themselves should change, inevitable that the complexity of the universe should enter into the heart of their poetry, and still more inevitable that nothing has changed, everything is as it was before when the lovers were singing in the earliest of the songs included here.

But it is well to remind ourselves that the wars have left their mark on Chinese poetry forever. Even today the Chinese scholar will sometimes find himself waking up at midnight and wondering what happened to the youths who were poured through the Yu Men Kuan on the northwestern frontier of Kansu; and these places on the edge of China have a significance for the Chinese that it is impossible for any foreigner to grasp. Those wars fought thousands of miles away, in a strange savage country, are indelibly impressed on their minds. We had no wars like this until recently. The images of splendor and desolation are nearly always images that arise from these far-flung territories—the green grave in the northwest where Chao Chun was buried, the yellow sands of the plains, the snows and the Yin mountains. Even now, the ghostly cavalcades of red-maned ponies and roughshod riders march along those deserted roads. We hear them. We see the pennons engraved with dragons and the banners engraved with gold; and because poetry was written about them, we see and remember them more easily than we see and remember the legionnaires who once guarded the northern forts of England. In some place unknown, along the shores of the Tsinghai or in distant Fergana, the hearts of the Chinese have their home.

War and the terror of war have left their mark on the Chinese race, but even more merciless than war has been the poverty of the people. They will not speak about it often in their poems, but it is always there. The threat of starvation is eternally real in this country, where floods and barren fields are as common as thieving officials, where life must be fought for and every grain of rice is precious. So death is present in these poems, as it was present in the poems of our Elizabethan ancestors, a grimacing skull, a thing to be feared, a claw coming out of the earth, a thing whose name can barely be whispered for fear that the ghosts will suffer on hearing their names. They had no rites by which they could exorcise the dead, and little enough faith in any future life. And because there was poverty, because death stood before them eternally like a threadbare ghost, they contrived all the more to enjoy the sparse beauty of life, and sharpened their senses until a single peach blossom could shine with the glory of a king's ransom. So they went on their pilgrimage, taking delight in little things, loving the sun and the colors of flowers above all things, people whose dust was so intermingled in the soil that they perhaps alone of all nations do not feel themselves strangers to the land. They may curse their land at times, thinking how barren it is and how unprotected from invaders; but it is theirs by a right greater than ours is ours.

For them death was so close that they were compelled like the Elizabethans to wring all the joy out of life by force. But they did not fear death, nor did they fear the ghosts—they feared more than anything else the frontiers of their land. No Chinese could have written, like the unknown priest who wrote *Everyman*:

O Death, thou comest when I had thee least in mind,

nor would he have seen the universe dressed in flames, like King Lear. Death for the Chinese poet is not an emotion: it is a thing that happens, like birth and marriage and the fall of the plum blossoms in early spring. There is no Christian apocalypse, no crucifixion, no final blaze of glory. They were more human than the Europeans, who from earliest times have hinted secretly that they were gods, or at least could become gods. And because they had no belief in a future world, they loved the concrete things of life passionately and with a kind of abandon, and where we will find glory in a dying youth on a wooden cross, they would find the same glory in a leaf, in the silence of the woods and the distant roaring of tigers. They lived in a settled world where things were what they were. In the end the warrior unarms, his task done, and finds sleep by the side of his bride—and his bride is the earth that gave him birth and sometimes nourished him; and he is as grateful to her in death as he is in life.

So much of Chinese poetry is foreign to us that we enter it with a sense of bewilderment. Here are no gods and angels, no superhuman forces, no "Accuser who is the God of this World." Since Babylonian times, the European spirit has been accustomed to the presence of vast and remote gods who ruled over the lives of all people with implacable scepters: their breath has filled our poetry for four thousand or more years. But the Chinese gods were always life-size, and exceedingly human, as anyone who has read Mr. Arthur Waley's excellent translation of the *Hsi Yu Chi* is aware. Their gods were playthings; beautifully decorative, and nearly always calm. Where our gods are youths striving in combat, theirs are generally old men, passionless and entirely preoccupied by the duties of benevolence. But it is necessary to note that these old men were projections of themselves, the men they would like to be if they could live long enough, if they could eat enough. And in a sense the old men were not so much projections of themselves as of their families, for individual life remains worthless—all must be trees, budding and giving forth fruit.

But if there is no death in Chinese poetry (there are comparatively few poems of grief, though innumerable poems of parting), there is always the unchanging sorrow that springs

effortlessly to the mind of the poet when he is least conscious
of betrayal. Sorrow is there—not in the shape of *la belle dame
sans merci*, who never appears in Chinese poetry, but in the
shape of the parched fields and flooded valleys of their home-
land, in the hysteria that is so close to the Chinese spirit, and
even in the irony. Let us take a simple poem by Tu Fu:

AUTUMN NIGHT

> Silver candles, autumn night, a cool screen,
> Soft silks, a tiny fan to catch the fireflies.
> On the stone stairs the night breathes cool as water.
> I sit and watch the Herd Boy and the Weaving Girl.

It is all so simple that it seems to flow out with the breath.
Nothing is concealed, a whole world, almost a whole civilization is revealed, but the concrete images of the first line are
whirled away among the stars in the last. It is not a trick: it
is something that came naturally to him, and we shall see it
again in Wang Wei and a thousand other poets—the concrete,
immediate thing slowly disappearing across the horizon, fading into ghostliness. The peach blossom follows the moving
water, the white birds fade into the faint emerald of the hills,
nothing is lasting, all disappears, and yet—the poet seems to
be saying—how delightful to watch the progress of the world.
Compare this with a poem written a few years ago:

AN OLD SOLDIER

> Riding on a skinny horse,
> he
> comes dimly from the wood
> and out of the morning mist
> and returns dimly into the mist.
>
> Day after day
> he is carried unsteadily,
> he knows not where:
> on his sword there is
> a little dust,
> a little rust,
> a little frost,
> a little brightness,
> a little blood shining in the morning sun.

It is demonstrably the same world, the same landscape, the
same kind of vision. The tautness of the T'ang dynasty is
absent, but something almost as precious has come to take
its place—a more complex arrangement of forces, a more in-
tensive understanding of suffering, a greater suggestiveness.
The poem, however, is not characteristic of modern poetry
in the sense that Tien Ch'ien's poetry is characteristic of our

time. The sadness remains, but over and above the sadness there can be heard during the present wars the sounds of battle and lamentation, a deeper and harsher note to remind us that the world has changed into the direction of steel. Though the current of the eternal river is the same, it is now dyed more deeply red with blood. So we can expect in the poems written in the last thirty years (and more particularly in the poems written in the last ten years), the harshness and dissonances we have come to expect in our own reiterations of a wasteland, where there is no sound of water and there are only red rocks. And what is curious is that the spiritual landscape of the West, the landscape in which T. S. Eliot has his home, is very similar to north China—the endless plains of loess, the huts dug in caves, the railway lines broken, and the eagles fastening on the bodies near the river; yet the Chinese poets, who live in such a landscape, are not conscious that they have been betrayed: out of the granite hardness and small comfort of their home they have built a world in which they have formed their own peace. Such a world can be seen in the poetry of Ai Ching, and even more obviously in the poetry of Tien Ch'ien. Out of sands and wind they have made a continent as colorful as any that poets have made before them.

The Western reader, reading Chinese poetry in a translation that must always fail to convey the sensuous quality of the Chinese characters, misses also the *color* of a Chinese page. Those large editions of the Chinese poets printed in the Ming dynasty, on a rich brown paper that fades a little, but only a little, with age; the large characters; the little red, blue, and yellow circles that describe the passages that elicited the admiration of famous commentators; the sheer sweep and magnificence of those crackling pages—all these are missing, in the same way that we miss the ragged miniscule printing and pulpy yellow paper of the wartime editions. There is a solidity in the Chinese page that is denied to us, and there is a peculiarity in the structure of the Chinese character that gives it the effect of being eternal, as a building sometimes seems to be eternal. If we could print translations of Chinese in the capital letters that appear on the Trajan column, we might approximate to their sense of permanence; but we shall never realize the beauty of Chinese poetry unless it is printed on a Chinese page.

There are other things we miss: the quality of their sensualities, which is more robust and at the same time more allusive than our own. There is a short poem in the *Book of Songs* called "In the Wood Lay a Dead Doe," which has had endless imitators and followers. Li Chin-fa, a Chinese sculptor who studied in Paris, wrote:

With my presumptuous fingers,
I felt the warmth of your skin.
Young deer went wandering in a wood:
Only the scent of the dead leaves remain,

and the contemporary poet Sun Chin-san wrote in a similar vein, using the same image, which derives from across the centuries:

Without any experience of hunting,
I do not know why there arises in my mind
A longing to hunt some wild fox in the night.
On such a snowy night hoofbeats are sweet and intoxicating:
Stealing in between the eyebrows like a sea gull,
Diving into the lake to catch fish,
A flake of snow pecks the curious quiver of the heart.[1]

Sensuality could hardly go further. Our own sensuality, which comes from a homosexual Greece and a passionately hetero-sexual Lebanon, is more confused, less direct, and not so menacing. The Chinese have no shame in using sexual images. The Entrance to the Female is a part of Taoism, and even the Peach Blossom Fountain can be read in other ways than a return to some primitive ancestral tribe. The *yang* and the *yin* remain, both powerful, both majestic and all-embracing. This is not, like ours, a male civilization, but one in which the male and the female are held in an unwavering equality, a civilization still based on the ritual of the seasons and on the communion of man and woman.

We miss too the compelling force of the Chinese characters, for though they no longer evoke in the Chinese mind the pic-tures on which they were originally formed, they can still sometimes produce an immediate image of the thing seen, especially when a string of nouns are joined together:

Dark room ghost green fire

Yin Fang Kuei Ch'in Huo,[2]

says Tu Fu, and there is no need for verbs or adverbs; the picture is there in all its fullness, possessing the primitive force of an incantation, so that we see the thing described with an immediacy that is denied to us when the page is filled with enclitics. So, but in a different sense, we

---

[1] Sun Chin-san: "The Snowy Night," translated by Yu Min-chuan.
[2] Occasionally in Latin something of the same effect is gained:
    nubila sol imbres nix venti fulmina grando
    clouds sun rain snow winds lightning (Lucretius: V, 1192)
but though there are other similar passages—there is one in Prudentius—the Western languages are usually unable to bear the weight of such heavy associations.

miss the sobbing sounds that come at the end of each short line of Ch'u Yuan. There is the color of the Chinese page, and the color of the high-strung Chinese voice, and both of these are denied to us.

But what remains is the spirit of Chinese song. Not all is lost in translation, and occasionally, as in the poems of Po Chu-i translated by Mr. Waley, something is indeed gained. The Chinese lyric is so close in feeling to ours, their feeling for the countryside is so much like ours, their best sharing so greatly the emotions that are shared by ours, that we are in danger of forgetting sometimes that we belong to different worlds, almost different universes. There are bridges between the two civilizations. There are paths we have traveled that lead inevitably to China. And since we share their sorrows, their griefs, and their hopes, there is no reason why we should not share their joys, even though their joys in the past were simpler than ours. We must make these bridges, or perish. We shall learn some of their secrets from their poetry. When, like Feng Fei-ming, a modern poet who is nearly always too tenuous to translate, we lay aside the books, the imagination becomes filled with the evocations of such simple things that we are surprised that we did not notice them before:

Studying at the dead hour,
Having laid aside the *Tao Teh Ching*,
I seem to have made away with fortune, and the evil and the
    remorse,

Which once assembled together in this room.
It is too strange—not like picking up a flower with a smile.
There was a fish in the water:
The cat did not catch the fish.
I remember one winter night a mouse walking on the carpet,
The cry of a night peddler like the music of the stars.
Again I think of the line that delighted my youth:
"A fish is the flower of water."
The light of the lamp itself seems to have written a poem
Of too great a solitude to be read by me.
Laughing: "I respect your illumination."
Then the lamp begs me listen to the watchmen of the night.[3]

Of such simple things, and of such quietness, is Chinese poetry made. The fish becomes a flower, the lamp writes a poem, and the mouse walks across the carpet, and at the same time battles are fought, men starve on the wayside, the corpses are piled high, and yet the simplicity remains. It is part of the secret—to find the simplest things of life and celebrate them. It is not always easy. We have nearly always aimed high in our poetry; the Chinese deliberately aimed at the earth, away

[3] Feng Fei-ming: "The Lamp," translated by Yu Min-chuan.

from the angelic hosts, and made something that is universal, because it is common to all men. There is a sense in which this is their greatest glory. They contrived to write poetry without dreaming, they saw clearly, and it was not their fault that they saw with so much sadness. The land was impenitent. No gods could make it richer. With their own strength they made the landscape, and their poetry for all its quietness is the sign of their spiritual strength.

And so it will go on, this poetry that is eternal, like the people, more lasting perhaps than ours, and in its humanity more vigorous. Out of a few things—the bodies and loves of men, the wheat growing, the white cliffs in the water—they have made their sacrifices. They complained of the impermanence of things, but they were themselves the most permanent. They cared only for humanity: their character for love or benevolence is two men standing together. The chain remains unbroken. From the earliest times to the present day, the same themes are repeated, the same images reappear, the same metal is hammered into shape. We who are constantly changing, at the mercy of every influx of scientific ideas, may do well to ponder sometimes the poetry of these people who are as unchanging as the stars.

ROBERT PAYNE

METHOD OF TRANSLATION

It has seemed best to translate the poems as simply and literally as possible, and to avoid footnotes wherever possible. The Chinese has therefore been translated line by line—without rhyme, for to have succeeded in rhyme would have necessitated padding out the lines or so changing their forms that they would have become unrecognizable. Legge's translations of the *Book of Songs* in his edition of the *Chinese Classics* are still a model for all translators, but his later attempts to put them into rhymed English verse are among the sorriest translations yet seen. Nor have we attempted, with Mrs. Ayscough, to seek out the original meanings of the Chinese characters and to attempt to introduce them into the translation; that the character for "autumn" contains the "grain" radical and the character for "fire" is not immediately perceived by the Chinese reader any more than we perceive the god Autumnus. The Chinese reader sees almost the same autumn that we do, hardly colored at all by thoughts of grain or scorching.

We have aimed, then, at literal translations, without paraphrases and without any attempt to recapture the sounds of the original or to follow the exact pattern of the syllabic line. Sometimes, as in the *Book of Songs* and the *Tao Teh Ching*, it has been necessary to insist on the shortest possible expression of the line, simply because the original is short and acquires much of its beauty precisely from the close-packed effect of the lines. Almost all of the *Book of Songs* is written in four-syllable lines; the length of lines in the *Tao Teh Ching* varies enormously, but it is evident that they are as close-packed as anything contained in Chinese poetry. To translate the third line of the first poem of the *Tao Teh Ching* included here with fourteen English words, as Mr. Waley does, suggests a delight in mere verbiage that is absent from the original, where there are only four characters. But occasionally, and more often than we would have wished, it has been necessary to translate the Chinese by far more words than there are in the original.

The Miltonic overflow is completely absent from Chinese poetry. Each line, or each couplet, has an identity of its own, almost self-sufficient. Such a pattern might in other hands make for dullness, but it is remarkable how even the long poems like Tu Fu's "Journey to the North," though written in single lines or couplets, are impelled forward by the movement of the poet's thought. A more static effect is produced by Li Ho's long evocation of his native landscape, but here it is deliberate.

The aim throughout was to have translations by skilled Chinese scholars rather than the adaptations that have been made by Western scholars. Chinese scholars were asked to translate the poems they believed they were most fitted to translate on the basis of their experience and scholarship; these were then revised by me and submitted to them, until final agreement was reached. My business was chiefly to be editor and reviser; for my knowledge of Chinese was rarely sufficient to allow me to act as arbiter in translating the delicacies of Chinese poetic speech. We have not employed rhyme, and we have attempted wherever possible to translate a line of Chinese into simple, accurate, and ryhthmic English prose, because it seemed better and more scholarly to be as accurate as possible. There are limitations in all translation, and we have made no effort to break through these limitations, but rather we have attempted to use them for our own advantages, which are delight in poetry and the understanding of a foreign soul.

ACKNOWLEDGMENTS

I am chiefly indebted to the Marquis d'Hervey Saint-Denys' *Poésies de l'Epoque des Thang* (Paris, 1862), which first led me to believe that it would be possible to produce an anthology of Chinese poetry from the earliest times to the present day, and to discussions with my friends Dr. Wen Yi-tuo, Dr. Pu Hsiang-hsing, and Professor Shen Yu-ting, who on one wintry night in Kunming were kind enough to suggest the outline that has since been followed. I am very conscious of a debt to James Legge's monumental edition of the *Book of Songs,* and to Mr. Arthur Waley's two excellent books *The Way and Its Power* and *The Book of Songs,* though I have occasionally differed from his interpretations.

I owe special gratitude to Professor Shen Yu-ting for his translation of the *Nine Songs* of Chu Yuan, to Professor Yang Yeh-tzu for his translation of Tao Yuanming, to Mr. Ho Chih-yuan for his versions of Li Ho, to Professor Pu Chiang-hsing for his translations of Tu Fu, and to Professor Yu Min-chuan for his translations of some of the poems of Ch'u Yuan, his translation of the texts from the Stone Drums and from Su T'ung-po. I have to thank many people in Yenan who were kind enough to verify the original text of the last poem included in this book, by Mr. Mao Tse-tung. I am grateful to Professor Yuan Chia-hua for his translations of Ts'en Ts'an, Miss Hsiung Ting for her translations from Li Ho Chou and others, Mrs. Sophia Chen for her translations of Li Ch'ing-chao, Mr. Ching Ti for his translations of Po Chu-i, Mr. Chu Chun-i for his translations of Tien Ch'ien, Mr. Chu K'an for his translations of Feng Chih, and Mr. Pei Wen-yu for his translations of Lu Yu. When the translators' names are not given, the translators were usually too numerous to be mentioned here.

THE CHOU DYNASTY
(*1112* B.C.—*249* B.C.)

THE BOOK OF SONGS

No one knows when the *Book of Songs* was written, or whether Confucius compiled them. We know that he read them and encouraged his son Po Yu to read them, paying particular attention to the *Chao Nan* and the *Chou Nan*, which are mostly love songs, and he went on to say that one who does not study them is like "one who stands with his face against a wall." All mystery, all mathematics were contained in them. Obeying their music, a man might enter heaven—he would assuredly never enter heaven without them.

No poetry could be simpler than these ancient odes. This is not folk poetry, but the poetry of enchanted experience, of a grave sadness and a delighted awareness in the beauty of earth. Here the rice fields are flowing with gold, the lovers bathe in the streams, there are white rocks and waterfalls and herons perching on cliffs, and it is as though the beginning of the world had come again—not dazzling, but quietly splendid, confronting us with the calm majesty of human lives lived to the full. Above all, they are human with an adult humanity. They are not afraid of sex, but delight in it with coarseness, with gentleness, with the grace of the supremely civilized. We see the same clear landscapes in the paintings of the Yuan dynasty, where nearly always there is a white horse or a white heron impertinently occupying the foreground, throwing the mountains and the mists into clear relief. There must always be something living in a Chinese landscape: you may look for an hour, but somewhere beneath those cliffs you will find a man walking. So it is with their ancient poetry: the men and women who wrote them were supremely alive.

Poetry here is stripped to the skin, not stripped to the bone. There is no hardness, nor any luxury. The girl lifts her skirt as she wades across the stream, pennons fly on the edge of the rice fields, even in those days there were seducers—but how charitably they are forgiven, and with what wealth of detail are they described; no more than a few brush strokes, but the fox is described to us forever. In the poem called *"Tsai Chou"* ("The Clearing of the Fields") the fruits of the earth and the fruits of man are curiously interwoven into a complete pattern of serene accomplishment. It was life lived according to ritual and the seasons, before men learned to conceal themselves in cities, a life that was so full that it bursts out of the page, as the seeds burst out of a pomegranate, three thousand years after they were first sung on the fields near the Yellow River.

We do not know even the exact meaning of words written a few years ago. Who can say what Dante meant by "love" when he wrote:

Tutti li mei penser parlan d'Amore,

since the meaning of love changes with every lover, and with every change of historical evolution? Love for the Egyptians was not the same as love for the Greeks. But the translator of Chinese poetry is faced with greater difficulties than the translator of Dante: *there is not one single word in these ancient poems whose precise significance we understand.* Anyone taking up, for example, Legge's edition of the *Book of Songs* is startled to find how much of the meaning and interpretations depends upon inspired guesswork. Inspired guesswork it must remain until the Pentecost descends upon us.

But if we fail in attempting to find an absolute interpretation of each character, we are helped by the simplicity of the poems. As always, the fewest brush strokes are the best. If we translate with the fewest possible words, attempting to give each word in English something of the living character of a Chinese symbol, and if we remember that all these songs were once sung, there is a chance that we may see these people as they were. They were more glorious in that childhood of their race than they are now; something of that glory survives in the famous nineteen Han poems, but it is already fading. These songs are the brightest things that came out of that bright landscape, where there are the brightest skies in the world.

They are the songs[1] of a people genuinely in love with life, still alive to the glitter of bright colors—nearly every poem contains a color adjective, and the colors are freshly seen and never described, so that we seem to be entering a world of pure yellows, pure greens, pure carmines, a world where no shadows fall and where everything is as it is, not clouded over with a suffused reflected glare from the earth but with the brightness of the sun shining at noonday—and in this world of harmonized colors, among rituals and delight in vegetation, the lovers appear to us, as they appear in the tapestries of Gobelin and in some early Italian paintings, with an immediacy that is almost bewildering. They sing like birds; they make love like adults; they are aware of all the simplicities that are enclosed within the hallowed conception of *Tien,* which is not the heaven we know, but the mysterious government of the blue sky at noon. It is a world comparable in its pure intensity

[1] Out of 311 recorded poems in the *Book of Songs,* the seventy that seemed to me to be most poetical are included here. The dynastic songs have been deliberately omitted with the exception of the very moving "Beginning of the People," which is placed at the end.

with the world of the scops and the trouvères, and it is perhaps not surprising that two of the poems included in the *Book of Songs* should seem to be echoes of one of the most famous *aubades:*

> *Il n'est mie jors,*
> *Saverose au corps gent,*
>   *Si me consent Dieus*
> *L'aloëte nos ment . . .* [2]

Here, too, in a country otherwise so strange, we see the pure skies of Provence and Italy, the gentleness and vigor of a new race awakening into awareness, the bird song, the nakedness, and the peace. Here are the same walled dikes, the same cartloads of peasants returning from a fiesta, the same eagerness and unchallenged vigor. Hölderlin, coming over the storm-swept Auvergne in winter, thought he saw in the descendants of the trouvères a godlike beauty and a divine skill; so may we, coming across the storm-swept heights of another language and another century, see these people in the untrammeled vigor of their youth.

We shall never know whence they came, and how they suddenly sprang into song. These songs are not the imaginations of a primitive people: the Chinese at the time of Confucius already possessed a consciousness of the ancientness of their civilization. There were wars before Homer; there is the same bitterness in these soldiers' songs that we have learned to read today. But chiefly they are songs of joy and the sadness that comes from joy. They are wholly Provençal, but they have something of the tenderness we associate with the English religious lyrics of the fourteenth century, when the lyrical feeling was still associated with prayer, and they have something too of the old English ballads:

> Maiden in the mor lay,
>   In the mor lay,
> Seuenyst fulle, seuenist fulle.
> Maiden in the mor lay.
>   In the mor lay
> Seuenistes fulle ant a day.

It is the heart speaking quietly and passionately and with full strength, before the heart was imprisoned. There was sadness in joy, and joy in sadness; and the language is not littered up with the names of complex emotions. A simplicity, as of pure sunlight, enters these poems and warms them until they are ablaze.

> [2] It is not daylight,
> O sweet one with the gentle body,
>   So God help me,
> The lark lies to us.

Those who know Provençal poetry will recognize the part songs, the *ballettes,* the *rondes,* and the *tensons;* they will almost hear the antiphonal voices, and see the colors of the women's gowns as they sing by their fires in winter. Occasionally they will notice a metallic brightness of color—somewhere under the trees a chariot is waiting. Like gypsies, the ancient Chinese liked bright things. Gold, silver, and copper were known to them. The ivory of elephants' teeth was sent in tribute by the tribes of central China. The tips of their lances were silvered or gilt, the ends of their bows were ornamented with wrought ivory. It was a society in which the unseen powers of heaven were felt to be continually present; their bronze vessels contained the portraits of thunderheaded dragons. It was a time of war, of unending battles against the wild tribes of the frontiers, but it was also a time of consolidation. They were growing conscious of themselves, but they were also growing conscious of that strange coherent thing that we were later to know as China.

It was a time also of leisure, of fantastic processions, of simple feasts and communal living. There is little of the allusiveness that characterizes T'ang dynasty painting, nor did they rend their passions into tatters. Already they possessed complex musical instruments; but their lives were simple and regulated according to the pattern of the seasons and the precepts of the philosophers. They liked riding in chariots, with bells hanging from the decorated bronze hoops—Confucius preferred charioteering to archery—and they delighted in ceremonies. It was an essentially feudal civilization, there was some kind of caste system, and sometimes there was great poverty. There is bitterness in some of the poems—we hear the unmistakable accents of some forerunner of Tu Fu in some of them. But afterward, when we have finished reading them, we remember only the serenity and the passion that brought this serenity into being.

As often in the history of poetry, the beginnings are the greatest. From this point Chinese poetry runs downhill. They were never to recapture this hallowed sense of the perfection of life. The fruit tree would be cultivated; the flowers would become more numerous, and possess other colors; there would be strange accretions, and still stranger cuttings implanted from the deserts of the northwest; but the garden would never be so beautiful again. We may regret its passing, and we may regret still more that the young Chinese of today are almost ignorant of these poems on which the whole of Chinese civilization rests, as a river rests within its embankments, but at least the songs still sing for us—they are here, Adam awake in the garden for the first time.

The White Pony

Pure is the white pony,
Feeding on the young shoots in my stackyard.
Keep him hobbled, keep him bridled,
Let him stay through all mornings.
So may my lover
Here take his ease.

Pure is the white pony.
Feeding on the bean sprouts in my stackyard.
Keep him hobbled, keep him bridled,
Let him stay through all evenings.
So may my lover
Here have his peace.

Pure is the white pony
Who comes to me swiftly,
Like a duke, like a marquis,
Let us enjoy ourselves completely,
Let us prolong our love-making,
Let us take our ease.

Pure is the white pony
Who lies in the empty valley
With a bundle of fresh hay.
He is like a piece of jade.
Oh, do not be like gold or jade.
Do not go far from my heart!

The Sun in the East

Heiho, the sun in the east!
This lovely man
Enters my chamber,
Enters my chamber,
And steps through my door.

Heiho, the sun in the east!
This lovely man
Enters my garden,
Enters my garden,
And steps over the threshold.

The North Wind

The cold north wind blows.
Down falls the snow.
Love me, be good to me,
Take my hand, go with me.
Why do you linger so?
Oh, let us go!

The cold north wind whistles.
Down whirls the falling snow.
Love me, be good to me,
Take my hand, go with me.
Why do you linger so?
Oh, let us go!

Only the red fox,
Only the black crow—
Love me, be good to me,
Take my hand, go with me.
Why do you linger so?
Oh, let us go!

The White Asters

She gathers white asters
By the pool, by the tiny islands.
She offers them
In sacrifice to her lord.

She gathers white asters
Down in the ravines.
She offers them
In the ancestral temple of her lord.

Her headdress is trembling.
In the early dawn she enters the prince's palace.
Her headdress softly trembling,
She returns to her room.

The Small Stars

The small stars are trembling,
Three or four in the east.
Reverently through the night we come.

In the early dawn we go from the prince's palace.
Our fates are not equal!

The small stars are trembling,
Orion and the Pleiades.
Reverently through the night we come
Covered in quilts and satins.
Our fates are not equal.[8]

My Lord Is Full of Delight

My lord is full of delight.
In his left hand he holds a flute,
With his right he summons me to play with him.
Oh, what sweet joy!

My lord is full of blessing.
In his left hand he holds dancing plumes,
With his right he summons me to dance with him.
Oh, what sweet joy!

Falling Leaves

Falling leaves, falling leaves,
The winds blow you away.
O uncles, O elders,
Set the tune and we will join you.

Falling leaves, falling leaves,
The wind makes you merry.
O uncles, O elders,
Set the tune and we will play.

The High Road

Once along the high way
I held you by the sleeve.
Do not hate me—
Old loves are not forsworn.

[8] The poem describes the concubines of the prince who return to their quarters in the early morning. According to later practice, which may still have existed at the time of the Chou princes, the concubines were taken by eunuchs, wrapped in silks, through the courtyards, and then laid at the foot of the prince's bed, the silks being taken away from them. The complaint is against the wife of the prince, while the small stars are of course both the faint stars of dawn and the concubines themselves.

Once along the high way
I held you by the hand.
Do not think me ugly—
Old loves are not forsworn.

The Rush Leaves

Green, green are the rush leaves,
White dew turns to frost.
That man I love
Is somewhere on the water.
I seek him upstream:
Hard is the road and long.
I seek him downriver.
Oh, he is there in midstream.

Thick, thick grow the rush leaves,
White dew not yet dry.
The man I love
Is on the margin of the water.
I seek him upstream:
Hard is the way and steep.
I wander downriver.
Oh, he is there in midstream.

Sweet, sweet are the rush leaves,
White dew not yet over.
The man I love
Is on the edge of the water.
I follow him upriver:
Hard is the way to the right.
I wander downriver.
Oh, he is on an island in midstream.

The Cock Crows

THE LADY: The cock has crowed.
            The sun has arisen.

THE LOVER: It is not yet cockcrow—
            Only the buzzing of the bluebottles.

THE LADY: The east is alight.
            The sun is aflame.

THE LOVER: It is not the dawn—
            Only the moon rising.

THE LADY: The bluebottles must be drowsy.
             It is sweet to lie by your side.

THE LOVER: Quick! Let me go from you.
             Do not let me hate you!

The Lady Says: "It Is Cockcrow"

The lady says: "It is cockcrow."
The knight says: "Dawn has not yet come."
She says, "Get up, look at the sky,
The morning star is glimmering.
Get up, lie-a-bed!
Harpoon the ducks, harpoon the geese!

"When you have harpooned them,
I shall serve them with dressing.
We shall drink wine together,
We shall grow old together,
With the lute and the pipe beside you,
There will be peace and happiness between us.

"When I know your friends are coming,
I will offer them girdle pendants.
When I know your friends are on the way,
I shall send girdle pendants to them.
When I know your sworn brothers are on the road,
I will bestow girdle pendants on them."

The Green Coat

Heiho, my coat is green,
Green coat with yellow lining.
Oh, the grief of my heart,
Will it never cease?

Heiho, my coat is green,
Green coat with yellow-green skirt.
Oh, the grief of my heart,
Will it never cease?

Heiho, the green threads,
How could I have sewn them?
Thinking of how he loved me,
I will not hold it against him.

Heiho, the coarse cloth,
The cold winds blow through it.
Thinking of the way he loved me,
How he held me to his heart.[4]

The Torches Are Bright

What of the night?
The night is not yet over.
The torches are blazing in the palace yard,
My lord is coming.
Ting-ling sound the phoenix bells.

What of the night?
The night is not yet over.
The torches are smoking in the palace yard,
My lord is coming.
Ching-ching sound the phoenix bells.

What of the night?
The night nears dawn.
The torches are dimming in the palace yard.
My lord is coming.
I see his banners.

Bound and Wound

The Firewood is bound and wound,
The three stars in the sky.
Tonight or tomorrow night
I will see my good lover.
Ay mi! Ay mi!
Who will be my sweet lover?

The Hay-sheaf is bound and wound,
The three stars on the edge of the sky.
Tonight or tomorrow night
I will see him.
Ay mi! Ay mi!
How shall we meet together?

The Wild-thorn is bound and wound,
The three stars near the door.
Tonight or tomorrow night
I shall see my darling.
Ay mi! Ay mi!
Who will he be?

[4] Presumably the song of an abandoned concubine. Until recently con
cubines wore green.

Ripe Plums

Ripe plums are dropping,
Now there are only seven.
May a fine lover come for me
Now while there is yet time.

Ripe plums are dropping,
Now there are only three.
May a fine lover come for me
While there is still time.

Ripe plums are dropping,
I lay them in a shallow basket.
May a fine lover come for me.
Tell me his name.

In the Wood Lay a Dead Doe

In the wood lay a dead doe
Covered over with white rushes.
The lady was sighing for the spring;
A fine knight lay over her.

In the forest of the oakenshaws,
In the wasteland lay a dead doe,
White rushes strewn over her:
O lady fair as jade.

"Please, sir, do not touch me.
Please, sir, don't take my kerchief.
Don't make my dog bark."

Debonair

She is fair and debonair:
She said she would meet me at the corner wall.
I love her, yet cannot see her.
I scratch my head and pace up and down.

She is sweet and debonair:
She gave me a red reed.
A red reed so red, oh,
I adore her beauty.

She went to the fields, threw me white corn,
So beautiful and rare.
Oh, but it is not the corn that is beautiful—
Beauty is the gift of a fair girl.

The Moon Is Rising

The white moon is rising,
O lady so lovely and bright.
Why am I enchanted?
Why am I consumed with grief?

The white moon in rising
Is like the splendor of my lady.
Why am I caught in these chains?
Why am I consumed with grief?

The moon rising in splendor
Is the light of my love.
Why am I forsaken?
Why am I consumed with grief?

The Young Peach Trees

The slender young peach tree,
The flowers ablaze.
The young brides are going home,
Bringing fruit to chamber and house.

The slender young peach tree,
How the fruit swells!
The young brides are going home,
Bringing fruit to chamber and house.

The slender young peach tree,
With glossy shining leaves.
The young brides are going home,
Bringing fruit to chamber and house.

Beyond the East Gate

Beyond the east gate
Are girls shining like clouds.
Though they are shining like clouds,
There is none on whom my heart dwells.
Plain cloth and gray kerchief,
This were joy enough for me!

Beyond the gate tower
Are girls lovely as rush wool.
Though they are lovely as rush wool,
There is none on whom my heart dwells.
Plain cloth and madder kerchief,
Such is my joy!

The Rainbow

There is a rainbow in the east.
No one dares to point at it.
The girls have run away
Far from father and mother, far from brothers.

A rainbow mounts in the west.
All morning the rain falls in showers.
The girls have gone away
Far from father and mother, far from brothers.

O you young girl
Who only desired to be married.
A boy has been false to you.
This is not heaven's will.[5]

The Plantains

Thick grow the plantains.
Now we go and gather them.
Thick grow the plantains—
Now they lie in our hands.

Thick grow the plantains.
Now we pluck the ripe ears.
Thick grow the plantains—
Look how they lie on the stems.

Thick grow the plantains.
Our skirts are piled high with them.
Thick grow the plantains.
We loop up our skirts over our belts.[6]

[5] Collective marriages were held when the rainbow was shining. (See Granet, *Danses et légendes de la Chine ancienne*, II, 503.) The rainbow, which bears the fertility symbol in the Chinese character, seems to have been a fetish, both feared and adored.

[6] The commentators say that the plantain was thought to assist child-bearing, but a much simpler interpretation remains possible.

The Mallards

Kwang-kwang cry the mallards
On the island in the river.
Such a noble young lady
Were fit bride for her lord.

There grow the tangled marsh mallows,
Left and right you will see them.
Such a noble young lady,
Waking and sleeping he will see her.

He sought her, could not find her;
Waking and sleeping, he grieved.
He longed for her with long thoughts,
And tumbled over on his side.

There grow the tangled marsh mallows,
Left and right you may gather them.
For this noble young lady
We will sing with small and great flutes.

There grow the tangled marsh mallows,
Left and right you may choose among them.
Such a noble young lady—
With bells and drums we will gladden her heart.

The Nest of the Magpie

Magpie has a nest,
Dove dwells in it:
This girl is going to be married—
Hundreds of chariots are driving to meet her!

Magpie has a nest,
Dove enters it:
This girl is going to be married—
Hundreds of chariots are driving to meet her!

Magpie has a nest,
Dove covers it:
This girl is going to be married—
Hundreds of chariots riding in splendor!

The Sun and the Moon

Ah, Sun, ah, Moon,
Which shine upon the earth below,
There is a man
Who will not keep faith.
How can he keep his oath?
Better if he had never seen me!

Ah, Sun, ah, Moon,
Which shadow the earth below,
There is a man
Who will not be true.
How can he keep troth?
Better if he had never sworn oath to me.

Ah, Sun, ah, Moon,
Which rise from the east,
There is a man
Who says no truth.
How can he be true?
Does he think he can forget me?

Ah, Sun, ah, Moon,
Which rise from the east.
O Father, O Mother,
Why was I ever born?
How can he keep his oath?
Loving me beyond all reason?

Ling-ling *Go the Hounds*

Ling-ling go the hounds.
Their master so handsome and good.
The hounds with the double ring,
The master so handsome and bearded.
The hounds with the treble ring,
The master so handsome and strong.

There Is a Fox

There is a fox ambling along
By the dam of Ch'i.
Oh, my heart is sad.
She has no skirt on.

There is a fox ambling along
By the deep ford of Ch'i.
Oh, my heart is sad—
She has no girdle.

There is a fox ambling along
By the banks of Ch'i.
Oh, my heart is sad—
She has no clothes on.

The Yellow Bird

O yellow bird, yellow bird,
Do not settle on the poppy,
Do not peck my millet seed,
For the people here
Do not want me to feed.
I must go back, I must go home
To my own people, my own land.

O yellow bird, yellow bird,
Do not settle on the mulberry,
Do not peck my maize seed.
With the people of this land
There can be no covenant.
I must go back, I must go home
To where my brothers are.

O yellow bird, yellow bird,
Do not settle on the oak,
Do not peck my wine millet.
With the people here
I cannot dwell.
I must go back, I must go home
To my own folks.

The New Tower

Bright shines the new tower:
The waters of the river are muddy.
She hoped for a fine gentle lover,
But received only coarse bamboo cloth.

Clean shines the new tower:
The waters of the river are dark and secret.
She hoped for a fine gentle lover,
But received only strips of old broadcloth.

The fish nets are sprung,
The wild geese fall in them.
She hoped for a fine gentle lover,
And received only "the stiff-necked one."[7]

The Cloth Cap

Oh, why should the sight of your cloth cap
Fill me with such longing?
My heart is aflame with grief.

Oh, why does the sight of your cloth coat
Spear my heart with grief?
Enough! I have fallen in love.

Oh, why does the sight of your cloth leggings
Tangle my heart in knots?
Enough! Let us be joined together!

Clearing the Fields

We clear the grasses and trees,
We plow and carve the land,
Two thousand men and women scrabbling weeds
Along the low wet lands, along the dyke walls.
The masters, the eldest sons,
The laborers, the hired servants,
They mark out the fields, they ply their colters,
Overflowing food baskets are brought to them,
They gaze on their fair wives
And press close to them.
They have sharp plowshares,
They set to work on the south acres,
They sow the many kinds of grain.
Each seed holds a moist germ;
Splendidly, splendidly the young grain shoots forth,
Sleekly, sleekly the young plants rise,
Tenderly, tenderly comes the young grain.
Thousands of weeders scrabbling among the weeds!
Host upon host of reapers!
Close-huddled stooks arranged in due order!
Myriads, many hundred thousands and millions of grains!

[7] The ancient commentators describe the poem as a satire on the marriage between Duke Suen (B.C. 718-699) and Suen Chiang. The "new tower" and the "wild goose" are of course the bride, the "muddy water" is the bridegroom. The bitterness in the poem may also arise from Duke Suen's wasteful wars, which depopulated the state. For a similar satire on a royal wedding, see "The frog he would awooing go."

From them come wine and sweet liquor,
Offering to the ancestors, the male and the female,
In fulfillment of sacrifices.
So glory shall come to the land.
They will have a sharp smell of pepper,
They will give comfort to the aged.
It is not only here that it is so,
It is not only now that it is so:
But in most ancient times ever and ever.

The Sharp Shares

Swee-swee go the sharp shares
There where they are working in the south acre,
Sowing the many kinds of grain,
Each seed holding a moist germ.
The women come to gaze at us,
They bring round and square baskets
Filled with fine millet,
Wearing finely woven straw hats.
They dig their hoes deep in the earth,
They slice away smartweed and thistle brier.
Where thistle brier and smartweed have grown rotten,
The millet grows to sheer heights.
Rustling of the reaping,
Plumping of fat sheaves,
Piling like a heaped wall,
Shaped like a toothed comb.
A hundred barns open to receive them.
When the hundred barns are brimming over,
The wives and children are at peace.
We sacrifice the yellow black-muzzled bull,
The bull with the crooked horns.
So it will be forever
According to the wisdom of the sages.

Thick Lies the Dew

Thick lies the dew.
The sun will suck it up to the sky.
Let us quaff long through the night
And not till we are drunk wander home.

Thick lies the dew
On the heavy grass.
Let us quaff long through the night.
Here in the palace drink to the end.

Thick lies the dew
On willow and thorn tree.
Pure are the lord's guests,
None without great virtue.

Cypress and yew
Hang down clusters of leaves.
Happy are the lord's guests,
None are without great fame.

The Red Bow

The springy red bow
Is taken and laid down.
He is my favorite guest,
With my whole heart I honor him.
With bells and drums ringing
The whole morning he shall be feasted.

The springy red bow
Is placed in its press.
He is the favored guest,
With my whole heart I rejoice in him.
With bells and drums ringing
The whole morning he will sit at my right hand.

The springy red bow
Is placed in its case.
He is my favored guest,
With my whole heart I adore him.
With bells and drums ringing
The whole morning I will pledge him in wine.[8]

The Gourd Has Bitter Leaves

HE: The gourd has bitter leaves:
      The river is deep at the ford.
      If the river is deep, I shall wade through.
      If the river is shallow, I will hold up my clothes.

SHE: The ford is in full flood.
      The pheasant cries out her complaint.
      The flood will not touch your axletrees.
      The pheasant is calling for her mate.

[8] In the Chou dynasty a red bow was given by the emperor as a mark of favor to his knights. Such a gift was offered by King P'ing to the Marquis of Ts'in (*Shu Ching*, V, xxviii, 4). Red was the color of honor in the Chou dynasty—hence the red bulls in other poems.

HE: *Soo-soo* comes the voice of the wild goose.
As the sun comes out of the east,
The knight must bring home his bride
Before the ice melts.

SHE: I keep beckoning to the boatman,
But others will cross the ferry before me.
Others will cross the ferry before me.
I pine for my lover.[9]

Chung Tzu

I beg you, Chung Tzu,
Do not break into my house,
Do not force a way through the willows I planted.
It is not that I care for the willows,
Only I fear my father and mother.
I love you, Chung Tzu, dearly—
Oh, but I am afraid, really afraid
Of what my father and mother will say.

I beg you, Chung Tzu,
Do not leap through my wall,
Do not force a way through the mulberries I planted.
It is not that I care for the mulberries,
Only I fear my brothers.
I love you, Chung Tzu, dearly—
Oh, but I am afraid, really afraid
Of what my brothers will say.

I beg you, Chung Tzu,
Do not come through my garden,
Do not force a way through the sandalwood I have planted.
It is not that I care for the sandalwood,
I am afraid of people talking.
I love you, Chung Tzu, dearly,
Only I am afraid, really afraid
Of what they will say.

The Green Thistles

Thick grow the green thistles.
I cannot fill my shallow basket.
I sigh for my lover,
And lay the basket on the road.

[9] In some parts of China today, among the Miao tribes especially, young lovers sing part songs to each other across streams, or the girl will sing from the hills to her lover in the valley. Often the girl will marry the man whose song pleases her most. See *The Chinese Earth*, by Shen Tseng-wen (London, 1947).

I climb the rocky cliffs,
My horse is weary.
I pour wine from the bronze ewer,
But still my heart pains me.

I climb the high cliffs,
My horse dribbles yellow foam.
I pour out wine from the horn cup,
Still my heart is overladen.

I climb the high uplands,
On a lame broken-down nag.
My lover is dying.
How can I cease sobbing?

Gathering Dolichos

He is away gathering dolichos.
For a single day I have not seen him.
The day is like three months!

He is away plucking southernwood.
For a single day I have not seen him.
The day is like three autumns!

He is away plucking arrowroot.
For a single day I have not seen him.
The day is like three years!

The Cock Pheasant

My cock pheasant is flying away.
Fling-fling goes the sound of his wings.
O my love,
Why are you separated from me?

My cock pheasant is flying away.
From above and below comes his song.
O my prince,
Why have you broken my heart?

Gaze on the sun and the moon:
No less enduring is my love.
The way is long—
How can I reach him?

O all you young princes,
You who have known his good deeds,
He has hatred for none, envies none,
What has he ever done wrong?[1]

Truly, the South Mountain

Truly, the South Mountain—
It was Yu who apportioned them.
The marshlands and highlands he prepared for the plow.
The descendants tilled them.
We drew the boundaries, we set up marking stones,
We made out the field shares on the south and east.

The heavens are an arch of clouds,
Multitudinous snow falls,
Small rain of spring falls.
All is made moist.
Abundance flows down to earth,
All kinds of grain arise.

The boundaries and marking stones are drawn clearly:
Millet seeds are sown in plenty:
They will be harvested by the descendants.
Thence comes wine and food
To be offered to the dead and to the guests.
For myriads of years, life without end.

In the midst of the field are shelters,
Along the boundaries gourds are set up.
We slice them, we pickle them,
We present them to the ancestors:
So shall the descendants live long,
Enjoying heaven's favor.

We sacrifice with pure wine,
We sacrifice the red bull,
We offer him to the ancestors,
We hold the bell knife,
We lay open the hair,
We receive the fat and the blood.

The fruit offering follows the flesh offering,
So strong-smelling, so sweet-smelling,
So hallowed, so shining an offering
To august ancestors,
Who reward us with blessings,
With long life never ending.

[1] The last two lines were quoted by Confucius (*Analects,* IX, xxvi) to describe the character of Tze-lu, his favorite disciple.

Harvest Overflowing

Harvest overflowing, millions of grains of millet and rice,
The granaries heaped to the roof beams,
Myriads and myriads and myriads of grains.
We will prepare wine and sweet liquor,
We will offer them to the ancestors,
We will consecrate them in the ceremonies:
Everywhere blessings will flow down on the people.

Do Not Follow the Great Chariot

Do not follow the great chariot:
You will only raise the dust.
Do not think of others' sorrows.
You will only be ill with grief.

Do not follow the great chariot.
The dust is dark and dim.
Do not think of the sorrows of others.
You will never escape from despair.

Do not follow the great chariot.
The dust hangs like mist.
Do not think of others' sorrows.
You will only be loaded with care.

The Crane Cries

The crane cries in the Nine Pools.
His voice is heard in the wild.
The fish sink in the deep
Or rest among islands.
There is delight in gardens
Where sandalwood flowers.
Beneath the trees are the withered leaves.
The stones on these hills
Are good for grindstones.

The crane cries in the Nine Pools.
Its voice is heard in heaven.
The fish rest among islands
Or sink in the deep.
There is delight in gardens
Where sandalwood flowers.

Beneath the trees are the withered husks.
The stones on these hills
Are good for working jade.[2]

O Minister of War

O minister of war,
We are the king's fangs and claws.
Why have you piled on us this misery?
We have no place in which to rest.

O minister of war,
We are the king's claws and teeth.
Why have you piled on us this misery?
We have nowhere to lay our heads.

O minister of war,
Truly you have behaved curiously.
You have piled on us this misery.
Our mothers lack food.

The Spirit Tower

When he measured out the spirit tower[3]
And drew up the plans,
Great throngs of people worked on it
And in no time it was made.
While it was being built there was no haste:
The people came in great multitudes.

The king was in his spirit garden.
The does and stags lay down.
They were so sleek and fat,
The white birds were gleaming.
The king stood near the spirit pool
Where the thick fish came shining.

[2] It is difficult to understand how this song became included among the *Songs.* Even in the Chou dynasty there was great poverty, and another song, not included in the selection made by Confucius, reads:

Rather than sink among men
It is better to swim the deep:
He who sinks in the deep
Should prepare to swim.
He who sinks among men
Can have no hope of safety.

[3] Mencius, in a famous passage, interprets the poem as an example of morality, but it is difficult not to believe that the poet was extolling the magic virtue of kingly *power*. The tower in the lake was built by King Wen, the founder of the Chou dynasty, near his capital.

He erected the toothed bars
On which hung great drums and bells.
These bells and these drums sang together.
There was great joy in the tower in the lake.
These bells and these drums sang together.
There was great joy in the tower in the lake.
Boom-boom went the lizard-skin drums.
The blind and visionless performed their tasks.

The Blind Musicians [4]

The blind musicians, the blind musicians
In the courtyard of Chou,
They have set up their pillars and crossbars,
With upright plumes and hooks for the drums and bells—
The small and large drums are hanging there,
The tambourines, the stone chimes, the batons and tiger
    clappers.
When all have been struck the music begins.
Then the pipes and the flutes sound shrilly.
Sweet is the music,
August as the song of birds.
The ancestors listen:
They are our guests.
Forever and ever they gaze on our victories.

The Turbulent Waters

Amid the turbulent waters
The white rocks stand clean.
With a white coat and a red lappet
I followed you to Yueh.
Now that I have seen my lord
Shall I not rejoice?

Amid the turbulent waters
The white rocks are washed clean.
With a white coat and a red lappet
I followed you to Kao.
Now that I have seen my lord,
Why should I be sad?

Amid the turbulent waters
The white rocks are dashed clean.
I have heard that you are wedded:
I dare not talk to you.

[4] Musicians in China are traditionally blind.

There Is a Girl in Our Coach

There is a girl in our coach.
Her face is like falling mallow blossoms.
Oh, they rustle, oh, they glitter,
Jades and cornelians hanging from her belt.
She is the eldest daughter of Chiang—
Demure and sweet and lovely is she!

She is traveling the same road.
Her face is like a falling mallow flower.
Oh, they rustle, Oh, they glitter,
Ting-ling go the jade girdle gems.
She is the beautiful eldest daughter of Chiang;
Her virtue is memorable.

My Husband

Heiho, my husband is brave,
One among millions.
Watch him swinging his pole—
Outrider to the king's chariot.

My husband has gone to the east:
My head whirls like flying thistledown.
Should I perfume and anoint my hair?
Why should I try to look pretty?

Let the rain come, let the rain fall:
Oh, the sun shines all day.
I am always dreaming of my husband.
My head is heavy, my heart is breaking.

Where shall I find the day lily
To plant in the north of my house?
In grief I dream of my husband:
My heart is forlorn.

The Greater East

Crooked are the thornwood spoons:
The road to Chou is like a grindstone
And built straight as an arrow.
The high officers ride along,
The commoners gaze at them.
Full of longing I gaze after them;
My tears flow down in streams.

In the lesser east and the greater east
Empty are the shuttles and spools.
Lightly, lightly go their woven shoes.
The people walk through the hoarfrost.
Tweet-tweet go the young bloods[5]
Who ride along the road to Chou.
Empty we come, empty we go.
My heart is full of sorrow.

Cold water flowing from springs,
Do not soak my bundle of firewood.
Sorrowfully when we awake, we sigh:
Alas, we are now deserted.
Bundles of wood, bundles of firewood:
I wish I could ride in a carriage.
Alas, we are now deserted.
If only there were peace!

The men of the east
Continually working, receiving no comfort.
The men of the west
Shining in their splendid garments.[6]
The sons of the boatmen
Wearing many kinds of bear fur.
The sons of the slaves
Taking what chance employment.

If they have wine,
They put up their noses at sauce.
Their girdle pendants are so long,
And yet they wish them longer.
The Milky Way in heaven
Shines on all brightly.
The Weaving Lady[7] sits on her stool.
Seven times a day she labors over her loom.

Seven times a day she labors over her loom,
Receiving no shining presents.
The Draft Ox glitters and shines:
He is not yoked to our carts.

[5] *T'iao-t'iao*, which I have translated *tweet-tweet*, is a satirically musical expression for the mincing gait of the young fops who have obtained wealth in the city.

[6] "Shining" is expressed by *ts'ao-ts'ao*.

[7] The Weaving Lady is in Lyra, the Draft Ox in Aquila. They lie on either side of the Milky Way, and once a year they are allowed to meet. The Draft Ox later became transformed into the Herd Boy. The Opener of Brightness is the morning star, the Lengthener of Roads the evening star. The Sieve is in the Hyades, and the Winnowing Fan in Sagittarius.

In the east is the Opener of Brightness,
In the west is the Lengthener of Roads.
Curved are the nets of heaven:
They have their appointed places.

In the south is the Sieve:
But it cannot sift grain.
In the north is the Ladle:
It cannot ladle out wine.
In the south is the Sieve,
The holes wide-open.
In the north is the Ladle,
The handle turned to the west.

The Precipitous Rocks

Oh, these precipitous rocks!
So high, so high!
The mountains and streams never end,
The journey goes on and on;
The soldiers who are sent to the east
Have no time to rest.

Oh, these precipitous rocks!
So high, so high!
The mountains and streams never end,
The journeys never end.
The soldiers who are sent to the east
Have no time to settle down.

There are swine with white trotters
Wading through the swollen stream.[8]
The moon is caught in the Hyades;
There will be great rains.
The soldiers who are sent to the east
Think only of this.

All Grasses Are Yellow

All grasses are yellow.
Every day we are out marching.
All our men taken,
Defending the frontier.

[8] Sometimes assumed to be an ill omen, but the trotters may be the soldiers themselves.

Take Up the Fish

Take up the fish in baskets,[6]
Yellow-jaw, red-ray.
Our host has wine,
Sweet and plenty.

Take up the fish in baskets,
Bream and tench.
Our host has wine,
Plenty and sweet.

Take up the fish in baskets,
White fish and carp.
Our host has wine,
Abundant and sweet.

The viands will be plenty,
All of them good.
The viands will be scented,
And of all kinds.
The viands will be piled high,
And all in due season!

The Rent Basket

Rent is the basket at the dam
Where bream and carp abound.
The lady of Ch'i has come home,
With a cloud of servitors.

Rent is the basket at the dam,
Where bream and tench abound.
The lady of Ch'i has come home,
With a rain of followers.

Rent is the basket of the dam,
The fishes go in and out freely.
The lady of Ch'i has come home,
Her attendants are like a stream.[7]

Wings of the Dragonfly

Wings of the dragonfly—
Robes shining in splendor.
My heart is grieving.
To whom shall I turn for rest?

[6] Probably the basket suspended beneath the slit dam.
[7] This would appear to be a song directed against some loose lady of rank.

Young wings of dragonflies,
Robes gaily embroidered.
My heart is grieving.
To whom shall I turn for peace?

The dragonfly bursts from the cocoon,
Hemp clothes white as snow.
My heart is grieving.
In whom shall I seek my love?

No Clothes

You say you have no clothes:
I will share my quilted gown with you.
The king is raising an army.
I will make ready my spear and lance.
I will be your comrade.

You say you have no clothes:
I will share my vest with you.
The king is raising an army.
I will make ready my spear and halberd,
And in the ranks join you.

You say you have no clothes:
I will share my quilt with you.
The king is raising an army.
I will make ready my jerkin and arms,
And march along with you.

The Woodman's Ax

Ting, ting goes the woodman's ax,
The bird sings *ying, ying*.
Leave the dark valley,
Climb the high tree.
Ying he sings again,
Looking for company.
See how even a bird
Searches after its mate.
How can a man dispense
With comrades and friends?
Spiritual beings are listening
Whether we are in harmony and peace.

Hoo, hoo go the hewers of wood,
I have strained my wine clear through the sieve,
I have a five-month-old lamb,
I have invited my father's brothers.
If they should not come,
It is not I who neglected them.
Oh, everything is swept clean—
Here are meats, here are eight dishes of grain,
Here a fatted ox.
I have invited my mother's brothers.
If they should not come,
Am I to blame?

They fell the trees on the slopes.
Such an abundance of wine has been strained!
The dishes are all ready.
Elder brothers, younger brothers—all of you come closer.
If people are wanting in strength,
Lay the fault to parched throats.
I strain the wine if I have it,
If I have none I buy.
I beat on the drum—*boom, boom.*
Swiftly I lead the dance.
When there is time on our hands,
Oh, let us drink pure wine!

The Good-Looking Boy

The good-looking boy
Is waiting for me in the lane.
Why should I not go with him?

The fair-looking boy
Is waiting for me in the hall.
Why should I not go with him?

In my embroidered coat, my cloak of lain,
In my embroidered skirt, my gown of lain.
My dear, my darling,
Take me in your coach!

In my embroidered skirt, my gown of lain,
In my embroidered coat, my cloak of lain,
My dear, my darling,
Take me with you when you go home!

Willows at the East Gate

The willows at the east gate
Have thick glossy leaves.
At dusk we were to meet.
Now the morning star glimmers.

The willows at the east gate
Have tufts of bright leaves.
At dusk we were to meet.
Now the morning star shines bright.

The Collar

Blue, blue is your collar[8]
My heart longs for you.
Even though I do not see you,
Why do you send no news?

Blue, blue is your girdle,
My heart grieves for you.
Even though I do not go to you,
Why do you not come?

So nimble, so changeful,
There on the tower on the wall—
One day without seeing you
Is like three months!

The Quince

He gave me a quince,
I gave him a jade pendant,
Not in repayment,
But to make our love lasting.

He gave me a peach,
I gave him an emerald,
Not in repayment,
But to make our love lasting.

He gave me a plum,
I gave him black jade,
Not in repayment,
But to make our love endure.

[8] Students wore blue collars up to the time of the Revolution. In the old days "blue collar" described a graduate of the first class. The poem would appear to be a lament by a wife when her husband goes up to take the imperial examination.

Shu Has Gone Hunting

Shu has gone hunting,
Driving a team of four horses.
He holds the reins like silk tassels,
The two outer horses are prancing.
Shu is in the marshlands,
The flames rise all around:
Stripped to the waist, grappling tigers,
He offers them at the prince's palace.
"O Shu, do not be rash!
Take care, they will harm you!"

Shu has gone hunting,
Driving his team of bays.
The two inside horses step high,
The two outside keep line like a flight of wild geese.
Shu is in the marshlands.
How well he shoots!
How skillfully he drives!
Now giving rein, now checking them,
Now flinging the arrows, now swinging the bow.

Shu has gone hunting,
Driving with four grays,
The two inside keeping abreast,
The two outside like hands.[9]
Shu is in the marshlands,
The flames are smoldering.
The horses move slowly,
Now he shoots rarely,
Now he lays aside his quiver.
Now he puts the bow in the case.

The Iron-Gray Horses

The sleek iron-gray horses
He holds with his six reins.
The duke's beloved boy,
Following the duke on the winter chase.

The boars in their seasons,
The boars running wild,
The duke says: "To your left!"
Bending the bow, he brings them down.

[9] I.e., moving together like the fingers of a hand.

In cavalcade through the north gardens
The teams come prancing,
Light chariots with bells at bridle,
Whippets and greyhounds running beside.

Our Chariots Are Strong

Our chariots so strong,
Our horses well matched,
With four lusty steeds each,
We yoked and drove eastward.

So gleaming the hunting chariots,
So sturdy the four horses.
To the east are the great grasslands.
We yoked and set out for the hunt.

The lords go on the foray
With picked men—*hiao-hiao!*
Our banners are unfurled
When we hunt in Kao country.

With teams of four horses,
So huge and so many,
With red leggings, gold slippers
They come to the Great Meet.

Thimbles and greaves are slipped on,
Bows and arrows are made ready;
Bowmen are assembled,
And serve to fire the brushwood.[1]

We drive the four bays,
The two outriders not swerving.
Faultlessly they gallop along:
Arrows fly—splitting asunder.

Softly the horses neigh,
Gently the banners wave,
Quietly go footmen and charioteers
That our kitchens may not be empty.

My lord is on his foray!
Quietly acclaim his fame.
Truly he is a great prince,
Stupendous is the bag![2]

[1] An alternative reading would give: And serve to pile high the game.
[2] Compare with the first of the "Stone Drum" poems.

The Beginning of the People

The beginning of the people
Came from Chiang Yuan.[3]
How did she give birth to the people?
She sacrificed and made offerings.
That her barrenness might be removed,
She trod in the footprints of God,
Was quickened, blessings came to her:
Early in the morning she became pregnant,
She gave birth, she brought forth.
This was Hou Chi.[4]

When she had fulfilled her months,
Her first-born came like a lamb.
There was no bursting, no rending,
Nor hurt, nor harm,
To make manifest his spirit power.
Did not God on high give her ease?
Did not God accept her sacrifices?
So she easily gave birth to a son.

He was placed in a narrow byre:
Sheep and oxen tenderly tended him.
He was placed in a low forest:[5]
The woodcutters came to the low forest.
He was placed on the cold ice:
A bird covered him with its wings.
When the bird winged away,
Hou Chi began to yell.
His cry was long and loud,
And could be heard from near and far.

When he could crawl,
How lithe and splendid his limbs!
As soon as he put food to his lips,
He learned to plant large beans.
The beans grew like waving banners.

[3] Chiang Yuan was the consort of the emperor K'u, the third emperor following the Yellow Emperor. He reigned around 2436 B.C.

[4] Hou Chi, the ancestral founder of the Chou dynasty, is here celebrated as the inventor of agriculture and sacrifices. It is possible, but not certain, that he is the same culture hero as Shen Nung, who was born on the river Chiang—which has the same Chinese character as Chiang Yuan. He became director of agriculture under the emperor Yao. Chi means "castaway."

[5] I.e., not in a forest on the mountains.

The rice rows were packed close together,
Riotously the hemp and wheat grew,
The young gourds crowding together.

The reaping of Hou Chi
Was such that it assisted the Way.[6]
He cleared the thick weeds,
He planted the yellow seeds,
Made the grain burst through its sheath,
So heavy, so tall,
So filled with goodness,
So juicy, so tender,
So strong and limber:
Thus he became Lord of T'ai.

He conferred lovely grains on us.
Black millet, double-kerneled,
Red millet and white.[7]
Everywhere the black was sown;
It was reaped and acred.
Everywhere the red and white were sown,
They were carried on shoulders and backs.
They were brought home for first offerings.

How shall we make our offerings?
We hull the grain, we pound it,
We soften it, we tread it,
We wash it till it crackles,
Distill it till the steam rises.
Then we consult the augurs, then we meditate,
Then we gather southernwood, then we burn
        the fats.
We sacrifice the rams to the spirits,
Roast flesh and broiled flesh—
So begins the fruitful year![8]

Altars are piled high with offerings,
Vessels of wood, vessels of earthenware.
As soon as a perfume ascends,
Supreme God is blessed with peace.
How great a fragrance in this auspicious time!
Hou Chi founded this sacrifice.
And assuredly there must be no change:
It has been handed down to the present time.

[6] I.e., worked together with heaven and earth.
[7] The black, according to the commentators, was used in sacrifices and
the red in offerings.
[8] The sacrifice was offered in the first month of winter.

FROM THE FOUNTAIN OF OLD POEMS

Shin Teh-ts'en, a scholar of the Ch'ing dynasty, was the first to collect together in a single volume, called *The Fountain of Old Poems*, the scattered verses that are to be found in the ancient writings of the Chinese. The poems come from different sources: the *Tso Chuan*, the *Shu Ching*, the Analects, Huai Nan-tzu, and others. Some pieces were found on tombstones, another was inscribed on a piece of old jade, a third on a bathing vessel. Most of these pieces are later than the *Book of Songs*, but no exact dates for any of them are known to modern scholars.

------ ～ ------

Song of the Splendid Clouds[1]

The emperor Shun announces his determination to resign the throne in favor of Yu

O splendid, glowing clouds,
Fill the world with color.
O sun and moon, make bright and fair
The dawn forever and ever.

Rejoinder of the eight ministers

Bright, bright is heaven above,
Splendid are the stars outspread.
The sun and moon made bright and fair
Only by the power of One Man.[2]

Rejoinder of the emperor Shun

The sun and moon have their paths,
The stars are held to their courses,
The four seasons observe the changes,

[1] The patriarch emperor Shun resigned the throne in 2010 B.C. at the age of ninety-four. In 1912, nearly four thousand years after the supposed composition of the song, it became the national hymn of the Republic.
[2] I.e., the Emperor, the "lonely one."

The ten thousand creatures are obedient.
Such music as I speak of
Corresponds to the spirit of heaven,
Leading to virtue and excellence.
Let all men listen to it!
Vigorously strike the drums!
Dance high to it!
My pure splendor has come to an end.
I lift up my robes and disappear.

Song of the Peasants

The emperor Yao was walking one day in the country when he came upon some peasants playing the game of yang *and heard them singing:*

We work when the sun rises,
We rest when the sun sets.
We dig wells for drink,
We plow the land for food.
What has the power of the Emperor
　　　to do with us?

Song of the White Clouds

There are white clouds in the heaven,
Great cliffs are lifted upward,
Interminable are the roads of earth,
Mountains and rivers bar the way:
I pray you not to die.
Please try to come again.

Song of the South Wind

The fragrance of the south wind
Can comfort the anger of my people.
The timely coming of the south wind
Can increase the gain of my people.

Song of the Wheat in Flower

The flowers of the wheat are in spike,
The rice and millet are gleaming wet.
Oh, the crafty boy,
Why is he not good to me?

Inscribed on a Jade Tablet of Yu

Chu-ying was lord of this place and produced this flower.
Bathed in the sun, washed in the moon, among the hundred
    precious things I grew.

The Cow-Feeders' Song

On the barren south hill
The white rocks gleam,
Born when neither Yao nor Shun resign their thrones,
Wearing a strip of cloth that reaches hardly to my knees,
From the sun's awakening to the mid of night I feed cattle.
Long is the night—when comes the dawn?
In the waters of Ts'ang Lang the white rocks are gleaming.
There is a carp a foot and a half long.
Wearing some tattered cloth that reaches hardly to my knees,
From the clear dawning to mid of night I feed the cattle.
O you yellow calves, go uphill and lie down.
I will be minister in the state of Tzu.
Going out of the east gate they rub horns on the rocks,
The splendid pines and the green yews above them.
My tattered clothes are frayed and raveled,
In my time there are no emperors like Yao and Shun.
My cattle, grow strong and eat the sweet grass.
There is a great minister among you.
I will go with you to the state of Tzu.

Song of the Emperor Yu on the Making of the Nine Tripods [3]

Gleaming, gleaming are the white clouds,
In the north and south,
In the east and west,
When the nine tripods are cast,
They will be handed down for the three dynasties.

A Prayer at Winter Thanksgiving

Earth, return to your place,
Water, flow back into ditches,
Insects, do not come swarming,
Let grasses and trees grow in the marshlands.

[3] The casting of tripods for presentation to the ruler was the traditional
mark of esteem by the people. The repetition of words like "splendid"
and "gleaming" in these early poems seems to suggest a delight in life
and color that the Chinese shared with the Greeks, who worshiped all
shining things—germ or sea or cloud.

A Warning by the Emperor Yao

Tremble, be fearful,
Night and day be careful,
Men do not trip over mountains:
They fall over earth mounds.

TAO TEH CHING

Of the author of the eighty-one poems included in the *Tao Teh Ching,* the classic of the Way of Virtue, we know almost nothing. According to the *Shih-chi,* he was "a native of Chu-jen hamlet, in Li-hsiang, in the district of K'u, in the state of Ch'u. His proper name was Erh, his courtesy name Pai-yang, his pseudonym Tan, and his family name Li. He was keeper of the state archives of Chou. After residing in Chou for a long time he perceived that the state was enfeebled and on its way to decline; thereupon he gave up his position and went away. No one knows where he died. It appears that he lived to be more than one hundred years old, and some say more than two hundred years old. . . ."

Almost certainly the book was not composed by one man: equally certainly someone who was called Lao Tzu took some part in it. We can recognize here and there in the accepted canon of the work the accents of a single individual, who was at once scholar, poet, and statesman—a man who liked quietness, and who saw in quietness the root of all things, the place where all things return. The idea of the "return" which is continually repeated through the book, is more important than the idea of the "way": for without the return of things to their roots, there would hardly have been any poetry in the book. The first poem included here introduces a theme that is absent from the *Book of Songs,* though henceforward we shall come across it continually in Chinese poetry. Here is the theme of Tao Yuan-ming's prose fragment called "The Peach-Blossom Fountain," and here is the theme of innumerable poems of Li Po. "There is no going without returning," says the inscription under the Tai Hexagram in the *Book of Changes.* It is out of such simple things that poetry is made.

But though the idea of the return is cardinal in the poems of the *Tao Teh Ching*—for it is perhaps necessary to insist that the book is almost wholly written in rhymed irregular verse—other and vaster themes are included, and it is through the interplay of a few dominant themes mercilessly repeated and examined that the book acquires its curious beauty. The Fountain, the Vast Simplicity, the Entrance of the Female, the nature of Quietness, the silent working of nature, the powers of the Sage—all these are examined critically and passed in review by a mind that is curiously transparent and curiously Chinese, hating war, delighting in simple things, attempting with all the powers at its command to reinforce rather than dominate nature. Man must not fight against nature. He must follow the Way—and the Way is not necessarily the path of least resistance, for the stars do not follow the path of least resistance. But the Way cannot be described in words, and the poet can only ceaselessly hint at it, inventing new images and discovering in a combination of many images the nature of the mysterious movements of all things.

The book was written at a time of war and shows signs at times of the strain of war. Always there is the implied lament for things past and things lost. In a passage almost certainly written in prose, Lao Tzu describes a vision of contentment:

The country is small, but has few inhabitants, only tens and hundreds. Even though they have all the trappings of the age, they do not require them. The people venerate death, they are not driven to welcome it or to migrate to distant places to avoid famine and misery. Even though there are boats and carriages, they do not need to travel. Even though they have coats of mail and weapons, they do not fight. Savory is their food, beautiful their clothing, simple their living, and happy their customs. They may see in the distance neighboring villages, and even hear the cocks crowing and dogs barking, and yet these people attain great age and live until death in such contentment that they do not go to see others.

So might a man have written in the trenches, seeing the whole world falling about his ears; and few things are more certain than that the book was written in the time of confusion known as the Warring States. But of everything else concerning the genesis of the book we remain ignorant.

I have included here the twenty-eight poems that seem to me to have the greatest poetic value. They have been taken out of their accepted order and arranged to show the development of the ideas of the "root" and the "return."

I

Go to the end of the Void,
Hold fast to Quietness!
All things are stirring.
I have beheld them in the place where they return.
See, all things are flowering,
But all return to the root.
The return to the root is called Quietness.
The return is destiny.
Constant is the destined return.
To know this constancy is to be illumined.
Not to know constancy
Is to run blindly into disaster.
He who knows constancy

Knows all things.
Justice is kingly,
Kingship is heavenly,
Heavenly is the Way,
The Way is eternal.
Though the body decays, such a man never dies!

II

The Way can only return.
All you can do is to become weak.
Though everything under heaven is born from being,
Being is born from nothingness.

III

The spirit of the Fountain never dies:
It is called the Mysterious Female.
The entrance to the Mysterious Female
Is the root of all Heaven and Earth.
Frail, frail it is, hardly existing,
But touch it: it will never run dry.

IV

Before Heaven and Earth were born
There was something formless yet complete.
Silent! Empty!
Changeless! Hanging on nothingness!
Pervading all things! Unending!
We say it is the Mother of all things under heaven,
But we do not know its real name.
We call it the Way.
We say it is Great.

To be Great is to go forward,
To go forward is to travel far,
To travel far is to return.

Great is the Way,
Great are Heaven and Earth,
Great is Man.[1]
Among the four great things
Man has his place.
Man follows Earth,
Earth follows Heaven,
Heaven follows the Way,
The Way follows itself.

[1] Some editions read "the emperor" for "man."

V

Away with learning! Away with grieving!
Between *wei* and *o*[2]
Where is the difference?
Between good and evil,
Where is the difference?
Must a man fear
What is feared by others?
Oh, pure idiocy!
All men are beaming with pleasure
As though feasting at the Great Sacrifice,
As though climbing the Spring Terrace:
I alone am silent, I have given no sign.
Like an infant who has not yet smiled,
Abandoned, like someone homeless.
All men have enough and to spare,
I alone seem to have nothing.
I am a man with the mind of an idiot,
A pure fool.
Everywhere men shine:
I alone am dark.
Everywhere men are gay:
I alone am disquieted,
Nervous as the sea,
Drifting, never ceasing.
Everywhere men have work:
I alone am stubborn, taking no part.
The chief difference lies in this:
I prize the breasts of the Mother.

VI

What the eye gazes at and cannot see is called "beyond vision,"
What the ear listens for and cannot hear is called "beyond
sound,"
What the hands feel for and cannot touch is called "without
substance."
These three can never be fathomed.
They become one thing.
Revealed, it is not dazzling.
Hidden, it is not dark.
Endless the things without name
Which return to where there is nothing.
They are called shapes without shape,
Forms without form,
Shadows, emblems.
Face them, you will see no front,
Follow them, you will see no back.

[2] Different forms of "yes"?

Lay hold of the ancient way:
Then you will possess the present.
To know the beginning of antiquity
Is to follow the thread of the Way.

VII

Be humble, you will be whole.
Bend, you will be straight.
Be hollow, you will be filled.
Be broken, you will be mended.
Possess little, you will have much.
Have much, you will be cast down.
Therefore the Sage holds to the One,
And measures all things under heaven.
He does not show himself.
Therefore he shines.
He does not proclaim himself;
Therefore he is clearly seen.
He does not praise himself;
Therefore he wins victories.
He is not proud of his handiwork;
Therefore it lasts forever.
He alone does not contend;
Therefore none under heaven can contend with him.
The ancient saying: "Be humble; you will be made whole"—
Wise words!
To reach wholeness one must return!

VIII

Would a man lay siege to the whole world and make it his own?
I have seen that he will not succeed.
All beneath heaven is a sacred vessel.
Do not tamper with it,
Do not make it your own.
Tampering with it you will spoil it,
Making it your own you will lose it.
For all creatures there is a time for advancing, a time for withdrawal,
A time for inhaling, a time for exhaling,
A time for growing strong, a time for decay,
A time for creation, a time for destruction.
Therefore the Sage avoids the extremes, the extravagant, the exalted.

IX

Where there is the Way under heaven,
Galloping horses fertilize the fields with their droppings.
When there is the Way under heaven,
War horses breed on the sacred mounds.
There is no enticement greater than envy,

No disaster greater than discontent,
No evil greater than covetousness.
He who knows the contentment that comes from content
Is ever content.

X

The Way is eternal and has no name,
An uncarved block, seemingly of little moment,
Yet greater than anything under heaven.
Should a duke or a prince cling to it,
Then the ten thousand people would render him homage,
Heaven and Earth would be in harmony,
Sending down a rain of sweet dew.
Peace and order would reign among the people.
Once the block is carved there are names,
But when there are names
Already it is time to stop.
Knowing when to stop prevents you from entering danger.
Into the Way come all things under heaven
As streams and torrents into rivers and the sea.

XI

Whatever is shrunk
Must first have been stretched.
Whatever is weak
Must first have been strong.
Whatever is thrown down
Must first have been set up.
Whatever is given
Must first have been taken.
This is called the dark illumination:
Soft weakness overcomes hard strength.
As a fish should not leap from the deep,
So should the sharp weapons of the nations
Never be shown.[3]

XII

If you hold the Great Form [4]
And go all over the empire,
There is no harm in your going,
There is peace and very quietness.
Music and good dishes
May make the stranger pause,
But the mouth of Tao,
So mild and flavorless—
Look in it, there is nothing to see,
Listen to it, there is nothing to hear,
Use it, it is never ending.

[3] The last three lines would appear to be later interpolations.
[4] I.e., the Way.

XIII

Silent words ripen of themselves:
A whirlwind does not last a whole morning,
Pelting rain does not last a whole day.
Who made them?
Heaven and Earth!
Heaven and Earth cannot make them last long.
How much less can man?
He who follows the Way
Becomes like the Way.
He who follows power
Becomes like power.
He who suffers loss
Becomes like loss.
He who conforms to the Way,
The Way joyfully welcomes.
He who conforms to power,
Power joyfully welcomes.
He who conforms to loss,
Loss joyfully welcomes.
If you are lacking in faith
Others will fail you.

XIV

The highest form of goodness is like water;
The goodness of water benefits all peoples, and does not strive:
Water is content with places detested by men.
So is the Way.

Earth makes good houses,
Depth makes good hearts,
Gentleness makes good friends,
Truth makes good speech,
Order makes good government,
Goodness makes good deeds,
Timeliness makes good actions.

Let there be no striving
Lest mistakes are made.

XV

Heaven is eternal, Earth enduring.
Why are Heaven and Earth eternal and enduring?
Because they do not live for themselves,
They live forever.

The Sage who desires to be last puts himself first,
If he desires to be outside, he finds himself surviving.
If he strives with no personal aims,
Everything he desires is given to him.

XVI

Those who in ancient days were the best commanders
Were those who were delicate, subtle, mysterious, profound,
Their minds too deep to be fathomed.
We can only speak of them as they appeared to the world.
Hesitant like one wading a winter stream,
Fearful like one seeing danger all round him,
Courteous like someone accepting an invitation,
Yielding like ice about to melt,
Vacant as an uncarved block,
Empty as a cave,
Dark as a muddy pool.
Who can become the dark pool, and in the end be so clear?
Who can become so dead, and in the end be so alive?
Those who follow Tao do not try to brim over:
Because they do not brim over,
They are like seeds and are eternally renewed.

XVII

The five colors lead to blindness,
The five tones deafen the ear,
The five flavors dull the palate.
Hunting and the chase have power to drive men mad;
Rare possessions tempt men to wrong deeds.
Therefore the Sage follows the belly,[5] not the eye:
He abandons "that" and takes "this."

XVIII

To know people is to be wise,
To know oneself is to be illumined,
To conquer others is to have strength,
To conquer oneself is to have power,
To be content is to have great wealth,
Devotedly to follow the Way is to fulfill all aims:
He who stays where he is is enduring.
To die and not to be lost—this is called "long life."

XIX

Can the moving soul be One,
Never losing hold?
Can you breathe light as a child?
Can your breath be controlled?
Can you cleanse the mysterious mirror,
Leaving no trace whatever?
Can you love people, rule nature,
Yet remain unknown?

[5] I.e., what is within.

At the opening and closing of the gates of Heaven,[6]
Can you take the part of the woman?
All-seeing, all-knowing?
Can you do nothing?

Rear them, then feed them!
Rear them, do not lay hold on them!
Subdue them, do not touch them!
Be their commander, but do not command them!
Here lies mysterious power.

XX

Away with sages! Away with wise men!
The people will gain a hundredfold.
Away with charity! Away with morality!
The people will return to piety and goodness.
Away with skill! Away with profit!
Then there will be no more robbers and thieves.
If these three revolutions are insufficient,
Then let men
Gaze on simplicity, hold the uncarved block,
Be selfless, have few desires.

XXI

Heaven and Earth are without benevolence.
To them all the creatures are but as straw dogs.[7]
The Sage has no benevolence:
To him the hundred families are but as straw dogs.
The space between Heaven and Earth
Is a blacksmith's bellows,
Vacant, inexhaustible.
Move it: plenty comes forth.
Many words cannot fathom it.
Look—it is in your heart!

XXII

That which no one knows is the Highest,
Next comes that which we love and praise,
Next comes that which we fear,
Next comes that which we despise.
When you are lacking in faith,
Others will be faithless to you.
How far away is the Sage, how few his words,
His task over, his work done,
The hundred families cry: Look, we did it ourselves!

[6] Perhaps the nostrils, but there may be deliberate imagery based on the
"Mysterious Female." See III and V.
[7] Straw animals used for sacrifices.

XXIII

Join together thirty spokes—you have a wheel:
Where there is nothing,
The wheel is useful.
Mold clay together—make a vessel:
There where there is nothing,
The vessel is useful.
Cut out doors and windows to make a house:
There where there is nothing,
The house is useful.
Though there are advantages in being,
Nothingness is useful.

XXIV

When the great man hears of Tao
Diligently he pursues it;
When the mediocre man hears of Tao
He cannot make up his mind.
When the small man hears of Tao
He laughs uproariously:
If he did not laugh, there would be no such thing as Tao.
The wise men say:
The bright way seems dark,
The way forward seems backward,
The smooth way seems rugged,
Highest virtue seems the deepest descent,
Pure white seems black,
Abounding virtue seems unavailing,
Steadfast virtue seems unfounded,
Complete virtue seems annihilation.
The Great Square has no corners,
The Great Vessel ripens late,
The Great Sound is silent,
The Great Form is without shape.[8]
The Tao is hidden and nameless;
Only Tao upholds all things
And brings them to fulfillment.

XXV

Tao gives birth to One,
One gives birth to Two,
Two gives birth to Three:
Three gives birth to all things.
All things are dark on one side and bright on the other:
Their breaths when blended together make a harmony.
Man hates most
Being helpless, being small, being pitiable:

[8] The Great Form, the Great Vessel, etc., are all names for the Tao
(the Way) seen under differing aspects.

Yet princes and barons call themselves by these names.[9]
That which increases diminishes:
That which diminishes increases.
What others have taught
I also will teach:
"The strong[1] man comes to a strong death."
Such a man I will have for my teacher.

XXVI

The great Tao is unanchored: goes left and right.
The ten thousand creatures are nourished by it and never
    denied.
It creates them, and makes no demands on them;
It clothes them, but has no mastery.
So it is called "humble."
The ten thousand creatures are fashioned by it, but it has no
    mastery:
So it is called "great."
Only that which does not know itself as great
Is able to assume greatness.

XXVII

He who would Tao in the service of a king
Does not conquer an empire by armed power:
It would turn back on him.
Where there are soldiers
Are thorns and brambles.
Where great armies pass
Are calamitous years.
Therefore the good general only protects:
He does not exploit his power.
Success does not make him boastful,
Success does not make him elated,
Success does not make him proud,
Success does not make him go further,
Success does not make him resort to power.
There is a time of youth and a time of decay:
This is not Tao.
What is not Tao soon perishes.

[9] It was the custom of the emperors from the most ancient times to
describe themselves as "the only one," "the lonely one." Lao Tzu (or
whoever is the author of the *Tao Teh Ching*) is here cynically taking
them according to their own words, and foreshadowing the doctrine of
"the rectification of names," which was later to be employed by Confucius. Much of the *Tao Teh Ching* contains a subdued but savage attack
on the state, deliberately setting the prestige of the sage against the
prestige of the emperor, and inculcating a kind of passive anarchism—
when the state rules according to the will of heaven, then government
will become as "easy as cooking little fishes."
[1] As opposed to the princes who call themselves weak. The real strength
lies in the Tao.

XXVIII

Know the male,
Cleave to the female,
Be the abyss of all things under heaven:
He who is the abyss of all things under heaven
Knows a power that is never exhausted,
Returns again to a state of infancy.
Know the white,
Cleave to the black,[2]
Follow the design of all things under heaven:
He who follows the design of all things under heaven
Knows a power that is effortless,
Returns again to the unbounded.
Know glory,
Cleave to ignominy,
Become the fountain of all things under heaven.
He who becomes the fountain of all things under heaven
Knows a power that is limitless,
Returns again to the uncarved block.
A block may be shaped into vessels,
But when the Sage uses it
He makes leaders of men:
"The great carver does not cut."

[2] I.e., the dark *ying,* or passive element of nature.

CHU YUAN (332–296 B.C.)

Like Confucius, Li Po, and Li Ho, Chu Yuan claimed descent from the imperial family, and there is a curious nobility and fantasy in his works. He is among the greatest of Chinese poets, but his death is remembered more than his life, and his sufferings are remembered more than his rare moments of happiness. On the fifth day of the fifth moon his death by suicide in the Milo River is celebrated all over China by dragon festivals and by offerings of rice thrown on the water. He would hardly approve of his popularity thousands of years after his death, for he seems to have possessed the soul of a recluse haunting the wild riverbanks, continually thinking of his own death and of a strange fairyland inhabited by the ancient gods and by the river nymphs of his imagination.

He lived at a time of remorseless wars, when King Huai (329–299) was busily attempting to extend the frontiers of his kingdom. Holding a high appointment at the court, Chu Yuan objected against the use of force, but without effect; in 303 he was banished, and never returned to power. Thereafter he wandered over the countryside, principally in the region of the vast inland T'ung-ting Lake in northern Hunan, collecting legends, rearranging the odes of the people, and writing the tragic complaint against the Emperor that is known as the *Li Sao,* until he could bear his fate no longer and drowned himself. He was not made for this world. He demanded of the imperial counselors more purity than they can have been expected to possess; but his haunting grief, his strangely brilliant imagination, and the grace of his poetry remain as perpetual reminders that purity is essential.

He did not always follow the legends. Liu Hsieh, writing in the sixth century A.D., objected that his falcon acting as a go-between was unscriptural, and his literary treatment of the two ladies of the Hsiang River was not in accordance with the *Tso Chuan,* the great historical work compiled by Confucius. Chu Yuan would hardly have cared: he found his legends among the people, and changed them to suit his convenience, and there is good reason for believing that he deliberately merged together a number of songs to produce his great hymns, which are included here. He would prefer to have known that a Han emperor would have fallen in love with *Li Sao* and that prince Huai Nan would have written his biography, now lost. Of his poetry, Liu Hsieh said in a famous rhythmical essay: "When he speaks of his sufferings, we are pierced to the heart, and when he describes mountains and streams, we hear their sounds and see them before us, and when he talks of times and seasons, as we unroll the poem, we see the times and seasons before us." And he concludes an astonishingly vivid essay by describing the poet's habit of genius: "His genius was so great, and the smoke of it curled so high, and there were such visions of illimitable mountains and streams, and such logic and feeling in his work, that I might say his face was of gold and his appearance of jade, his beauty outshining all things and as light as a hair."

His influence was immense. Not only the Han dynasty poets, but poets of much later ages worshiped him until he was regarded as a kind of god of poetry. Like Vergil, he acquired magical legends after his death. He was always spoken of in hyperboles. Even the historian Ssu-ma Ch'ien, usually so critical, described him as "a man who, though cast in mud and filth, was touched with no impurity; and with such a heart he may be said to rival the sun and moon in giving brightness." The reader of an English translation of his work may not be expected to agree, but it is hoped that he will at least agree on the dazzling quality of the poet's imagination.

———————— ❧ ————————

The Nine Songs[1]

The Nine Songs may not be entirely the work of Chu Yuan; there is increasing evidence that he did little more than adapt and perhaps put in order some songs that he found during his wanderings. Even Wang Yi, the earliest editor and commentator of the songs, held this opinion, and recent scholarship has done no more than reinforce the earlier opinion. It seems probable that the songs were originally composed in the language of the state of Ch'u, which was not Chinese but a form of Tai, belonging to the Indo-Chinese group of languages. But even though the original songs were neither Chinese nor composed by Chu Yuan, the imagery is so distinctly his, and the feeling so evidently springs from the same sources as the *Li Sao,* which has been translated here as *Encountering Sorrow,* that it is difficult not to believe that he changed them according to his purpose, and gave vent to his own feelings.

They would appear to be shamanistic songs sung by young and beautifully dressed priestesses, perhaps over tripods that contained scented herbs, and perhaps in a state of trance. The

[1] Though they are called *The Nine Songs (Chu K'o),* they are nine only by Chinese mathematics; eleven have come down to us. The last two may have been inserted later.

continual use of flight imagery, the references to the soaring
and swooping of the gods, suggest the kind of imagery and
the kind of imagination that occur in dreams or intoxication
by gods. In their present state, the colloquies between the gods
and the ministrants have a headlong speed that is entirely lacking in the more muted *Book of Songs*. And even the deliberate
eroticism seems to be foreign, entirely unlike the more
deliberately unsuggestive verses of the Ch'u dynasty, where
love affairs and the woman's longing for the man are treated
with a quiet compassion and a grave tenderness.

The poems to the two arbiters of fate suggest that two
different tribal songs have been incorporated. The relationship
between the two arbiters, or why there should be two arbiters
at all, is never clearly stated. The commentator of the *Hou
Han-shu* says: "The Arbiter of Fate is a spirit, the superior of
the destroyers. He measures eight feet, has a small nose, is
farsighted, has much moustache, and is lean"—a description
that hardly tallies with Chu Yuan's description. Once Chuang-
tzu talked in a dream to a skull and said: "If I could induce the
Arbiter of Fate to restore your body to life, would you wish
for this?" Wang Yi comments: "As master of the Yin he kills.
As master of the Yang he gives life. The Arbiter of Fate always mounts the clear atmosphere of heaven and directs the
destiny of everyone's life and death"—a commentary that adds
nothing, as usual, to the original. What is remarkable is that
the erotic tinge, which occurs throughout the poems, should be
most evident in the hymns to the two arbiters of fate.

For a further elucidation of the complex problems involved
in the hymns, see Eduard Erckes, *The God of Death in
Ancient China, Tung-pao*, XXXV, 1–3.

I. THE GREAT UNITY, THE SOVEREIGN OF THE EAST[2]

On this auspicious day, at the felicitous hour,
Joyously we entertain the Sovereign Lord.
With long swords and jade guards in our hands,
With girdles of lapis lazuli tinkling *ling-lang,*
We offer jade gifts on mats of fairy grass.
Holding up fragrant grasses and jades,
We pour libations of pepper juice and cinnamon wine.
The drumsticks are raised: we beat the drums.
Psalters and zithers unfold in a great harmony.
The ministrants dance in flowing silks and resplendent robes.
A wafting fragrance fills the spaces of the hall,
And the five tones in crowded chorus sing:
Glory and gladness to the happy lord!

[2] The Lord of the East, *Tung Huang T'ai I*, is supposed to have been the
autochthonous god of the eastern part of the state of Ch'u, of which
Chu Yuan was at one time prime minister.

II. THE LORD WHO DWELLS IN THE CLOUDS

He bathes among orchids, washes his hair in the scented streams;
Adorns his embroidered coat with flowers from the sunset tree.
This Spirit comes with leisurely steps and stays:
The splendor of his glory is never ending.
He rests and remains in his eternal palace,
Equal in brilliance to the sun and the moon.
In a chariot drawn by dragons, wearing regal garments,
He wanders over the boundless plains of Heaven.
In a shining glory this spirit has descended.
Suddenly he soars high among the clouds,
Seeing the whole province of Ch'i and even beyond,[3]
Spreading over the Four Seas in the interminable distance.
Thinking of this Lord I sigh deeply;
Sorrow weighs heavily upon my heart.

III. THE LORD OF HSIANG [4]

LADY: The Lord comes not, and stays his steps.
    I am waiting for him on the island
    With sidelong glances and with gleaming smiles.
    Come swiftly on a boat of sandalwood,
    Oh, make the Yuan and Hsiang to have no wave!
    May the waters of the river flow gently.
    So I gaze for the lord who has not yet come,
    Playing on my flute and dreaming of his presence.

LORD: In a chariot drawn by feathered dragons and hornless
        serpents,
    I wander the winding paths of the Tung-t'ing Lake.
    A pennant of creeping fig leaves bound with aloes,
    My standard of irises garlanded with orchids.
    Gazing northward upon the distant shores of Ts'en,
    I give forth light which spreads over the great river.
    The beams of my light are never ending.
    The Lady moans and deeply sighs.

LADY: My tears flow in endless streams:
    In sorrow and sadness I dream of my lord,
    Who sails with oars of cinnamon and sweeps of cassia,
    Breaking through ice and the heaped-up snow.
    Like someone gathering irises in a lake
    Or plucking hibiscus from the top of a tree,

[3] One of the seven states then contending for power. The others were
Ch'in, Ch'u, Yen, Han, Chao, and Wei.
[4] The division of the speeches is conjectural. It is clear that the Lady of
Hsiang is waiting for her Lord; but the Chinese is so close-packed that it
is not always possible to know the exact moment when the Lady ceases
speaking and the Lord begins.

So does the marriage broker[5] labor among alien hearts.
Your love for me is not deep, but easily broken.
The river drools over the stone shallows.
Flying dragons flap feathery wings.
Unfaithful love brings continual murmurings.
You broke your promise when you said there was no
    more time.

LORD: By morning I wander along the river,
During the evening I approach the northern island.
Birds build their nests in the housetops.
Water purls beneath my temple walls.
I cast my jade ring in the tide;
I drop my girdle pendant on the shores of Li.
I gather azaleas on the fragrant island.
These flowers I shall bestow upon the lady.
The time may never come again.
Meanwhile I wander, composing myself at my leisure.

IV. THE LADY OF HSIANG[6]

LADY: The son of the Supreme Lord descends the northern
    stairway:
My eyes are alight with melancholy gazing.
Soft fall the autumn winds,
The leaves are falling in the ripples of the Tung-t'ing
    Lake.

LORD: Treading amid white duckweed, I gaze in the far dis-
    tance,
Awaiting the beautiful one under the curtains of
    evening.
Why should the birds gather among duckweed?
What use is a fish-net on a tree?

LADY: In the Yuan River there are angelicas, in the Li there
    are orchids:
Thinking of the prince, I dare not speak aloud.
With wildly beating heart I gaze afar.
I gaze at the river flowing peacefully away.
Why should the deer search for food in a garden?
Why should the scaly dragon live in a small pool?

LORD: In the morning I ride my horse along the banks;
In the evening I arrive at the western shore.
I hear the beautiful one summoning me.
I hasten to her on my galloping courser.

[5] The suggestion is that the labors of the marriage broker are as difficult
as plucking the hibiscus from the topmost branches.
[6] Hsiang Fu-jen, the collective name for the two daughters of the emperor Yao. The elder was called Wu Huang, the younger Nu Ying. They
became simultaneously empresses and consorts of the emperor Shun.

LADY: I will build my house in the water,
      There will be a roof of lotos leaves,
      A trellis of iris, carpets of purple shells,
      Juice of scented pepper seeds strewn on the walls,
      Rafters of cinnamon, beams of orchids,
      Pillars of magnolia, joists of white angelica;
      With woven fig leaves I will make a tapestry of curtains.
      With bundles of split orchids I will make lattices.
      The weights shall be of white jade,[7]
      Wild orchids will exhale their perfumes.
      Irises will be woven in the lotos roof.
      Asarums will compose the binding straw.
      Thousands upon thousands of herbs shall fill the gardens,
      Sweet herbs will hang over the fragrant door.

V. THE SENIOR ARBITER OF FATE[8]

LORD: May the gates of Heaven be opened wide!
      In ecstasy I ride the black cloud.
      I command the whirlwind to be my herald,
      I summon the rainstorm to lay the dust!

MINISTRANT: You who swoop down to the earth (continually) swaying,
      Grant that I may follow in your train to the Hollow Tree.[9]

LORD: How manifold are the people of the Nine Provinces,
      Whose lives and deaths depend on my power!
      I ride the pure air, I command the dark and the brightness.
      Soaring high, I float in the serene heavens.

MINISTRANT: I hasten toward the Lord, preparing for the journey,
      To accompany the Great Sovereign to the Chiu Mountains.

LORD: My clouds of scarves are waving and billowing.
      My jade girdle pendant sparkles in bewildering light.
      Amid the alternations of dark and brightness,
      There are none who have known the extent of my power.

---

[7] I.e., to hold down the carpets.

[8] As before, the division between the characters is conjectural. The ministrant would appear to be Chu Yuan himself.

[9] The K'un-lung Mountains, regarded as the place where the sun sets, the abode of the gods, and the center of the earth. From the white waters that flow from it, it was also known as the place of the dead.

MINISTRANT: I pluck the white flowers of the life-giving poppy.
I shall bestow them upon one who is far away.
Old age, white beard, draw imperceptibly nearer,
Yet we are drawing further and further apart.

LORD: I ride the roaring chariots of dragons,
Soaring high into the serene heavens.

MINISTRANT: My desire increases, my heart is aching
For those things which can no longer be accomplished.
Twining laurel twigs, I gaze for a long time.
Grant that I might remain without diminishing beauty.

LORD: Man's destiny is ordained. What shall be, will be.
Who can arrange his own meetings and partings?

VI. THE JUNIOR ARBITER OF FATE[1]

LADY: The autumn orchids and the silver pennies
Grow in rows beneath the temple door.
Green leaves and white flowers
With melting fragrance overpower me.
Always men have possessed beautiful women:
Then why are you so grief-stricken?

LORD: Oh, riotously grow the autumn orchids!
Green leaves and purple stems—
The temple hall is filled with beautiful women:
Suddenly our eyes meet in betrothal.
On entering you are silent, on leaving you bid no farewell.
I ride the whirlwind, bearing pennons of cloud.
Nothing is sadder than parting from the living,
Nothing more joyful than making a new friend.

LADY: With a cloak of lotos and a girdle of aloes,
Suddenly you came and suddenly you went away.
When you rest at night near the heavenly palace,
Whom are you waiting for among the clouds?

LORD: With you I would wander the Nine Rivers,
The whirlwind and the waves rise.
With you I would bathe my hair in the Hsien Pool,[2]
I would dry your hair on the slopes of Yang.[3]
Waiting for the beautiful one who has not yet come,
Facing the wind I sing my mad strains aloud.

[1] The presence of two arbiters would suggest that the legends of two different states were later fused together. Here, too, the divisions are conjectural.

[2] Where the sun bathes.

[3] Where the sun sets.

LADY: With a roof of peacocks, pennons from kingfishers,
          Ascending the Nine Heavens, waving comet tails,
          Grasping a long sword and protecting the heavenly
              virgins,
          Oh, you alone are fitted to be the leader of the people!

VII. THE LORD OF THE EAST

I arise in the east in all my immensity,
Shining among palisades of colored cloud,
Quietly I ride, stroking my charger.
Night shines: daylight comes breaking through.
My chariot has dragon shafts, wheels of thunder,
Cloudy pennons winding and frolicking.
Long do I sigh before I mount the chariot,
Deep in thought, pawing the ground.
My colors and music throw people in ecstasy;
Beholders are bemused, they forget their homes.
The tight strings of harps play in unison,
Jade bells hanging from the bar are made to sound.
To the tune of pipes and the playing of the flageolet,
Thinking of myself, beautiful and beneficent servant of
      Heaven,
I soar and sweep through the air like a kingfisher.
The hymnals are open, the people gather for the dance,
Following the tune and the beat of the drum.
So many ministrants that the sun can hardly be seen.
With my mantle of blue cloud, in my white-dappled skirt,
With my long arrow I shoot at the wolf star.
Then, taking my bow, I step back and descend.
Grasping the North Ladle, I scoop up the laurel-scented wine.[4]
Joining my reins, I ride and soar into the heavens.
Hidden in darkness, I make my way to the east.

VIII. THE GOD OF THE RIVER

With you I wander the Nine Rivers.
The whirlwind and the waves arise.
Riding the water chariot with the roof of lotos leaves,
I am drawn by two dragons and a hornless serpent.
Climbing on K'un-lung Mountains I look in the four directions.
My spirit wanders over the face of the deep.
The day is waning. Bemused, I forget my home.
I am dreaming of a distant shore.
In a fish-scale house, in a hall of dragons,
Under a purple shell gateway, in a palace of pearl,
O spirit, why do you dwell in the waters?
Riding the white tortoise, chasing the spotted fishes,
I wander with you among the small islets.

---

[4] The Ladle is the Dipper imagined as a wine scoop; the wolf star probably Sirius.

The swift-flowing freshet comes swirling downriver.
With a gentle bow you turn toward the east.
So I escort the beautiful one to the south anchorage.
Wave after wave comes to welcome me;
Multitudes of fishes bid me farewell.

IX. THE SPIRIT OF THE MOUNTAIN

LORD: There seems to be a spirit on the mountain
    Clad in creeping fig, girdled with ivy,
    Smiling with drooping lids and shining teeth;
    She longs for me, makes enticing gestures.

LADY: Riding a red leopard and led by a striped fox,
    In a chariot of magnolias bound with cassia banners,
    Clad in orchids, girdled in azaleas,
    I cull sweet flowers for my beloved.

LORD: I dwell in a dark grove, the sky unseen.
    The road is steep; I have come too late in the year.
    I stand like a pillar alone on the mountaintop.
    Clouds hover and float beneath my feet.

LADY: Darkness and gloom spread around; the day lies dim.
    The east wind rages, the spirits send the rain.
    I am waiting for my beloved. Bemused, I forget my
       home.
    The year is drawing to a close. Who will now honor
       me?

LORD: I pluck the three kinds of larkspur on the hillside,
    Amid the craggy rocks and luxuriant vines.
    Complaining of the princess, I am sad and loath to
       return.
    She is thinking of me and yet has no time to comfort
       me.

LADY: I am the spirit of the mountain, crowned with alpinias,
    Drinking from the rocky fountain, in the shade of firs
       and pines.
    I half wonder whether you still think of me.
    Thunder rumbles. Sheets of rain darken the earth.

LORD: The gibbons howl and monkeys mourn all night.
    The whistling wind whispers among falling leaves.
    Thinking of the princess in vain can I lay my sorrow.

X. THE PATRIOTS WHO DIED IN BATTLE

We grasp our *wu-k'o* shields; we put on rhinoceros hides;
The wheels of our chariots interlock; our short swords touch.

Our banners obscure the sun; our enemies rise thick as clouds.
Arrows twine in the air; warriors race headlong.
The ranks are thrown back; the lines are menaced.
A near wheel horse dies; an off wheel horse lies wounded.
Two wheels are buried deep; four horses are entangled in reins.
I raise the jade stick and beat the sounding drum.
Heaven's hour grows dark; the august spirits are enraged.
The dead lie on the field; they are abandoned in the wilderness.
They go their way without returning; depart without seeing
　　their homes.
The battlefields are afar; the journey home is long.
With long bows at their sides, Ch'in bows at their shoulders,
Their heads were slashed from their bodies, yet their hearts
　　were undaunted.
They were courageous and bold, they were filled with martial
　　ardor.
Unyielding to the end, we cannot contemn them.
Their bodies are dead, their spirits still powerful.
Their souls were resolute, they were heroes among the ghosts.

XI. THE SACRIFICE

Now the rites are over, the drums are joined:
Among sweet-smelling herbs they dance in turn.
The lovely girls sing to a solemn measure.
In spring there shall be orchids, in autumn chrysanthemums
Lasting to eternity, forever and ever.

All translated by Shen Yu-ting.

From *The Nine Declarations*

This is the beautiful dress
I liked best in my youth;
Now that I am old
I like it no less:
My headdress touching the cloud,
Shining long sword in my hand,
Bright pearls decorating my back,
Precious jade hanging from my belt.

In this covetous chaotic world
No one understands me—
I gallop at full speed
Though they pay no attention to me,
Having harnessed my chariot,
A blue dragon and a white one.
I go with the emperor Shun
Traveling through the Jade Garden.
I mount the K'un-lung Mountains,

I eat pure flowers,
I am as old as heaven and earth,
I compete with the sun and moon in brilliance.

Ah, none of the south barbarians
Understand me.
I will cross the Hsiang River
Early tomorrow morning.
When I have landed at the island of Ngo
I will look back and sigh
At the lingering winter wind.
My horse will have paced the hillside bank
Before my chariot arrives at Square Wood;
Then I shall take a barge up the Yan River,
All the oars striking the waves together,
But the barge will go its own way, not pushing forward,
Hesitating, remaining in the whirlpools.

I shall start from Crooked Beach in the morning,
I shall lodge at Bright Time late at night.
What is the harm of living in a waste space,
If my heart is sincere and upright?

Slowly I wander the bank of the river,
Not knowing where I should go:
The dark forest so endless,
The habitation of apes and monkeys,
The mountains so high that the sun is hidden,
Wet with rain mists, the valleys so dark and dim,
The heavy sleet and snow falling at random,
The flossy clouds embracing roofs and eaves.
I regret I have no happiness all my days
And am compelled to lead a separate life
Among these mountains, in utter desolation;
But never shall I change my mind
To fit it into the vulgarity of the world:
Therefore I am destined to die
A poor, pained, and grief-stricken man.

Tsieh-yu had his whole head shaved,
Sang-hu went out of his house naked:[5]
A loyal minister is often dismissed,

[5] Tsieh-yu was a contemporary of Confucius who pretended to be mad,
so that he might not be appointed officer by the Duke of Ch'u. Sang-hu
was a hermit, of whom little is known. Master Wu (Wu Tzu-ssu) was a
loyal general of the Chou dynasty. He served the Duke of Wu, and
begged the Duke to invade the kingdom of Yueh; but refusing to listen
to this advice, the Duke of Wu ordered him to commit suicide. Pi-kan
was the uncle of the profligate Chou, the last king of the Shang-Yin
dynasty. He offended the king by advising him to forego his immoral life,
and in consequence was executed and his body cut open.

The virtuous are not often appointed.
So calamity befell Master Wu
And Pi-kan was made into mincemeat.
So it has been since ancient times:
Why do I complain that men are blind today?
I shall follow the straight path without hesitation,
Bearing up against chaos till my last breath!

Epilogue

The phoenix flies farther and farther
As the hours fly.
Crows and sparrows build their nests
Above the ancestral altar in the hall.
The magnolias stretch out of the jungle
And die in entanglement.
When rancid smells are liked,
Fragrance cannot come near.
The Negative in the place of the Positive—
This is the time of great evil.
Embracing loyalty, but forlorn,
I commence my journeys.

Translated by Yu Min-chuan.

Encountering Sorrow

I am a distant descendant of Kao Yang Ti,[6]
My late and noble father was named Pai Yung.
Arcturus had just come into the sky
On the day of Ken Ying,[7] when I descended to earth.

My father reviewed the horoscope of my early life,
And conferred on me an auspicious name:
The name he gave me was Perfect Legality.
I also acquired the name of Ministrant of Harmony.

Already I possessed innumerable excellencies;
Great powers of understanding were given to me.
I was clad in angelica and nightshade,
From my girdle hung autumn orchids.

I cannot keep pace with the years.
I fear the years will escape me.
In the morning I gather cedar branches from the hills,
At night I pluck the evergreens on the islands.

[6] The dynastic title of Chuan Hsu, grandson of the Yellow Emperor. He reigned from 2598 B.C. to 2514 B.C.
[7] The cyclic year.

The sun and moon will not suddenly delay:
Spring and autumn move in their accustomed order.
Now the parched grass and leafless trees decay,
I fear my beloved lingers on the road.

Even when she was of age, she could not refuse evil gifts.
Why does she not mend her erring ways?
By riding pure thoroughbreds, she might course ahead,
And show the way that lies before us.

The three good kings were unendingly virtuous:
The scented herbs lay in their proper order.
The pepper of Shen was mingled with oleander,
But how shall angelica blend with wood orchids?

The emperors Yao and Shun were stern and shining,
They obeyed the Tao and renewed the Way.
The wild encounters of Chieh and Chou—
How soon the easy pathways lead to pitfalls!

Yet there are places where men assume these pleasures.
Shady is the way, dark and dangerous the passages.
Why should I fear danger for myself?
I only fear the imperial chariots will be ruined.

Swiftly I wander in all directions
In search of the footprints left by ancient kings.
The scented flowers are indifferent to my motives:
They utter scandal: they are consumed with rage.

I know my words have power to anger you:
My fortitude is such, I cannot cease.
I call the Nine Heavens to witness my honor.
I only seek the good of my adored.

At yellow dusk we were to meet.
Alas, you came halfway, then turned aside.
Time was when we shared our lovers' oaths,
But now you hide from me, have commerce with other men.
For me there is no terror in leave-taking.
I am wounded by my lady's change of heart.

Already I have planted nine acres of orchids
And a hundred acres of valerian,
Ten acres each of moss flowers and white rumex,
And many sun apples and sweet spirit grass.

I want the branches and leaves to be luxuriant and tall,
I shall wait for the proper time of reaping.
If they are nipped and withered, why should I grieve?
I weep for sweet herbs among foul weeds.

They go stampeding in search of money and grain.
Surfeited, they are not afraid to come for more.
Alas, they forgive themselves and blame only others.
Their hearts swell with life, swayed by envy and greed.

They ride roughshod in pursuit of their ends.
My heart does not hunger after such things.
Gradually old age will fall about me;
Perhaps I shall never establish my good fame.

At dawn I drink the dropping dews of magnolias,
At dusk I eat fallen chrysanthemum petals.
If I respect only the good and the virtuous,
Why should I grieve over their interminably hungry jaws?

I bind the valerian petals with tendrils,
I thread the fallen buds of lily flowers,
I wreathe the hibiscus with mallows
And rope the ivy into threaded sheaves.

Therefore I shall behave like the men of old,
Though the world may never admit my claims.
They say such thoughts[8] are out of fashion,
But I shall follow the path of P'eng Hsien.

I sigh deeply and wipe my tears away,
Grieving for the many sufferings of the people.
Loving virtue I curb myself with bit and bridle;
Day and night they curse and vilify me.

Now in my disgrace I wear the yellow orchid,
And wear also the flowering angelica,
And all these things seem good to me.
Though I die nine deaths I shall never repent.

I hate the wantonness of my adored,[9]
Who never searched the hearts of the people:
Because all women envy my moth eyebrows,
Slanderous tongues accuse me of being dissolute.

Truly in these days the art of the craftsman
Is to prepare everything without compass or squares.
The crooked is made straight without line or ink.
Toleration of all things has become the law.

[8] I.e., suicide. P'eng Hsien was a former sage who committed suicide under the same conditions as Chu Yuan.

[9] King Huai of Ch'u, under whom Chu Yuan was at one time minister.

Oppressed and saddened, I remain irresolute:
This time I am alone in my deep sufferings.
Far better to drown and perish utterly—
I can no longer allow myself to endure these things.

The hawks do not fly in flocks.
This has been so since the beginning of the world.
How can the circle ever be squared?
Going such different ways, how can we ever reach harmony?

I will cleanse my heart and cool my fever,
I will endure the forfeit and accept abuse.
To yield with a pure heart and die righteously,
This is what the men of old always commended.

I regret only, I never knew a peaceful life.
For a while I temporized; then I returned.
Now I wheel round my chariot and discover a new road:
I have not gone too far down the wrong lane.

I pace my horse amid the orchid marshes,
I climb the pepper hill and rest betimes.
I went straight forward, but not to encounter sorrows:
Withdrawing from the world, I mend my old clothes.

I'll wear a cloak of lotoses and water chestnuts,
My vest will be woven of hibiscus flowers.
If men know me not, I shall have no care:
My thoughts are pure and scented like flowers.

My cap will be lifted even higher,
My girdle pendant longer, studded with jewels.
They will be scented and many-colored—
Ah, my brightness shall not grow less.

Swiftly I look back and gaze in the distance,
My glance scours the four wildernesses,
My girdle pendants shining with glittering colors,
Their scent dispersed, filling the air.

Every man has his own opinions:
My desire is to remain eternally virtuous.
Though my limbs were torn from me, I would not change.
How then may my heart repent of its sins?

The beauty of my sister Hsu[1]
Now and always comes to my mind.
She says: "Kun[2] died because he was virtuous.
For this he was killed in the wilds of Yu.

[1] The elder sister of Chu Yuan.
[2] A famous minister under the patriarch emperor Shun.

"Why should you be outspoken in the cause of virtue?
You alone are possessed of a sense of moderation.
Thistles and wild bamboos grow in the houses of others,
You have encountered those who have no principles.

"I cannot go from house to house entreating:
There is no one who knows the depths of my confiding heart.
The world creates its own peculiar friendships.
Why are you still alone, refusing to listen to me?"

I follow the temperate ways of the ancients,
With trembling heart I wander the marshlands.
I cross the Yuan and Hsiang as I journey south.
I intend to lay my claims at the feet of Shun.[3]

Ch'i[4] sang the Nine Songs and Nine Colloquies,
Hsia K'ang rejoiced in tossing his kingdom away.
They made no plans, cut sheer through all warnings;
Thereby the five brothers lost their inheritance.[5]

Yi[6] was a restless pander, a lost huntsman,
Loving nothing better than chasing the great fox.
How could such a ruler come to a fair end?
It was Cho who coveted his master's wife.

Chiao possessed the strength of an ox:
He too was abandoned by the wayside.
He threw his life away in daily dissipation,
And then at last he forfeited his head.[7]

Emperor Hsieh[8] transgressed all rules;
Flagrant indulgence led to disaster,
For the emperor Hsu made him a meatball:
The House of Yin could not long endure.

[3] I.e., to the grave of the emperor Shun.

[4] The eldest son of the emperor Yu.

[5] Hsia K'ang was the son of Ch'i. His name means "summer peace," and he was noted for his profligacy, through which he and his four brothers were ruined.

[6] Yi, minister of Yu, murdered one of his two sons with the help of Cho, who finally killed the minister and married his widow, whose name appears to have been "Great Fox." For a discussion of the whole legend, see Granet, *Danses et légendes*, II, 513.

[7] Chiao was the surviving son of Yi.

[8] The last and most profligate emperor of the Hsia dynasty (2205-1766 B.C.).

Yu and T'ang alone were reverently stern:
The dynasty of Chou taught the unmistakable way.
Helping the virtuous, assisting the wise,
They followed consecrate laws impartially.

The august heavens are not moved by pity:
Eternally they watch over and reward men's virtues.
The saints and the wise walk in the paths of freedom—
Surely they will receive the blessings of the earth!

I gaze on the past and on the future;
I have delved deep, meditating the fate of the people.
To what profit are those who have no thought of goodness?
How owe allegiance to those devoid of virtue?

In mortal peril I accept all danger—
Never shall I regret the things I have done;
The blade was not measured to the shaft.
So, in the old days, were men minced into meatballs.

Therefore in dark despair I go lamenting;
I weep because the times are out of joint.
Plucking the yellow orchid, wiping away my tears:
Like waves, like waves, they wet the lapel of my coat.

Crablike I kneel on the mat[9] and abjure Heaven:
"Always have I espoused the middle way."
Teams of jade dragons draw my phoenix chariot—
Suddenly in a sandstorm I ascend in the air.

At dawn I strike the linchpin and drive to Blue Tree;[1]
Before evening comes, I shall reach Hsien Garden.
Then I shall rest awhile beside the carved gate,
There where the sun falls with shattering suddenness.

I command Hi Ho[2] to drive slowly,
Bidding him not hurry over the outermost mountains;
The way is long, the journey wearisome;
I shall search high and low, continually praying.

I shall water my horse at the lake of Hsien,[3]
Hitch the bridle reins on the Tree of the Sun;
Flicking the sun's face with a sprig of *jo-mu* leaves,
I will wander along at my own sweet will.

[9] In the attitude of complete prostration.
[1] The burial place of the patriarch Emperor Shun, supposed to be in modern Wuchow, Kiangsi.
[2] The guardian attendant of the Sun.
[3] A lake in whose waters the Sun bathes.

The spirit of the moon heralds the way;
The spirit of the wind urges me forward;
The phoenixes shall ride out before me;
The thunder god is not yet prepared.[4]

I command the phoenixes to rise in the air.
Day and night they must fly without resting.
A whirlwind gathers, the storm is upon me,
The clouds and rainbows attend my progress.

Vastness of clouds thundering above me!
So many colors continually melting!
I order the gatekeeper to open the gates,
But he only leans on the door and gazes at me.

In obscure light I look for a place of rest:
I gather orchids in the shade, biding my time.
A world in confusion, good and evil made one—
Virtue concealed in the pangs of jealousy.

When morning comes I ride over White Waters,[5]
I climb the High Winds and tether my horses.
Suddenly I look back and tears flow:
I am sad there is no woman with me on these heights.

I wander through the palace of the Green Emperor;
I cut the red-veined leaves, I lengthen my girdle pendant.
The lovely flower is not yet plucked:
At last I see the girl who will obey me.

Commanding the spirit of rain to ride the clouds,
I go in search of Fu Fei's[6] hiding place.
I unloosen my girdle—sign of the pledged word.
I order Chien Hsu to arrange the matter propitiously.

Oh, the confusion of the world and of women!
Perversity upon perversity confounded!
In the evening I return to my humble rock,
At dawn I rinse my hair in Weipan stream.

So arrogantly she guards her beauty:
Yet daily she offers herself to anyone she pleases.
She is beautiful, but knows nothing of proprieties.
I shall abandon her and seek elsewhere.

[4] The god of death is not yet ready.
[5] A vast river in the K'un-lung Mountains on the edge of the world. "To go to the white waters" often means "to die."
[6] The guardian spirit of the streams.

I gaze to the four points of the compass.
I wander over Heaven and come to earth again.
Looking up, I see Chienti in her Emerald Tower:[7]
Behold the wanton concubine of Emperor K'u.

I command the red-billed falcon to be my go-between.
The falcon says: "Nothing good will come of it."
Sparrows twitter and offer their services instead.
Oh, how I hate the artifices of their cunning ways!

The frisking puppy plays, the fox is cautious.
Were I to press my suit, there would be dangers.
The phoenixes have received the marriage offerings:
I fear the High Emperor has been there before me.

I love my wanderings, but have no aim in view.
I roam amidst the outermost regions.
As long as Hsia K'ang remained unmarried,
The two lovely daughters of Yu remained virgin.

My arms are weak, the go-between is stupid;
I fear her arguments have little weight.
The world in turmoil envies the virtuous;
Loving to conceal virtue, it praises vice.

The chamber of virgins is deep, inaccessible.
The wise king has not yet seen the light.
My desires must remain forever unappeased:
How can I continue to live in misery?

I will employ spirit weeds, auguries of bamboo,
I will command the sorceress to tell me my destiny.
They say: "Two handsome ones should be united."
But whose pledged word is worth anything in love-making?

They say: "Somewhere there are nine vast provinces,
But you remain altogether alone.
Go into the distance. Avoid cleverness.
Then in your search for a girl, no one will leave you alone."

Where is a place where there are no scented herbs?
Why do you sorrow after your old home?
In this dark world I am dazzled by brightness.
Who knows what is good and evil in me?

All people are not equal in good and evil.
Why are those farmers so strangely unlike?
Some taste bitter herbs to excite their loins—
Why should I not wear orchids in my girdle pendants?

[7] The concubine of the emperor K'u, who gave birth to Chieh the Tyrant,
when a swallow dropped a brightly colored egg in her mouth.

Though they gaze on plants, they canot name them.
How should they prize the beauty of flawless jade?
They would fill a bag of flowers with excrement.
They say: "The pepper of Shen is tasteless."

I will accept the auguries of the sorceress,
Yet my heart remains crafty as a fox.
In the evening Wu Hsien[8] will descend to me.
I will offer him pepper and the finest rice.

Descent of angelic hosts darkens the sky;
On the Mountains of Nine Sorrows we are greeted by flapping
      wings.
Revealing auspicious auguries.

They say: "Ascend to the heights, descend to the depths,
Seek that which is square and harmonious."
T'ang and Yu were benevolent; they also sought wives:
Chih and Chih Yu were their accomplished servitors.[9]

If the sentiments within you are true,
Why then should you seek a go-between?
Yueh[1] was the architect of the Learned Cliffs:
Wu Ting, who employed him, never doubted his skill.

Lu Wang was clever in using a knife:
King Wen exalted him after a chance meeting.
Ning Ch'i sang simple country songs:
Ch'i Huan, hearing him, desired to give him honor.

You have not reached old age;
Your laboring days are not yet over.
I fear the voice of the butcher bird when it sings:
In time all flowers lose their perfumes.

Splendid the red veins of my girdle pendants.
In the shade of trees all is concealed.
The fawners have no sincerity;
I fear they will shatter my girdle pendants with their jealousy.

[8] Wu Hsien would appear to be the guardian of the tomb of Shun.
[9] T'ang and Yu were acknowledged good emperors; Chih and Chih Yu
the types of good ministers.
[1] Of Yueh it is recorded that the emperor Wu Ting of the Yang dynasty
dreamed of him, and awakening the next morning, discovered that he
had been exiled. He was thereupon recalled to high office. Lu Wang,
minister under King Wen of Chou, was chiefly responsible for the overthrow of Chou Hsin, last ruler of the decaying Yang dynasty.

O world in confusion—change everywhere—
Why should I not utterly disappear?
The orchids and peonies are no longer sweet-scented;
Hyacinths and bluebells have changed to weeds.

How is it the sweet-scented flowers of the past
Now give off such evil odors?
Surely the reason lies in this—
The good and virtuous are weighed down by evils.

I thought at least I could rely on flowers.
Alas, I wronged them: yet how fair they seemed!
Men destroy beauty simply for the sake of wronging her.
How shall they find what they desire among flowers?
Chiao, the pepper flower, ripe with obscene flattery,[2]

Filled a bag of flowers with dogweed!
He forced upon her a deliberate entrance.
Where is the perfume he could offer to a bride?
The stream of time pours everything away:
What is there that remains unchanged?
The pepper plant and orchid are changed utterly,
And so too are harebells and fritillaries.

My girdle pendants are pure and flawless;
Yet sometimes even virtue comes to be destroyed.
No, these faint perfumes shall never fade,
Nor shall their sweetness ever vanish away!

I order my life harmoniously; I rejoice;
I search hither and thither for the hidden one.
While these adornments remain, I shall be steadfast
In my far-flung pursuit up and down the world.

The sorceress foretold a happy augury:
I must choose an auspicious day for departure.
I cut the red-veined leaves for food.
For me the ghost of these leaves will be as rice.

I will be driven by a team of flying dragons,
My chariots will be adorned with jade and ivories.
How can the wounded heart find peace?
Still for interminable miles I must wander.

Even now I have not reached the K'un-lung Mountains;
Long is the way, there are whirlwinds and sandstorms.
Among dark shades, rainbow-colored clouds arise.
Ting-ting ring the phoenix bells.

[2] Perhaps a pun on the name of Ssuma Tzu Lan, the minister and prince chiefly responsible for Chu Yuan's dismissal.

In the morning I start from the Ford of Heaven,
In the evening I will reach the outermost west.
Banners wave on the wings of phoenixes
In peace and harmony soaring and hovering.

Suddenly in front of me I see Shifting Sands,
Slowly I pace the banks of the Red River.
I wave to the Scaly Dragon to ferry me over,
I crave from the August West propitious journeying.

Long is the way, innumerable the pitfalls,
Calmly I ride within my chariots.
The road to Po-chou[8] winds and twists to the left.
I appoint the West Ocean to be our meeting place.

I collect my chariots together, a thousand in number.
Their linchpins are jade, they ride abreast,
Eight dragons yoked to them in curving teams
With banners of colored cloud like waving snakes.

I shall restrain my zeal, dispatch all haste.
My spirit shall fly through the boundless heavens.
I sing the Nine Songs, I dance to the music of Shun.
My days are spent in refreshment of pleasure.

So shall I ascend to Heaven's uttermost glory:
Suddenly, looking down, I shall see my home.
My charioteer laments, my charger is filled with sorrow.
They prance and curvet, but do not advance.

So I have come to the end—
No more can be told.
There is no good man in the state,
There is no one who knows me.
Why should I still devote myself to my country
Since there is none to rule her virtuously?
I shall follow P'eng Hsien to his grave!

[8] Po-chou is fairy country, lying to the northwest of the K'un-lung Mountains.

THE STONE DRUMS

These poems were engraved on the ten stone cylinders found around A.D. 600 in the southern part of Shensi province and removed in 1126 to Peking, where they are now preserved in the Confucian temple. They were long ascribed to the reign of the Chou dynasty King Hsuan (828–762 B.C.), but recent research has proved almost conclusively that they belong to the Ch'in dynasty (255–209 B.C.). The character of the calligraphy, which is often exceedingly beautiful, lies between the "greater seal" and the "lesser seal." A large number of the characters are no longer decipherable, and rather less than half of the original poems can be seen today, though a few characters are still preserved from rubbings made during the Sung dynasty. The present translation is based on the text and notes of Professor Tan Lang, of Lienta University.

YU MIN-CHUAN

I

Our chariots are strong,
Our horses well matched,
Our chariots are beautiful,
Our teams are sleek,
The lords so many and shining
Go hunting with banners waving.
The does and deer pressed hard,
These are what the lords are seeking.
The lords are holding fast
To splendid horn bows.
We drive against the bulls,
Which come with thundering hoofbeats
In clouds of hot dust.
We defend ourselves and watch
For when the stags run fast.
We struggle against the wild bulls
That come so huge and so rough.
When the wild bulls come out alone,
Oh, we shoot, we shoot.[1]

[1] Compare with the poem "Our Chariots Are Strong" in *The Book of Songs*.

II

The Chian River brimming over[2]
Falls into a deep gulf,
Where the lords are fishing
All kinds of carp.
In the clear shallows
Small fish are swimming idly:
In the shoals these silvery ones
Are striving for a bite.
Yet in muddy waters
There are herrings and perch and dories,
Whose flesh is greasy and choice.
Oh, how fast they run,
The throwers of nets!
What kind of fish is it?
It is carp and trout
Which can be strung together
On aspen or willow twigs.

III

Our waters are clean,
Our roads are even,
Our land has been divided,
Decorated with beautiful plants . . .
Our emperor will be forever at peace. . . .

IV

Safe in our chariot,
Drawn by four portly horses,
Reined with bridles of copper,
The right horses stout and strong,
The left floating like waving banners. . . .
Now we gain the wild plain,
Here our chariots pause,
We climb from the boxes,
We hold up embroidered bows,
We aim, we shoot the innumerable boars,
The hares, the pheasants, the stags, the roes. . . .

V

The sweet[3] rain falls.
Furiously the current rushes along,
The river brims over its banks,

[2] A river in the southwest of Shensi province.
[3] *Ling*, which has been translated as "spirit" in the poems of Chu Yuan, here has the meaning of "benevolent," "according to the auguries," "auspicious." This fragment may be the concluding piece of the series, describing the return of the huntsmen by boat from the foray, but no definite order of the poems inscribed on the drums is known.

The lords ride on horseback
And are about to wade in the stream.
The Chian River is overflowing,
The water is cold.
They turn back in their warships:
From Mei [4] they start westward.
Many are these men with horses,[5]
Who fasten their ships together and go downriver,
Sailing on the south limit or the north.
Their oars and paddles go deep
. . . one side of the river
And never . . . ceasing,
Rowing or resting, resting or rowing
. . . the affair.

Translated by Yu Min-chuan.

[4] A place in southwest Shensi province.

[5] The horses were apparently shipped in galleys, and the servants rowed their masters home. The last line may have indicated the successful conclusion of the affair.

THE HAN DYNASTY

(206 B.C.—A.D. 221)

LIU PANG, KNOWN AS THE
EMPEROR KAO TI
(REIGNED 206–194 B.C.)

Liu Pang was born near Hsuchoufu in northern Kiangsu, and when still young raised the standard of revolt with the help of a descendant of the old royal house of Ch'u, who was at that time only a shepherd. The revolt succeeded in 206 B.C., but the prince of Ch'u was assassinated, and Liu Pang founded the dynasty alone, naming it after an obscure river where he had once been stationed. He established his capital near Ch'ang-an, the modern Sian. He was the grandfather of the famous Prince of Huai-nan.

The Great Wind

The great wind rises, clouds are scattered;
Master of all seas, I return to my home.
Where are my warriors who guard the four frontiers?[1]

---

[1] This short poem sets the key for much that happened afterward. There is a weightiness in Han dynasty poetry that comes from the remorseless wars and from the solidity of the kingdom. The five-word lines, in which the following selections from the *Nineteen Songs* were composed, are supposed to have been first written by Su Wu and Li Ling, two military generals under the emperor Wu Ti of western Han, and the seven-line verses are supposed to have been initiated by the Emperor himself, and both were modeled after the examples of the barbarian tribes with whom Su Wu spent nineteen years of imprisonment, and Li Ling spent the remainder of his life. The greater part of the poems in the *Book of Songs* were composed in four-word lines, though occasionally lines of two, three, five, six, seven, and eight words occur.

Up to this moment poetry was song, and it was not till the end of the Han dynasty that poetry was completely divorced from music. The four-syllable lines were to be used again by Tao Yuan-ming, but this was probably a deliberate attempt to recapture the ancient mood of the songs. In 150 B.C. the emperor Wu Ti instituted the Yo Fu, or Musical Academy, which encouraged verses with four, five, and seven syllables, but it was the last two that remained most characteristic of the period.

FROM THE NINETEEN
HAN POEMS

It was inevitable that the themes of the *Book of Songs* should become more complex, and the anonymous *Nineteen Poems* composed in the Han dynasty (206 B.C.–A.D. 221) provide a commentary on the development of Chinese lyrical feeling, written and sung probably a thousand years later, but continuing and deepening the tradition. They lack the color and the gaiety of the *Songs,* but for the first time perspectives become visible, an ampler music is heard, and there is an increasing richness in the original Chinese, which cannot be conveyed in the English. The poems are all written in five-character lines, were probably based on folk songs, and have had an enormous influence on subsequent poetry, particularly during the T'ang dynasties, when all that concerned Han was deeply studied, imitated, and explored—sometimes *ad nauseam.* What is important is that the poems define an attitude to life more adult and with a deeper melancholy than the *Songs.*

I

No end to this marching, forever and ever. . . .
In life we are separated from one another,
Parted by a thousand and ten thousand li,
Each to a different corner of the sky,
The road so long, so perilous.
Who knows when we shall see each other again?
The Tartar horse rejoices in the north wind,
The bird of Yueh rests on the south branch,
The time since we parted is already far away:
Daily my clothes hang looser upon me,
Floating clouds hide the bright sun.
Now the wanderer does not care to return.
A year and a month have passed—too late!
Needless to talk again of abandoning me—
Just make an effort to take care of yourself.[1]

II

There are emerald herbs by the riverbank,
There are thick-leaved willows in the garden,

[1] Literally: make an effort to eat more food.

There is a weeping lady in a tower.
There she sits palely beside the window;
Her beautiful face is powdered with rouge.
Delicately, delicately she puts out a pale hand.
Once she was a dancing girl,
Now the wife of a man in exile:
The wanderer went away, he never returned.
Oh, bitter it is to lie in a bed alone!

III

So green are the cypresses on the hills,
So shapely are the rocks in the stream . . .²
Man's life between Heaven and earth
Is like the wayside trysting of a traveler.
A pint of wine drunk together gives great joy,
And surely friendship never did one harm.
I yoke my chariot, urge on my stippled steeds.
There is amusement to be found in Wan and Lo.
O luxuriance of Lo!
Nobles and mandarins tripping over one another,
So many royal dukes having their mansions,
Two palaces gazing at one another from afar,
Twin towers each rising a hundred feet in the air.
Here at my leisure I may rejoice my heart and soul,
And never will sadness ever come to me!

IV

Let us now enjoy a famous feast
With indescribable pleasures and delights,
With plucked lutes rending perfect harmony
And new songs entertaining a beauty that is divine.
Such virtues may our high words express,
That listening to the tunes, we recognize a truth within them.
May all our hearts express but a single desire,
A secret that is never openly admitted.
Man's life as it is accomplished in the world
Vanishes as swiftly as dust in a whirlwind.
So may we be vivid and high-stepping,³
And may we be ourselves the first to tread "the highways and
  the fords";⁴
For there is no use in being poor and humble,
Or always sighing over griefs and sorrows.

² The first two lines are borrowed from another song. It was the custom to set the tune to an older song, and to insert the opening lines of the song.
³ Oddly enough, "high-stepping" is an absolutely literal translation of the Chinese and means exactly what it does in English.
⁴ This is probably a reference to high positions or great wealth.

V

There in the northwest lies a lofty mansion
That floats above the flying clouds.
The softest silken curtains hang from windows;
The storied tower is reached by a triple stairway.
From high in the air come sounds of playing and singing.
Oh, but how sad the songs!
Do they not say it is the widow of Ch'i Liang?[5]
The note of autumn[6] follows the dance of the wind,
And then halfway the song grows hesitant.
Listen, after the first note—three sighs!
Nor does her complaint make an end to her grief.
I have less sorrow for the grief of the girl singing
Than pity for her song, which remains unheard.[7]
May our voices be joined like two wild geese,
And with beating wings may we climb the sky.

VI

I have crossed the river and gathered hibiscus:
In the orchid marshes are many scented herbs.
To whom shall I send the flowers I have plucked?
The one who fills my thoughts has gone afar—
Does he gaze in thought upon this ancient land?
No end, no end to these interminable pathways.
We parted from each other though our hearts are one.
My grief will never end till my last breath comes.

VII

The splendid moon shines on the fiery night,
Making the house cricket sing on the east wall.
The Jade Scales[8] point to the beginning of winter.
Scattering of a million stars across the sky!
Already the fields are white with hoarfrost;
Now comes the sudden change of season.
The autumn cicada chirrups among the briers,
But where have the black swallows gone?
Once I had a friend who shared my studies.
He fanned his wings and rose clear to the sky,
Forgetting how once we walked hand in hand.

[5] Ch'i Liang had neither father, husband, nor son, and drowned herself
in the river Chu. Her grief was so great that ten days after her death the
walls of the city fell in sympathy with her.

[6] *Ching chang* is an ancient song of autumn.

[7] Or: despised.

[8] The first of three stars (Alioth, Mizar, and Akhair) that form the tail
of the Great Bear, but here used to signify the whole tail.

He left me, like one who leaves only footprints behind.
South lies the Winnowing Fan, north lies the Ladle,[9]
The Herd Boy whose oxen have never been yoked.
A friend who is not constant as a rock
Is unworthy of the name—utterly unprofitable.

VIII

Frail is the bamboo that thrives in solitude,
Pushing its roots into the slope of the Great Mountain.
I dedicate new loyalty to my lord,
I am the ivy clinging to the wall:
There is a time for ivy to grow,
And a time for lovers to meet.
You have gone far away beyond the mountains.
My lord, thinking of you has made me old.
Why is your chariot so late in coming?
My complaint is for the sweet-smelling orchid,
Whose flower opens and brilliantly shines.
The time has passed when it may be plucked,
And like the winter grasses it will perish.
My lord, if you would keep your high trust,
How profitless would be this humble servant of yours.[1]

IX

In the courtyard grows a rare tree
With green leaves and a splendid flowering.
Lifting myself to the branch, I cut down some blossoms;
I shall send them to him on whom my heart dwells.
The sweet smell fills my sleeves and lap.
The distance is too great for it ever to reach you.
Moreover, such a gift would hardly please you.
Now I know how long you have been away.

X

Infinitely apart lie the Herd Boy star
And the streaming whiteness of the Lady of the Han River.[2]
So delicately she plies her white fingers,
Click-click go the spindles of her loom.

[9] The Winnowing Fan is part of Sagittarius. The Herd Boy corresponds
to three stars (Beta, Alpha, and Gamma) in Aquilon: the reference is to
the closing lines of one of the songs in the *Book of Songs:*

> In the south is the Winnowing Fan,
> But it cannot be used for sifting grain:
> In the north is the Ladle,
> Which cannot scoop wine or liquor.

[1] It is not always clear in these poems whether they are love songs or
complaints against a lord. Cf. Chu Yuan's *Encountering Sorrow.*

[2] Vega and two other stars in Lyra. The Han River is the Milky Way,
which, except on the seventh day of the seventh moon, separates the
Weaving Lady and the Herd Boy.

When the day ends, her task is not done,
And her bitter tears flow down like rain.
The Han River is shallow and clear,
And yet how great a distance separates them.
Always a river yawns before them:
Forever gazing, never being able to speak.

XI

Turning my chariot, I yoke my horses and drive
Deeper and deeper down the eternal road.
Everywhere so desolate and barren!
The autumn winds blow on a host of grasses.
There where I go, everything is new.
How should I not feel the coming of old age?
Ripeness and decay, each have their season.
Success is bitter when it comes too late.
Man cannot endure like metal or stone,
Nor can he prolong his days forever.
As with all that changes, life disappears.
A glorious name is the only prize that endures.

XII

At the beginning of winter a cold chill falls.
Oh, bitterly cold the north wind blows,
As sorrows increase the nights seem longer.
I raise my head and look at the starlit sky.
The moon is full on the fifteenth day,
On the twentieth day the "toad and hare" are waning.[8]
A stranger comes from a far land,
Bringing me a single sealed scroll.
The first words read: "I am sick for love."
The last words are: "I shall go forever."
Carefully I place the letter in the folds of my dress.
For three years the words shall not fade.
Oh, with what passion my heart is burning,
I fear you will never know.

XIII

How pure and bright is the moon,
Shining down on the silk curtains of my bed.
When sorrow will not let me sleep,
Waving my gown to and fro, I pace my room.
Sometimes a journey brings you joy,
But the greatest happiness is to remain at home.
Outside the door I roam alone:
To whom shall I tell the sorrows of my heart?
Lifting my head, I return to my chamber.
Falling tears wet my mantle and robe.

[8] These can be seen in the moon, and are used to personify the moon.

XIV

I drive my chariot down through the East Gate,
From afar I see the graveyard below the North Wall.
The white aspens are sighing, sighing.
Pines and cypresses line the broad road.
Under the earth are men who died long ago.
Dark, dark are their long nights of rest.
Far, far below the Yellow Springs
For a thousand years they lie in unchanging sleep.
The *yang* and the *yin* change in their seasons;
Like morning dew are our destined years.
The term of life has not the strength of metal or stone;
The mourners themselves become mourned.
Neither saint nor sage can escape this evil.
Seeking the food by which to become immortal spirits,
Many have suffered from strange medicines.
Better to relish fine wine
And clothe our bodies in silks and satins.

XV

They have departed, there is no speech with them.
For those who have come[4] we should have affection.
I go from the city gate and look before me,
And I can see only mounds and tombs.
The old graveyard is a plowed field,
The pines and cypresses are cut down for timber.
In the white aspens the winds are sighing.
Their interminable soughing fills me with sadness.
I want to see the gate of my own village.
I want to return, but there is no way.

Soldier's Song

Anonymous

I joined the army when I was fifteen,
I returned only when my hair was gray.
On the way I met some villagers.
I asked them who was living in my home.
"Far away, over there is your house.
Tombs are built among the pine trees.
The rabbits run in and out of the dog holes,
And pheasants are flying from the roof beams.
In the courtyard grow the wild rice shoots;
The sweet ferns[5] flourish by the wellside."

---

[4] I.e., the living.
[5] A plant with yellow flowers, much resembling the sunflower, and edible.

I cook rice in the grain,
And prepare a soup of ferns.
As soon as dinner is ready,
I do not know who to call.
When I stagger out and look to the east,
Tears fall and wet my clothes.

Translated by Ho Yung.

South of the City We Fight

South of the city we fight,
North of the wall we die:
Dying in the field unburied, the crows feed on us.
"Tell the crows we have no fear:
We died on the fields, no one has buried us.
Crows, how shall our bodies escape you?"
The waters flow deep;
Dark are the reeds in the pool.
The riders fought and are dead,
Their chargers are whinnying.
Once near the bridge stood a house—
South or north, no one knows.
Harvest ungathered,
How can you make offerings?
Though you served your prince truly,
Nothing remains.
O you, faithful soldiers,
Your accomplishments will not be forgotten:
One morning you went to battle,
One night you did not return.[6]

South of the River We Gather Lotos

South of the river we gather lotos.
How round, how round are the lotos leaves.
Fishes sport among the lotos leaves.
They sport to the east of the leaves,
They sport to the west of the leaves,
They sport to the south of the leaves,
They sport to the north of the leaves.[7]

[6] This is purely an academy piece.
[7] Perhaps the most famous of all academy pieces. It was often repeated, and the opening words, *Chiang nan keh ts'ai lien,* became a drug on the poetic market. No one knows what ti means.

The Song of Lo-fu

The sun rises in the east,
Shining on the high chambers of the house of Ch'in.
In the house of Ch'in a lovely girl dwells:
Lo-fu is her name.

Well does she tend her silkworms,
Gathering mulberry leaves south of the city.
She carries her basket by a thread of blue silk:
The loops of her basket are made of cassia.

Her hair is dressed in loose plaits,
Moonstones hang from her ears.
Her petticoat is made of yellow silk,
Her jacket of purple.

Anyone gazing on Lo-fu
Drops what he is carrying, strokes his cheek.
Young men when they see Lo-fu
Doff their caps, show their red scarves.

The plowman forgets his plow,
The farmer forgets his hoe.
Perturbed, they wander away
And squat gazing at Lo-fu.

The Governor drives from the south,
The five horses slacken their pace.
The Governor sends his men to ask
To whose house belongs Lo-fu.

"I am the daughter of Master Ch'in.
I am called Lo-fu."
"Tell me how old you are."
"I am not yet twenty,
Yet I am more than fifteen."

The Governor calls to Lo-fu:
"Will you ride in my chariot?"
Lo-fu bows and replies:
"What a fool my lord is!
My lord has a wife,
I also have a husband.
Over there are horsemen riding,
Over a thousand, my lover leading them."

"How shall I know your husband?"
"White horse followed by black colt,
Blue threads in the horse's tail,
Pennons of gold in the horse's mane,
At his waist a squirrel sword
Worth more than a fortune in gold.

"At fifteen clerk to the court,
At twenty he was made chamberlain,
At thirty he attended the Emperor,
At forty he was governor of a city.

"He is beautiful and white:
Soft as silk the down on his cheek.
Proudly he walks through the palace hall,
Where a thousand courtiers await him,
And all offer him great fame."

Old Song

She went up the mountain to gather sweet orchids,
She came down the hill and met her old husband.
Long she knelt before him, and asked him:
"How is your new wife?"
"Though my new wife talks well,
She is not so charming as the old.
They are alike in the color of their faces,
But the work of their hands is not the same.
The new wife comes down through the gate to meet me,
The old wife came down from her tower.
The new wife is clever at embroidery silk,
The old wife worked well over cotton spools.
With embroidered silk an inch can be done in a day,
Of cotton cloth more than five feet.
If we compare silks and cotton,
The old wife is not less than the new."

WU TI (REIGNED 140–87 B.C.)

He was the sixth emperor of the Han dynasty and an enthusiastic patron of literature. In his reign the wild tribes of Yunnan were pacified, cash came into use, he instituted the degree of "Scholar of the Five Classics," and toyed with Taoism. The following verses were written in the state barge when returning from celebrating the sacred rites.

The Autumn Winds

The autumn winds rise and the white clouds fly,
The grass grows yellow, leaves fall, wild geese return to the south.
The orchids are blossoming, sweet-smelling are the chrysanthemums.
I think of the lovely girl I can never forget.

My dragon boat dips swiftly over the Fen River.
Over these rapids white waves arise.
Flutes and drums beat time, I sing the song of the rowers.
O revel, O feasting, why do these sad thoughts come?
Youth is so brief and death so strong!

SOUTHEAST THE PEACOCK
FLIES . . .

An anonymous ballad of the later Han dynasty written in
five-word lines like the *Nineteen Poems*. The commentators
relate that during the period Chien-an (A.D. 196–220) the
wife of a certain Chiao Tsung-ch'ing, magistrate of Luchiang
in Kiangsi, was driven away from the house by her mother-in-
law. In sorrow and weariness she drowned herself, and the
husband, hearing of her death, hanged himself on a tree in the
courtyard, thus avenging her and at the same time putting a
curse on the ill-tempered mother. Such an action was hardly
Confucian, for it was not one of filial piety. The common
people rejoiced in the song, which is probably more famous
and enduring than any other ballad composed in China. The
peacock and the title are totally irrelevant to the story, but it is
not necessary to believe that the first two lines set the music
of the song on some other song—they may have been inserted
deliberately for artistic effect.

———————⟆⟅———————

Southeast the peacock flies,
Every five li he whirls around. . . .
"When I was thirteen I could weave silk,
At fourteen I learned to make clothes,
At fifteen I could play the zither with twenty-five strings,
At sixteen I knew the classics and the songs.
In the center of my heart are often sorrows and cares.
My lord went away to be magistrate in a city.
I remained behind with perfect constancy,
I remained alone in an empty bride chamber.
It was not often that we could see each other.[1]

When the crowing of the cock came, I went on with my
  weaving.
Night after night I ceaselessly awaited you—
In three days I could finish five strips of cloth,
But the Great One[2] found me too slow.
It was not at all that I was too slow,
But among your family—how hard to be a wife!
I won't allow them to drive me away,
But what is the use of staying with them?
So I beg you to ask your old parents
In a proper time to return me to my home."

[1] These two lines are probably spurious.
[2] The mother-in-law.

When the magistrate heard the words she spoke,
In the great hall he spoke to his mother:
"There are no good auguries written in my stars.
By good fortune this girl was given to me.
Our hair was plaited, we shared pillow and mat,
We swore friendship until the Yellow Springs.[3]
We have been together only two or three years,
No more than this—only a little while.
She has not deserved any punishment.
Why then do you treat her unkindly?"

The mother replied to the magistrate:
"Such a strange babbling from your lips!
Your wife has no manners or graces;
In all she does, she thinks only of herself.
For a long while I have been filled with indignation,
Thinking how best you may better yourself.
Our neighbors in the east have a fine daughter,
Who is known as Ch'in Lo-fu.
She is worthy of your love, has lovely limbs;
Your mother will ask for her to be your wife.
Let the other be dispatched from the house:
Send her away: do not let her stay here."

For a long while the magistrate knelt before her:
"There is only one thing I can say, my mother.
If you send my wife away on this day,
Never again will I take another wife."
Hearing these words, his mother
Beat on the bed in overwhelming anger.
"Little son, have you lost all shame?
Dare you so impertinently defend your wife?
Now and forever I shall have no affection for you,
And remember that nothing will break my desire."

The magistrate made no attempt to reply.
Twice he bowed low, then went to his chamber.
Lifting his voice, he addressed his young bride,
Choking with sobs, barely able to speak:
"If it remained with me, I would not drive you away—
My mother is always harassing me.
Just for a little while return to your home.
Now I must go to my business in the city:
It is not for long; I will return in a little while,
And then in a little while I will come to you.
Do not be cast down,
And never forget these words I have spoken."

[3] I.e., of death.

The young wife replied to the magistrate:
"Please—no more of these entanglements.
There was a time when my years were awakening.
I left my family and came to your great home.
I performed my duties, was submissive to your parents,
In nothing at all exercising a will of my own.
Day and night trouble stared in my face.
I have come into so great a misery:
Never with words have I committed a crime,
And have always labored in return for their kindness.
But when, as now, they try to drive me away,
Why do you speak of my returning?
Your servant possesses delicately embroidered gowns,
And girdles that seem to sparkle like fire,
And hanging bed curtains of red gauze,
And scented sachets at the four corners,
Sixty or seventy small coffers,
Bound with green silk, with jasper hinges,
And many, many other things, all different—
Nothing that cannot be found among them.
So humble I am, and these things so valueless,
Hardly worth offering to your future wife,
Yet keep them—perhaps they may be of use to her.
Never, never shall we meet again,
But for all time I beg you enjoy happiness,
And through all years never forget our love."

The cock crowed: dawn was rising.
The young wife rose, and delicately prepared herself.
She donned an embroidered silk-lined gown,
Four or five times returning to each task.
So she stepped in her satin shoes,
In her hair put gleaming tortoise-shell combs,
With white silk enfolded her waist;
From her ears dangled moonstones,
Her fingers were like pared onion skins,
Her lips redder than red sulphur stones.
Delicately she walked, with minute steps,
More perfect in her beauty than any the world has seen;
She went to the hall to take leave of the mother,
Whose anger still remained unappeased.
(The girl said:) "In my girlhood,
I was brought up humbly in the country,
And never received any education.
How could I hope for a husband of good family?
You have given me many gifts of silks and money,
But even so I cannot bear to be driven away.
Today I shall return to my family,
Afraid if I stayed you would have sorrow in the house."

Then she bade farewell to her husband's young sister,
Her tears falling like a necklace of pearls.
"When newlywed I first came to this house,
You were learning to walk by leaning on chairs.
Today, now that I am being driven away,
You, little sister, are as tall as I am.
Put all your heart in serving your old parents.
On the seventh and twenty-ninth days,
When you are on holiday, do not forget me."

She passed through the gate, mounted her carriage, rode
        away,
Her tears falling in more than a hundred streams.
The magistrate rode away on horseback before her,
The young wife rode in a carriage behind.
Thunder of wheels and hoofs along the road!
They met each other at the mouth of the great road:
He jumped from his horse and went into the carriage.
With head inclined, he whispered in her ear:
"I swear on oath that I shall never leave you.
Now for a little while return to your home.
I am going now to my office,
But in a little while I shall come back again.
I swear to heaven that I will not forsake you."

The young wife answered the magistrate:
"I know, my lord, there is great affection between us.
I know too that you hold me in high honor.
My lord, do not let me await too long your coming.
Be steadfast as rock.
Your servant is like a reed,
And a reed is as soft as silk.
The rock must remain immovable.
I have a father and an elder brother,
And both of them are wild as thunder.
I fear they will not let me perform my desires.
And if they oppose me, they will make my heart bleed."
With hands outstretched they bade their endless farewells,
Both filled with love and overcome by sorrow.

She passed through the gate into the family hall,
Stepping so delicately, so fearful of the future.
With a great noise her mother clapped her hands:
"We did not think our child would come so soon.
At thirteen we taught you to weave silk,
At fourteen you could make clothes,
At fifteen you played the zither with twenty-five strings,
At sixteen you knew the ritual and the ceremonies,
At seventeen we gave you to wife,

Demanding that you should always keep faith,
But now you seem to have committed a crime.
Without anyone going to fetch you, why have you returned?"

"Your Lan-chih stands ashamed before her mother,
And yet your child has committed no crime."
Hearing this, a deep pity welled in her mother's heart.

Since her return, about ten days had passed,
When the mayor of the city sent a go-between:
"Our Master has a third son," he said.
"None so charming in the whole wide world.
He is eighteen or nineteen years old,
Gifted with fine words, possessing many excellencies."
The mother spoke to her daughter:
"Go, my child, accept this invitation."
Her daughter replied in tears:
"That time when Lan-chih left her husband's house,
The magistrate looked kind and swore on oath
That never would anything be allowed to separate us,
But if I were to break these sacred vows
I am afraid I would be guilty of a crime.
Therefore, I beg you, have no converse with them:
Perhaps later we may speak about it to them."

The mother said to the go-between:
"To our great sorrow we have a daughter
Who was married, but now returns to her parents.
Unworthy of being married to a magistrate,
What use is she to the lord's son?
Seek in a better place a worthy daughter,
For we cannot agree to make her his bride."

The go-between had already gone some days,
When the mayor summoned him again.
"They say there is a lady of the Lan family,
Who comes from a long line of mandarins.
I have five sons, and the fifth
Is not yet married, but has excellent parts.
I shall send one of my aldermen as go-between,
And one of my clerks to act as secretary."
Immediately they betook themselves to the family.
"Our lord has five sons," they said.
"And one of them wishes to be bound in the Great Alliance,
Therefore we come as messengers to your house."
The mother thanked the messengers for coming.
"Our daughter has already made her vows.
I am her mother—what else can I say?"

Suddenly the girl's brother, hearing the words,
His heart downcast, and filled with sorrow,
Raised his voice and yelled to his sister:
"Indeed, you are an unreasonable girl.
You were married first to a magistrate,
And now you are to be married to a lord.
You climb from the earth to the sky,
Such splendor anointing your body;
If you do not accept this young and talented man,
What in the future will come of you?"

Lan-chih raised her head and answered:
"Brother, you have good reason to say this.
I left my family, and served my husband well,
But then, halfway, I returned to my home,
And now must follow my brother's desires.
I can no longer follow my own pleasure.
Though the magistrate has made his formal vows,
Never on earth shall we meet again;
Therefore tell them they have my consent,
And this marriage may truly be brought about,"
The go-between rose from the ceremonial couch,
Repeatedly nodding his head in agreement;
So he returned to the yamen to tell the Governor:
"Your servants have fulfilled your command,
Our conference has been crowned with success."

When the mayor heard these tidings,
His heart was filled with an immense joy.
He consulted the calendar and the almanac:
"There will be propitious events within this moon,
The six stars will be in harmonious conjunction,
On the thirtieth day good omens are announced;
Today is already the twenty-seventh,
Therefore, my son, it is time to conclude your marriage!"
Then he gave orders to hasten the nuptials.
Endlessly, like floating clouds, the servants were on parade.
Blue tits and white doves decorated the prows,
At the four corners waved the dragon banners,
Gently, gently, trailing in the wind,
Gold coaches with jade-encrusted wheels
And pied horses prancing, prancing,
Bearing long plumes, saddles threaded with gold,
And for wedding gift three million pennies
Strung together on blue silken threads,
And three hundred strips of colored silk,
And the strangest fish from Chiao-kuang,
And three or four hundred servants
Marching in grand procession to the Governor's yamen.

The mother said to her daughter:
"A letter has just arrived from the Governor,
Saying that tomorrow you will be taken in marriage.
Why are you not making your clothes?
I beg you, do nothing to spoil the ceremony!"
The girl uttered no word,
But sobbed through the kerchief that covered her mouth,
And the tears flowed down like a sea.
She moved her bed of glazed stone
And placed it beneath the garden window.
In her left hand she held scissors and shears,
In her right hand her embroidered silks.
While morning passed, she sewed an embroidered coat,
And in the afternoon completed a damask robe;
And the dying day came to its end,
And sad in heart she went outside and wept.

When the magistrate heard of these things,
He took short leave and came back to her.
He had hardly gone two or three li,
When his horse began to whinny plaintively.
The young wife recognized the whinnying horse,
And hurriedly she ran to meet her lord,
And sadly at a distance saw him there.
Knowing full well that he had come indeed,
She lifted her hand and tapped the horse's saddle,
And sighed and sobbed as though her heart would break:
"Since my lord went away from me,
Many strange things have happened to me,
And they are not such things as we expected,
And hardly could you conceive them.
I have my parents, a father and a mother,
And with them also were joined my brothers:
They have forced me to marry another.
And you, my lord, why do you come?"

The magistrate answered his young wife:
"You have done well to climb so high!
The great rock, foursquare and strong,
Can endure for a thousand years:
The humble reed, by being bent,
Disappears in a single day.
May you shine in splendor like the sun,
While I alone go down to the Yellow Springs."

The young wife answered the magistrate:
"How can you utter such words?
Together we have suffered this constraint.
First it was you, and then your humble servant—
Down to the Yellow Springs let us both go,

And let our words of today not be forsaken!"
They held hands and went on their ways,
Each one returning to his proper home.
The living have made their mortal farewell,
But how shall we speak of their immeasurable sadness?
They think only of leaving this world:
A million things will not make them return.

    The magistrate returned to his home,
Entered the hall, and bowed low to his mother:
"Today a great cold wind has arisen,
An icy wind that scatters the petals,
A cold frost stiffens the orchids.[4]
Darkness, darkness—such is the day of your son,
And after me there will only be you alone;
For it was you who laid this evil—
Cease tormenting the ghosts and the demons.
May your life last as long as the South Mountain
And your four limbs be firm and strong!"
When his mother heard him speak,
Bitter tears flowed down with each word.
"You are sprung of good family,
With the rank of mandarin at the court,
How could you die for the sake of such a wife?
Between the high and low is there no difference?
Our eastern neighbor has a fine daughter,
Whose grace and charm are known to all the town.
I, your mother, will go and fetch her.
All things will be arranged between morning and evening."

    The magistrate went away, making the double bow,
And for a long while sighed in his empty room,
More hardened than ever to his plan.
Then he turned his eyes toward the door,
Heartbroken, with a grief that only increased.
During that day the horses and oxen lowed,
The young bride entered her green marriage tent.
Darkness followed on dusk.
Silence was spread over the sleep of men.
"On this day the term of my life descends.
The spirit goes, only the body remains."
Then she lifted her skirt and removed her silk shoes,
And hurled herself into the blue lake.

    The magistrate heard of it.
He knew in his heart an eternal parting had come.
For a while he wandered beneath the trees of the yard,
Then hanged himself from a branch at the southeast.

[4] Referring to the young wife, Lan-chih, whose name includes the character for orchid: *lan*.

The two families desired they should be buried together,
A common grave on the slopes of a flowering mountain.
East and west they planted firs and cypresses,
Left and right they planted *wu-t'ung* trees.
The boughs were intertwined,
The leaves were joined together.
Two birds nest there who only fly together.
These birds are known as True Felicity.
With raised heads they call one another
All night long to the time of the fifth watch.
The passers-by stay to listen to them;
Lonely widows pause as they wander their rooms.
May there be a grace for those who follow after:
Learn of this story and never forget it!

PERIOD OF TRAVAIL

(A.D. 222–618)

YUAN CHI (A.D. 210–263)

Yuan Chi was born in Yu-chih in Honan and rose to high office under the emperor Wen Ti of the Wei dynasty, but later exchanged the post for one where there was a better cook. Living during the time of vicious wars between the Three Kingdoms (A.D. 221–265), he deliberately withdrew from the court and founded with six others the famous group of scholars known as the Seven Sages of the Bamboo Grove, who threw piety to the winds, drugged themselves with wine and herbs, and were constrained toward a bitter coarse-grained humor in defiance of the warlike times. He was a Taoist and a musician, but is known now chiefly for his poetry and for some excellent stories told about him. He died of grief after hearing of the execution of his close friend Chi Kang.

Strange Bird

The strange bird makes its abode in the woods:
Its name is "phoenix."
In the morning it drinks at the honeyed spring,
At night it seeks rest on the hillside.
Throughout the land there rings its shrill note.
Neck-craning, its eye reaches all corners of the earth.
There sweeps along a gust of west wind,
Wherefore it causes the plumage to be impaired.
Then it flies westward toward the K'un-lung Mountains,
And who knows whether it will ever return?
Now a great regret seizes upon my mind—
If only I had my home in a different place!

Translated by Yang Chi-sing.

Speaking My Mind

When I was thirteen or fourteen
I delighted in the study of history and the odes.
My plain clothes covered a heart of jade.
In morals I was greater than Yen and Ming.[1]
Always I gazed from the window in all directions;
I climbed up mountains to greet what I so piously expected.
All I saw were tombs and mounds on the hills.
Ten thousand ages passed in a single moment,
A thousand autumns, ten thousand days passed.
A glorious name is of no worth.
I occupied myself with the study of great books,
And now I laugh at this folly.

[1] Yen Shu Tzu, a recluse of the Lu State in the fourth century B.C., who, when a neighbor's house was blown down and a girl took refuge with him, sat up until dawn, holding a lighted candle in his hand.

TAO YUAN-MING
(A.D. 372?–A.D. 427)

He was a hermit who wrote with a studied gravity and careless indifference to fame, content to plow his farm and watch his children playing in the farmyard, so quietly observant and meditative that when we read him we can almost touch him, so close he is even now to our most meditative moods. There is nothing histrionic here. He is silence speaking to itself, and yet there is nothing tenuous in his writings—they are quiet, but they are etched deep, and the smoldering passion of the hermit who deliberately divorced himself from official life and celebrated the contentment of the farmer's progress is even more characteristically Chinese than the passion of Tu Fu or the dancing delight in life that pours through the poetry of Li Po. He wrote with a kind of sad, troubled perfection. He said once: "The highest pleasure in life is playing jokes with children." At another time, resigning from his post as magistrate at Peng-tse in Kiangsi, he said: "I will not crook the hinges of my back for five pecks of rice a day." Thereafter he returned to his farm, his chrysanthemums, and his lute, and lived out his days in a cloudy serenity, never quite understanding the world, troubled and afraid of death, determined to have nothing to do with politics, a pure lonely scholar desperately anxious to do what was right, half Confucian, half Taoist or Buddhist, a man who was never entirely at home in the world but intensely human, so human indeed that we know him better than we know any other Chinese poet—his likes, his dislikes, his terrible scorn for all officialdom.

He was born into the troubled times that followed the downfall of the Han dynasty, but no one knows the exact date on which he was born—it may have been in the first year of the reign of Tai Yuan (A.D. 376) or in the second year of the reign of Hsien-an (A.D. 372). It was a time of political experiment, of reorientation and vast corruption, and he hated all these things. His great-grandfather, the celebrated Tao Kan, once held the post of Minister of War, and even then died poor. His father and grandfather were both magistrates, while his mother's father was appointed General of the Western Marches. The family should have been rich—there were great opportunities for acquiring wealth—but they were always poor, refusing to be corrupt, following a family tradition. Tao Yuan-ming wrote of his maternal grandfather: "He behaved always correctly, and never boasted of his deeds. You could

129

hardly detect from his expression whether he was angry or
pleased. He was fond of drinking, but only in moderation, and
when he indulged his fancy, he would look as peaceful as
though he were alone, even if he was surrounded by many
people."

Partly it was heredity and the family tradition, partly his
own innate contempt for the shows and ceremonials of life.
There is always robust good sense in him, an underlying gravity of manner, and a queer streak of humor. He praised all the
seasons, but seems to have preferred autumn, when the chrysanthemums blossom. He painted in thin light colors, and for
this reason has been called the poet of old people, but in fact
he is the poet's poet, his verses possessing in the original
Chinese a classic perfection of idiom. He is the nightingale
rather than the skylark, and if he can be compared with any
Western poets at all, we must go to the Vergil of the *Georgics*
and the more recent poems of Robert Frost. He would deliberately select the most colorless words, not because he disliked
color, but because he was intent on describing things as they
are without adventitious aids, in the same way that Yeats,
in revising his poetry, would search for the starkest, not the
most evocative adjective. He was almost the first Chinese poet
to describe nature intimately. He was the herald of a more
accurate dawn.

And yet there was passion underneath. You can feel it in
nearly all his poems, a controlled passion that smolders and
only rarely bursts into flame, but nevertheless continually present—the passion of a man who had seen much, who feared the
barbarians massing on the north and the incursions of the
Sung armies, and who lived at a time when immense changes
were sweeping over China—the vast southern movement of
the population, the desperate and nearly always unavailing
attempts toward political stability. He was too practical to take
refuge in the mountains like the *rishis*—there remained farm-
ing and the consolations of a farmer's beggarly existence. In
a long preface to "Returning Home," he wrote:

My family is poor, and it is difficult for me to support my family
by cultivation. The room is full of children, but the cask of wine is
nearly always empty. When I lacked means to get sustenance, many
of my acquaintances advised me to serve in the government. And
even though this did not suit my interest, still it was not easy to gain
such a post. But the world was busy with its affairs, and princes and
dukes vied with one another in employing men of ability, and so
through the recommendation of my uncle I received an appointment as a chief official in a small district. The country remained
in confusion, and upon my soul I was sick of serving in a distant
place. Peng-tse is only some thirty miles from my home, and in
addition there were the advantages of official fields, which assisted

my income: so I undertook these duties. But after a few days I was overcome by a feeling of homesickness. Why? To serve there was against my instinct, and could not be put right by affectations. Hunger and cold can cause physical suffering, but to do things against my conscience still tortures my spirit. There is a precious lesson that I have derived from hard experience: one who indulges himself in worldly affairs merely satisfies his mouth and his stomach. But even then I conceived the desire to wait for the next crop, and then leave my office silently. A few days later my sister died in Wuchang. I was eager to go to her funeral, and so I resigned of my own accord. I have been an official for little more than eighty days.[1]

He had spent, according to the commentators, exactly eighty-three days in office, but from that moment he entered into a life of seclusion. The Taoists and the Ch'an Buddhists have claimed him as their disciple, and the story is told that one day Tao Yuan-ming and Ling Ching-hsiu, a Taoist monk, called on Hui-yuan, a famous Buddhist scholar who lived alone on a mountain. They were deep in conversation as they passed beyond the bridge over the Tiger River; suddenly a lone tiger roared aloud. They looked at one another, and laughed. The story, like so many Ch'an Buddhist stories, is quite deliberately pointless, but it illustrates the affection in which Tao Yuan-ming was always held. On the place where they had laughed a temple called the San-hsiao T'ing was erected to commemorate their laughter.

He loved nature and wine, children and chrysanthemums; he loved walking desultorily through the countryside; he delighted in the seasons. He grimaced sometimes against the cold and against death, but he knew they were inevitable, and took comfort in birds. Of his poetry Su T'ung-po wrote: "There is no poet I treasure more than Tao Yuan-ming; he alone pleases me. He wrote few poems: they are plain yet beautiful, rich and yet not ornamented. Tu Fu, Li Po, and all the others are inferior to him," whereupon Su T'ung-po proceeded to model over a hundred poems on those of Tao Yuan-ming, following the rhyme scheme and deliberately imitating them. Chu Hsi, the great philosopher, said that his poems were so plain, peaceful, and unaffected that they seemed to have been composed by nature herself.

He made no demands on fame, or even on life: he seems to have been contented with the world as he saw it—the world of valleys and plains, of a deliberate simplicity and an incurable nostalgia. As Su T'ung-po imitated his poems, so he imitated poems of the earlier Han period. He so loved chrysanthemums that even now, fifteen hundred years after his death, it is almost impossible for a Chinese to see a chrysanthemum

[1] Translated by Yen Whai-sheu.

without summoning his name. He is the poet of quietness and solitude, and described himself perfectly in prose:

The Scholar of Five Willows is a native of I know not what place; and no one knows his name or surname. Because there were five willows beside his house, he was known simply as the Scholar of the Five Willows. He was quiet, even taciturn, had no desire for riches or fame. He amused himself with books, but never to such an extent that he would trouble himself with exact interpretations. When he found a passage that particularly delighted him, he was so happy that he went without food.

He had a passion for wine, but sometimes he was so poor that he could obtain none. His friends realized this, and they never forgot to invite him over for a drink. He always emptied his cup, determined whatever else happened to get drunk. After he was drunk he retired, and cared nothing at all where he found himself. The four walls of his house were bare and tattered, and did not shelter him from wind or sun. Wearing a short flax-cloth jacket, all torn, and carrying an empty rice bowl, he was perfectly content.

He amused himself by writing occasional poems, wherein his aspirations are revealed, having no interest in worldly success or failure. And so his life passed to its end.

The prose fragment "The Peach-Blossom Fountain" has been included here, partly for its sheer beauty, but also because of its deep influence on all the poetry that comes afterward. Once again the image of "the return," which dominates some of the most superb Han poems and which is visible throughout the *Tao Teh Ching*, achieves a perfect expression.

The Peach-Blossom Fountain

During the reign of T'ai Yuan of the Tsin dynasty, a fisherman of Wu-ling was pushing his boat up a stream, forgetting to notice how far he was going. Suddenly he came upon a forest of peach trees that lay for several hundred paces along both sides of the river. There were no other trees. Beautiful were the fragrant herbs, and the petals were continually dropping from the branches. Wondering at the place he had come to, the fisherman went on to see where the forest ended, and found that it ended at the source of the river, and there he saw a mountain with a small cave with a crack of light gleaming beyond.

Leaving his boat, the fisherman went through the opening of the cave. At first it was so narrow that he found difficulty in passing through, but after several tens of paces he suddenly came into broad daylight; he saw the open plains, the tidy farmsteads and rich fields with delightful lakes, mulberries, bamboos, and suchlike things. Paths threaded across the fields. He heard dogs barking and cocks crowing, and saw men and women walking about or working; and they wore clothes exactly like those worn by people outside. The old men had yellow hair and the young wore their hair in loops, and all seemed joyous and contented.

But when they saw the fisherman, they were alarmed and asked where he came from. He answered all their questions; they invited him to their homes, and brought wine and killed chickens for supper. Soon other villagers heard of his arrival, and came to inquire about him. Of themselves they said that in an ancient time their forefathers, in order to avoid the disasters that fell on the Ch'in dynasty, had fled with their wives and their children and their neighbors into this secluded country. They never came out again, and so they had been separated from the other world. They asked who was reigning: they had never heard of the Han dynasty, and still less had they heard of Wei and Tsin. The fisherman told them all he knew; they sighed to hear it, deeply moved.

Each in turn invited the fisherman into his house, spreading out food and wine. After staying several days, he bade them farewell. The people of the place said to him: "It is not worth while to speak of us to outsiders." When he came out of the cave, he found his boat and returned along the way he came, and all the while he attempted to remember landmarks.

When he reached the city, he went to the governor and related his discovery. The governor sent some men to go with him. They looked for the landmarks, lost their way, and never found the road to the place.

Liu Tse-chi, a high-minded scholar of Nan-yang, heard of the story, and joyfully made plans to make the journey. But nothing came of it, and soon afterward he died after an illness. Since that time no one has sought to find the ford.

Translated by Yang Yeh-tzu.

Substance, Shadow, and Spirit

High and low, wise and simple, all are busily preserving their moments of life. In this they err greatly. So I shall expose the sufferings of Substance and Shadow, and speak of the perceiving Spirit and Nature as offering a solution. May the well-disposed reader understand my intentions.

Substance says to Shadow

Heaven and Earth endure eternally,
Mountains and streams will never change;
The plants know their natural course,
They wither and flourish in frost and dew.
Man should be above them in intelligence,
But he alone is unlike them:
A while ago he was living,
Now he is gone and will never return.
No one ever awakes from the dead;
Friends and relatives will not long remember him.
Looking at the things he used in his life,
Our eyes fill with tears.
I have no mortal magic to overcome death:
Certainly death will overtake me.
I hope you will take my advice.
Whenever you have a chance, never refuse a drink.

Shadow says to Substance

Immortality is beyond comprehension,
And it is hard to preserve life.
I would wander on the heights of the K'un-lung Mountains,
But closed is the road to that place.
Since the day I met you we have shared
The same joys, the same sorrows.
In the shade we seem to part for a while,
But in the sun we are always together.
We cannot keep company forever:
Together we shall vanish in the darkness.
The name dies when the body comes to an end.
Such is the painful thought that consumes my heart:
Our descendants will love a virtuous man,
So why should you not exert yourself?
Though wine may melt our sorrows,
Nothing compares with deeds well done.

Spirit expounds

The Great Potter is always righteous.
All creatures appear in fullness and clarity.
Man takes his place between Heaven and Earth—
Is it not on account of me?
Though I differ in nature from you both,
Ever since birth we have been together
With intimate sharing of good and ill.
I could not but speak to you.

The Three Emperors were great sages,[2]
But where are they today?
P'eng Tsu[3] enjoyed a grand old age:
If he had desired it, he could not stay.
Old and young meet the same death,
So do countless wiseacres and fools.
Only ceaseless drunkenness brings forgetfulness,
Yet it hastens our end.
Virtuous deeds bring happiness,
But how can we be certain of praise?
Ponder how all this harms our life.
We should resign ourselves to fate
And drift on the waves of Great Nature,
Neither joyfully nor fearfully:
When the end comes, let it come,
And no more cares beset you.

The Beggar

Hunger drives me along my road:
I do not know where I am going.
Drifting about in this neighborhood,
Embarrassed I knock on a door.
The master knows why I have come;
His gifts are such as I had hoped.
So we chatter to the day's end,
Each cup drained and replenished,
And happy in our new friendship
We begin to compose poetry.
"You favor me like the washerwoman,[4]
But I am not a future hero.
How can I show you my heart's gratitude?
I will requite you from the dark shades."

The Empty Boat

Softly and unhampered an empty boat glides on
To and fro along the stream of eternity.
Scarcely has the year begun
When we are halfway among the constellations.

[2] The legendary patriarchal emperors, Yao, Shun, and Yu.

[3] A great-grandson of the legendary emperor Chuan Hsu, B.C. 2514. He had ninety wives and was over eight hundred years old when he disappeared in the west.

[4] Han Hsin, marquis of Huai-yin, once went fishing in the river outside the city; a washerwoman, seeing how hungry he looked, gave him food. He thanked her, saying that he would one day repay her kindness, but the washerwoman answered him angrily, saying she wanted no reward. He helped Liu Pang to bring the Han dynasty into being. As the result of a plot he was later seized and beheaded in B.C. 196.

Beyond the south window everything blossoms,
The north forests are well wooded and luxuriant.
Down to mysterious pools pours timely rain,
Winds from warmer climates ruffle the early dawn.
Whoever comes must go.
Mortal destiny commands that we shall leave.
Remain with your proper destiny to the end;
Leaning on elbows we shall not harm the inward wholeness:
Whether the changing current is foul or fair,
The ups and downs can never touch our freedom.
To behave in this way shows a lofty spirit—
What need is there to climb high mountains?

Moving House

There was a time when I wanted to live in a south village,
But not because I was guided by the auguries.
I had heard that many simple men lived there—
With them I would be glad to spend my mornings and evenings.
For many years this was my desire,
And now today I shall accomplish my task:
So wretched a cottage need not be spacious,
All I want is a bed and a mat.
Often the neighbors will come to see me,
We shall argue vociferously about the ancient times,
Rare writings we shall enjoy reading together,
And we shall clear up all doubtful interpretations.

Retrospect

When I was young I remained aloof from worldly affairs,
Devoting myself to my books and my lyre,
Wearing rough clothes I was happy
And content with utter poverty.
But there came a time of change,
Of drawing reins and straying on the highway.
I threw aside my scrolls, prepared my baggage,
To be for a while separated from my garden and field.
In the far distance the solitary boat disappears.
Like a winding thread spin my thoughts for home.
Have I not traveled far and wide,
Rising and descending over a thousand li?
My heart remains with the house near the lakes and hills.
Looking at clouds I am ashamed by the high-flying birds,
Seeing fish swimming I stand abashed near the water.

The perfect ideal is locked in my heart,
No outward appearances will ever defile it.
I shall follow the dispensation of nature
And at last return to a hermit's cottage.

A Fire Burns Down My Cottage

So I lived in a thatched cottage on a narrow lane,
Always content, as long as I could avoid coaches.
Fiercely the wind blew in midsummer,
Suddenly my house was burned down.
Of the whole house not a room was left.
I went to live in a boat in front of the door.
Far away, herald of a new autumn,
The clear moon will soon be at the full.
The herbs in the garden are now sprouting again,
But the frightened birds have not yet returned.
I stand here at midnight, my thoughts afar off;
A glance embraces all the nine heavens.
I, since my youth, have been proud and stubborn—
Forty years and more have passed away.
Appearances follow their destined paths,
But the abode of the spirit is always calm:
Firm and steadfast is my character:
Not jade nor stone could be as hard.
I think of the Golden Age
When the produce of fields was never stolen,
When people could fill their bellies carelessly,
Rising at dawn, returning to sleep in the evening.
But since I cannot live in that age,
I prefer to water my garden.

Remembering the Ancient Farmstead

in early spring of the dynastic year Kwei-mao

I

In ancient times I heard of the south acres,
And yet I never once put foot on them.
There have been men with often empty bowls,
But can we avoid rising in the spring?
In the early morning I prepare my yoke,
At the beginning my mind has already traveled afar off:
The birds sing in welcoming the new season,
The mild winds bring added blessings.
Cold bamboos cover wild paths;
The land is remote—few visit it.

Therefore the old man who planted his staff[5]
Lightly went away and did not return.
Believing this, I feel inferior to one with a broad view:
The truth it preserves is not in the least shallow.

II

The Ancient Master left us a precept:
We should care for the Tao, not for poverty.
I looked eagerly toward him—he was too far to be reached:
So my purpose is to return to my arduous toil.
Wielding the plow, joyfully I ply my trade;
Laughing, I urge on the farmers.
Winds from afar sweep across open fields,
The young corn also is refreshed.
Though the harvest is not yet brought in,
What we have now gives us great happiness.
The plowman and the sower sometimes rest;
No strangers ask about their ways.
Together at sunset we return home,
And with a jar of wine I reward my neighbors.
Singing verses, I close the cottage door:
I am half as contented as a countryman.

Drinking Songs

I. CHRYSANTHEMUMS

I built my cottage among the habitations of men,
And yet I heard neither horses nor carriages.
Would you know how these things come to pass?
A distant soul creates its own solitude.
I pluck chrysanthemums under the east hedge.
Easily the south mountain comes in sight.
So wonderful is the mountain air at sunset,
And the birds flying in flocks homeward.
In all these things are secret truths:
Though I try to explain it, words are of no avail.

II. DRUNK AND SOBER

A guest resides in me,
Our interests are not altogether the same.
One of us is drunk:
The other is always awake.

---

[5] One day when Tzu-lu was walking behind the Master, he fell behind and met an old man carrying a basket over his staff. Tzu-lu said: "Sir, have you seen my master?" The old man answered, saying: "You who do not work with your four limbs, nor sift the five grains—who is your master?" Thereupon he planted his staff in the ground and began weeding, while Tzu-lu stood there with hands folded together in respect. *Analects* of Confucius, XVIII, vii.

Awake and drunk—
We laugh at one another,
And we do not understand each other's world.
Proprieties and conventions—
Such folly to follow them in earnest.
Be proud, be unconcerned;
Then you will approach wisdom.
Listen, you drunken old man,
When day dies,
Light a candle.

III. THE ORCHID

The lonely orchid grows in the courtyard,
Retaining its fragrance till the coming of the wind:
Then of a sudden a fresh breeze stirs,
And the orchid rises clear from the weeds.
Continuing the road, he has lost the old pathway;
With faith in reason he may find the way out.
Once awakened, let him think of returning.
When the birds are all killed, the bow is thrown away.

In Imitation of Old Poems [6]

I. FRIENDSHIP

Orchids blossomed beneath the window,
Thickly the willows shaded the hall:
When first I took leave of you,
I did not intend to go on a long journey.
This wanderer a thousand li from home
Met on the way a good friend:
Before we could speak our hearts were overcome.
Not that we had lifted our wine cups.
The orchids were withered and the willows wan:
Our words are not redeemed.
I bid farewell to my youthful friends.
We have not been true and steadfast.
In our passion we wished to risk our lives.
After we have parted, where is our pledge?

II. THE HERMIT

There is a worthy man in the east
Whose garments are seldom perfect.
In thirty days he will take nine meals,
And he will wear out a hat in ten years.
No one leads a more bitter life,
Yet his countenance is always fresh.
I want to visit this old man.

[6] Written in the same versification as the *Nineteen Poems*.

In the morning I start, crossing streams and mountains:
Evergreen pines border the path on both sides.
White clouds linger near eaves.
He knows why I have come,
Takes down his lyre and plays for me.
The first note startles the departing crane,
The second note sings of the solitary pheasant.
I wish to stay with you here
From now on to the end of the bitter-cold year.

The Poor Scholars

All things have their own shelter,
But the lonely cloud has nothing to lean on:
Faintly it vanishes from the sky.
When shall I see again its shedding light?
The rosy morning opens the night mist,
Innumerable birds flutter along.
One bird stirs slowly from the forest
And returns before the fall of evening.
To keep the measure and stay in old pathways
Would mean to suffer cold and hunger.
If no one knows my character,
Let it be—why should I grieve?

Reading The Book of Strange Places and Seas [7]

In early summer the woods and herbs are thriving,
Around my cottage thick sway the branches and shades.
The numerous birds delight in their sanctuaries,
And I too love my cottage.
After I have plowed and sown,
Then I return to read my books.
The narrow lane which has no deep ruts
Has often turned back an old friend's coach.
Joyfully I pour my spring wine,
And pluck the lettuce growing in my garden.
A fine rain comes from the east
And a sweet wind follows it.
Idly I read the legends of King Chou
And glance at the map of the strange places.
In a moment I am flying through the universe.
How could such a man ever be unhappy?

All translated by Yang Yeh-tzu.

[7] *The Book of Strange Places and Seas* was a book of legends supposedly compiled by Prince Huai Nan Tzu.

In Early Morning

In early morning someone knocks at my door.
Throwing on my unbuttoned clothes, I open the door myself.
"Who are you, my friend?" I ask.
There is an old, kind, good-hearted man,
Bringing with him a wine pot,
Believing that I have fallen on evil days.
"Under an old straw roof, my friend,
Humility does not go well with your life.
All the generations are the same:
I beg you not to let your legs be caked in mud."
I was so deeply moved by the old man's words,
For my soul is fashioned otherwise than theirs.
Perhaps I shall learn to walk in the dust of their wheels,
But to be false to myself—how shall I expose myself?
"Let us drink and enjoy the wine you have brought,
For my path is already laid out and cannot be altered."

Living in the Country

At the foot of the south mountain I sow beans;
The weeds tangle them, the bean shoots are weak.
I rise early and scratch in the wilderness.
Under the moonlight I return with my hoe on my shoulder.
The footpath between the furrows so narrow, the grasses so
    long
That my clothes are moistened with dew.
Why should I care when my clothes are wet?
I only hope to make myself a hermit.

The Cold Year

The bitter-cold year comes to an end.
In my cotton gown I look for the sun in the porch.
The southern orchard is bare, without leaves.
The rotting branches are heaped in the north garden.
I empty my cup and drink to the dregs,
And when I look in the kitchen, no smoke rises from the
    hearths;
Books and poems lie scattered beside my chair,
Yet the light is dying, and I shall have no time to read.
My life here is not like the agony in Ch'en,[8]
But sometimes I suffer from bitter reproaches.
Then let me remember, to calm my distress,
That the sages of old suffered from the same melancholy.

[8] Where Confucius nearly starved to death.

An Elegy for Myself

Where there is life, there must be death:
Dying early—even this may not be a short life.
Last night we were human beings,
But today we enter into the lists of the spirits.
Where are our souls going?
Are they attached to our withered bodies?
My adorable children will weep for their father,
And some good friends will caress my dead body with tears.
As for myself, I shall entirely have lost sensation;
There will be no difference between right and wrong,
When a thousand years have gone past.
None will remember the glory and humility of today.
Now that I live in the world,
All I regret is that I did not drink like a prodigal.

What I could not drink during my life,
They will not give me after my death.
The ants only have wings in the spring:
Let us enjoy life while there is still time.
It will be too late when they are weeping round my deathbed,
When my eyes see no longer and I am underground,
On the day when, having been laid out in the morning in the
        main hall,
At night I sleep for the first time in a wilderness.
The tall grasses will wave round my tomb,
The wind will moan in the shading poplars.
Autumn: a white frost covering the ground,
The horses browsing and neighing all round me.
There in my small underground chamber, alone,
I shall be imprisoned for thousands of years.
A thousand years without seeing the light again:
A thousand years without speaking to a human being.

Those who brought me here in a procession
Have gone again, each one to his home.
Some weep, and others sing.
I am nothing, buried deep in the earth.

Chrysanthemums

The autumn chrysanthemums have the loveliest colors,
Flowers and leaves all moistened with the dew.
I drink this cup of all-forgetful wine,
And so drive all my earthly cares away.
Alone I lift the cup to my lips:

The wine is poured when the cup is empty.
And everything is silent at the setting of the sun;
While the homing birds flock to the woods there is chirping.
Under the east balcony I shout boisterously:
Satisfied now that my humble life can go on.

All translated by Yang Chi-sing.

Return to the Country

I

When I was young, I had no taste for worldly affairs,
And naturally I grew up to love the mountains.
By mistake I fell into the traps of the world;
And there I wasted thirty years.
Imprisoned birds long for their ancient woods,
Fish on shore long for their former waters.
I cultivate the land in the south region.
So, like a peasant, I return to my native fields.
I possess no more than ten mu[9]
And no more than eight or nine rooms.
Birch and willows shade the eaves of my house,
Peach and apricot grow in the courtyard.
Far in the distance are the huts of men.
Above their roofs comes the faint smoke.
Dogs bark in the deep lanes,
Cocks crow on the tops of mulberry bushes.
Inside the house no sounds come to disturb me;
I live alone, perfectly at leisure.
There, for a long while, I was imprisoned in a cage,
But now once again I return to myself.

II

The affairs of men are absent in the country.
No bustle of wheels in the poor, solitary lanes.
By the clear light of day doors are half closed.
In the empty house all worldly desires fade away.
There are times when peasants meet together,
Wearing rough clothes; they wander at leisure,
And though together, never speak a word,
Except to give their best regards to the hemp and mulberries.
Each day the mulberries and hemp increase,
And every day my acres are enlarged.
But always I fear the coming of sleet and frost,
When all is ruined—nothing but brushwood!

[9] About one sixth of an English acre.

The Return

I must return. My fields and my orchards
Are invaded by weeds.
Why should I not return?
Since I have made my soul the slave of my body,
Why should I wait, moaning dreadfully?
No, I shall not waste my sighs on the past,
I shall lift my spirit toward the far future.
I have not wandered too far from the path.
     Still I know
I am once more on the road to my home.

Lightly, lightly, the boat glides lightly,
My gown fills with wind and flies in the air.
I discover the road as I go forward,
And curse the faintness of sunset and dawn.

Ah, then, my door and my house will appear to me,
I shall exult and run like a boy,
The servants will press forward to greet me,
My children will be waiting before the door.
The three pathways are almost overgrown,
But the pine trees are still green,
And the chrysanthemums will spread their blossoms.
I take the children by the hand and enter.
Wine is brought to me in full bottles.
I empty the cup and lean on the window
And joyfully contemplate my favorite branches,
And joyfully savor the peace of my cottage.
Sometimes I wander in my garden
Where there is a door that is rarely open.
I lean on my staff at my leisure
And sometimes lift my head and look around.
Idly, the clouds climb the valleys;
The birds, weary of flying, seek for their nests.
Light thickens, but still I remain in the fields,
Caressing with my hands a solitary pine.

               I must return!
I shall have no more friends to amuse me.
The world and I have broken apart.
What have I to do with men any longer?
I shall forget myself in the peace of my family,
And the hours will pass, and the music of my lyre. . . .

And the peasants say that spring is coming,
And in the western fields we must seek out our plows.
I shall ride out in a carriage
And drive over the sharp hills of my estate.
I shall row a small boat into the wilderness
Of leaves in search of a quiet grotto.
The trees, splendidly gleaming,
Climb higher with the coming of spring,
And the fountains and the springs
Steal from their caverns of rock.
Ah, happy is life in the spring,
But my life is slowly coming to an end.

How long shall I stay in the world?
Why do they not leave my heart in peace?
Why do I torment myself so vainly?
Shall I stay, shall I go?
I have no love for honors,
I have no love for riches.
Paradise is beyond all my hopes.
And therefore in the clear daylight
I shall walk among my fields and among my flowers,
Singing a little and sighing,
And climbing the mountains of the east
To the accompaniment of a liquid stream,
Chanting a few songs,
Till the time comes when I shall be summoned away,
Having accomplished my destiny, with no cares in the world.

THE T'ANG DYNASTY

(A.D. *618–954*)

LI SHIH-MING (A.D. 597–649)

Li Shih-ming, the second emperor of the T'ang dynasty, was one of the most glorious figures of Chinese history. He was born in A.D. 597, twenty years before the T'ang dynasty came into being. He was still a young man when he ended the age-old struggle with the Turks and sealed the treaty of friendship by the sacrifice of a white horse on a bridge over the river Wei, which separated the two armies. In 621 he was nominated to the post of Chief Guardian of the Empire, and in 627, on the abdication of his father, he ascended the throne, taking the title of Chen Kuan. He was a contemporary of Theodosius, whose ambassador reached Ch'ang-an in 640. He was a great administrator, a lover of poetry, handsome in youth, and splendid in all the achievements of peace. The first Christian missionaries arrived during his reign; he gave refuge to Firouz, son of Yezdegard; he allowed the Manichaeans and the Zoro-astrians and Moslems to build temples in his country. *The Journey to the West*, which Arthur Waley has admirably trans-lated under the title *Monkey*, gives a disarming and perhaps inaccurate report of him. He was canonized under the name of T'ang T'ai Tsung, "Great Ancestor of the T'ang," by which he is now better known.

To the Tune of "Horses Drinking by the Great Wall"[1]

Beyond the frontiers lie the hard winters and the raging winds;
The waters of Chiao Ho are frozen over with huge icebergs.
On the Han Lake come the hundred layers of waves.
Over the Yin Mountains lie thousands of li of snow.
The garrisons live hard, gazing out for beacon fires.
On the highest peaks, the banners of the commander are
    unfurled,
But the soldiers fold theirs: the hunt begins.
They water their horses at the foot of the Great Wall.
Interminable the footprints of horses over endless cold sands.
Hear on the frontier the howling of the north wind.
We entered the land of the Huns and subdued them in their
    desert strongholds.

[1] A song that was sung during the last years of the Han dynasty (B.C. 206-A.D. 221).

148

To the west were the natives of Chiang, who played on flutes
    and cymbals to welcome us,
Here the Huns themselves laid down their arms and surren-
    dered.
The soldiers of Han returned in triumph.
High in the air flew the banner of victory.
A tablet was engraved with their names, for the sake of
    posterity.
In battle with barbarians peace was assured,
And on the altar of heaven we sang our victory.

Translated by Wang Sheng-chih.

CHEN TZU-ANG (A.D. 656–698)

He came from a wealthy Szechuanese family, and spent his life up to the age of seventeen gambling and drinking, but suddenly changed his habits and set to studying, becoming a *chin shih* at the age of twenty-eight. Once he purchased a costly lute and went to the market place, offering to sing on it, but at the moment he was about to sing, he dashed it into a thousand pieces and handed round copies of his poems instead. He became intimate with the empress Wu Hou, but on the death of his father the local magistrate threw him into prison, hoping to obtain the wealth his father had left behind. Chen Tzu-ang died in prison at the age of forty-two.

The Ancients

I look before, and do not see the ancients.
Looking after I do not see the coming ages.
Only Heaven and Earth will last forever:
Alone I lament, and my tears fall down.

Men of Affairs

Men of affairs are proud of their cunning and skill,
But in the Tao they have still much to learn.
They are proud of their exploitations,
But they do not know what happens to the body.
Why do they not learn from the Master of Dark Truth,
Who saw the whole world in a little jade bottle?
Whose bright soul was free of Earth and Heaven,
For riding on Change he entered into Freedom.

WANG WEI (A.D. 699-759)

Like Campion, he was a physician as well as a poet, but when he lived he was more famous as a painter. "In his poetry," said Su T'ung-po, "there is painting, and in his painting poetry." His ancestors came from Taiyuan in Shansi, but during his father's lifetime the family moved to Yunchi in the same province, and it was there at the age of nineteen that he began to write his most famous poems.

He was made *chin shih* at the age of twenty-one. When, in the fourteenth year of T'ien-pao, An Lu-shan raised the flag of rebellion, Wang Wei was captured and imprisoned in a monastery in Loyang—it was said that An Lu-shan wanted to see what kind of animal a poet was. He remained in Loyang, compelled to act as censor, until the death of his captor, when he was released. He was accused of being a collaborationist, and like many poets seems to have cared little enough for either of the contending powers—he lived in considerable luxury and honor in his captivity. He was later reappointed to high position by the emperor Su Tsung, chiefly as a result of the influential connections of his brother Wang Chin, a Buddhist who possessed quite fantastic influence at one time on the emperor T'ai Tsung and who was later banished. He did not remain long in court. His wife died. A settled melancholy sent him into the hills, where he lived quietly until he died at the age of sixty in a monk's gown.

He was a superb painter, and wrote as delicately and convincingly as he painted. Like Wu Tao-tzu, the greatest of all Chinese painters, he would say before beginning to paint: "I have it all in my heart." It was not necessary for him to paint while gazing at scenery, and some of his most subtle evocations of landscape were clearly written in the library. His poetry, which follows the almost impossibly strict form of *chueh-chu*, is very similar to the little we know of his painting —the moon is always rising, the plum blossoms are always falling, and the forest is empty. He was a firm believer in Buddhism, and there is a Buddhist clarity in his poems that is absent in the *chueh-chu* of the later poets of the T'ang dynasty. More than anyone except Tao Yuan-ming and Tu Fu, he can evoke a whole landscape in a single line.

Morning

The peach blossom is redder because rain fell overnight,
The willows are greener in the morning mist.
The fallen petals are not yet swept away by servants.
Birds sing. The guest on the hill is asleep.

The Cold Mountain

The cold mountain turns dark green.
The autumn stream flows murmuring on.
Leaning on my staff beneath the wicket gate,
In the rushing wind I hear the cry of the aged cicada.

Beside the Lake

While the flute played on the edge of the water,
At sunset I bade farewell to my husband.
For a while I gazed upon the lake,
And there was only a white cloud rolling among green hills.

After Long Rain

The long rain falls on the empty forest. Smoke rises
Over the cooking pots where they are preparing to feast the
    neighbors.
With immense wings the heron flows over the rice fields.
In the deep shade the yellow heron is singing.

In a Bamboo Grove

Lying alone in this dark bamboo grove,
Playing on a flute, continually whistling,
In this dark wood where no one comes,
The bright moon comes to shine on me.

Verses

You who come from the old village—
Tell me what is happening there.
When you left, were the chill plum blossoms
Flowering beneath the white window?

A Song for Wei City

The morning rain of Wei city wets the white dust,
The inns are green, the willows are in spring.
May I advise you to empty one more cup,
For west of the Yuan-kuan hills you will find no friend.

Desolation

There was no sight of man in the immense mountain,
Yet human voices were continually being heard.
The sun reflects the distant scenes into the thick woods,
Forming patterns on the green moss.

Translated by Li Fu-ning.

Thinking of My Brother in Shantung on the Ninth Day of the Ninth Moon

To be a stranger in a strange land:
Whenever one feasts, one thinks of one's brother twice as
     much as before.
There where my brother far away is ascending,
The dogwood is flowering, and a man is missed.

Meditation

Red beans grow in the south country,
In autumn flourishing on many boughs.
I beg you gather them in great quantities,
For I love nothing better than these.[1]

Translated by Li Fu-ning.

Departure

I have just seen you go down the mountain.
I close the wicker gate in the setting sun.
The grass will be green again in coming spring,
But will the wanderer ever return?

On Going Away

Dismounting from my horse to drink with you,
"Where are you going?" I asked.
You said: "Because I cannot go where I want to go,
I shall return to the south mountain border.
There I shall not care what happens outside.
The white clouds flow on forever."

[1] The red beans, the seeds of *Abrus precatorius*, grow wild in some
parts of Hainan. One half of the bean is bright red, the other half black.

Walking at Leisure

Walking at leisure we watch laurel flowers falling.
In the silence of this night the spring mountain is empty.
The moon rises, the birds are startled
As they sing occasionally near the spring fountain.

In the Hills[2]

White pebbles jut from the river stream,
Stray leaves turn red in the cold autumn:
No rain is falling on the mountain path,
But my clothes are damp in the fine green air.

Translated by Li Fu-ning.

[2] Su T'ung-po regarded this poem as the best example to demonstrate Wang Wei's genius in painting in words instead of in colors.

THE SONG OF EXPERIENCING
THE TAO

For some reason few purely Chinese Buddhist poems have been preserved. There are lines in the *Lotos Essence*, translated from Sanskrit, which possess an entirely Chinese flavor, as for example the description of the blessed:

> The flesh and hair shine,
> Even the forehead shines,
> And whitened hairs shed light.
> It is because all virtue
> Was planted long ago.
> The body is immovable,
> Having entered into ecstasy.
> Extraordinary virtue brightly burns
> And shines with glory.

But for the most part Chinese Buddhist poetry follows the Sanskrit, and though the persevering reader will find among the Ch'an patriarchs a curious foreshadowing of some of the evanescent poems of Wang Wei, he will find little of permanent value, and much that is merely puzzling. There exists, however, a curious collection of songs composed by the southern school of the Ch'an Buddhists known as the School of Shen-hui. According to tradition the songs were composed by a monk from Yung-chia in Chekiang called Hsuan-chueh, who was known to be alive in the year 713. But whether he was the real author of the forty-six Buddhist songs attributed to him is still uncertain.

For this selection from the *Yung-chia Cheng-tao-ko* I am indebted to Dr. Walter Liebenthal's admirable translations and commentaries published in *Monumenta Serica*, VI, 1941.

I

The roar of the lion is the fearless man speaking:
When the beasts hear it, their skulls crack open.
Hearing it, stampeding elephants lose their majestic powers.
Only the gods and dragons rejoice when it is heard in meditation.

II

He meditates when walking and when sitting.
Silent, speaking, moving, resting, his body is at peace.

In the face of pointed swords he remains eternally calm.
Many Kalpas ago our Master met Dipamkara,[1]
But already he was the "patient sufferer."[2]

III

Purify the five eyes, possess the five powers.
If once you have known truth, you know the unknown.
In a mirror the body's shape is easily discerned,
But in vain can you grasp the moon on the water.

IV

They walk alone, and yet they are together—
Along the road to Nirvana, the Perfect Ones
With antique minds, pure-hearted, high-spirited,
With sunken cheekbones, despised by the common people.

V

Wander the streams and oceans, cross mountains and rivers,
Search for the Way, call upon masters, desire to enter the Tao.
No sooner have you come to Ts'ao-hsi,[3]
You will know that neither birth nor death has any meaning.

VI

The moon shines on the river, pines sigh in the wind.
What happens in the quietness of eternal night?
My heart is confirmed in its pure Buddhahood.
My body is clothed in dust, dew, clouds, and sunset.

VII

An alms bowl subdues a dragon, a stick defeats tigers.
The two sets of gold rings sound *ling-ling*.
The priest does not carry his stick to no purpose.
It is the stick of the *tathagata*,[4] a holy relic.

VIII

In the forest of sandalwood, only the trees grow.
The lion runs wild in these thickets.

[1] In former times the Buddha in the incarnation of Sumedha met the Buddha Dipamkara. He spread his hair on the ground, that it might be used as a carpet by the Buddha. Dipamkara prophesied his future for him.

[2] The story of the "patient sufferer" is told in the *Vajracchedika Sutra*. The ascetic is sitting in meditation in a wood. Near by a king is hunting, accompanied by the ladies of his harem. After the hunt the king, tired, goes to sleep. Awakened, he asks for the women, but they are found in the company of the meditating ascetic. The king takes his sword and cuts the ascetic into pieces, but the ascetic feels no resentment at all.

[3] In Shao-chou, Kwangtung, where there was the monastery of Hui-neng, the sixth Ch'an patriarch.

[4] I.e. the Buddha.

In the silence of the forests none dares oppose him.
The birds fly away, the animals run from him.

IX

The baby lion was ahead of the common herd.
When three years old, he roared tremendously.
Though the jackals compete with the King of the Law [5]
And shout for a hundred years, they exist to no purpose.

X

Let them slander me: I remain unmoved.
Who tries to burn the sky only wearies himself.
I drink the words of the slanderer as though they were dew.
They purge me; suddenly I enter the Ineffable.

If you find any virtue in evil words,
Then the slanderer becomes your spiritual guide.
Let neither offense nor slander provoke hatred in you.
How otherwise can the power of divine endurance be beheld?

[5] *Fa wang:* the King of the Law, or Dharma.

LI PO

We do not know whether he was born in Kansu or in Szechuan, or even the date of his birth, or how he died. Like Chu Yuan, he claimed royal ancestry—from the emperor Li Kao of the state of Liang—but this too is uncertain. We know that before he was born, his mother dreamed that a star had fallen into her arms, and from the great white (*Tai-po*) star of Venus he derived his name. There is a legend that his immediate ancestors were thieves and murderers who had taken refuge in the frontier districts, and since everything is possible in the life of a poet who lived in a continual fairyland of the imagination, it is not improbable that his ancestors were equally immune to criticism. There may have been tribal blood in him. He was tall and powerfully built; he had a loud screeching voice; he ate like a tiger and boasted that he could drink 300 cups at a sitting. He married at least three times, and seems to have been as irreverent toward women as he was to the Emperor. He met Tu Fu, and though he was at least ten years older than the younger poet, they slept under the same coverlet and walked hand in hand in the sunlight, and the friendship between them remained long after they had separated. He was a good swordsman, an excellent musician, and a connoisseur of good wines; he was a debauchee and a drunkard and perhaps even a murderer; he was once sentenced to death and he was three times under arrest, but it is doubtful whether any of these things meant much to him. He cared for none of his great accomplishments, and amused himself by writing poems and then throwing them into a stream and watching them sail away. He was the spirit of freedom walking in a bloody land.

It is usual to describe him as a Taoist, but he would never have accepted the description. Ho Chih-chang called him "a god in exile"; he called himself the *tai-peng*—the great phoenix, whose wings obscure the sun like clouds. Like Chu Yuan, he liked to wear a garment made entirely of flowers, and then, with his bright hungry tigerish eyes, his black hair flowing over his shoulders, his arms akimbo, he would recite poetry deliriously, as though the gods were speaking through him. Like Blake, he would speak in the most matter-of-fact voice imaginable of his encounters with the angels, and describe how the heavens opened to receive him; but sometimes, and perhaps as a result of his extraordinary intoxication with the mere sights and sounds of the world, he would fall into profound fits of melancholy. "At fifteen," he wrote, "I ran after gods and goblins," and though he enjoyed his brief visits to fairyland.

he was often inextricably caught up in a world where there was only bloodshed, avarice, corruption, and despair. For long periods he disappeared from the world, wandering through half the provinces of China—once he was banished to the distant southwest province of Yunnan, then known as Yeh-lang. He seems to have liked flowers and water most, and in a line that echoes a famous prose essay by Tao Yuan-ming, he combined the two things he loved most in a single litany:

> The peach blossom follows the moving water.

The evanescence of the world tormented him, drove him to frenzy; he would dam the water and make an everlasting flower of imperishable metal if he could, and yet he knew that the sheer beauty of the world lay in its evanescence. He seems to have been shortsighted—the objects in the foreground of his poetry are brilliantly illuminated, but the background is always misty and hardly discernible—and for him everything seems to be colored more deeply and splendidly than it has ever appeared to anyone else except perhaps Ezekiel. He had no knowledge of the restraints of poetry. Once he asked Tu Fu whether he was growing thin from the hard labor of composing poetry; he himself composed as easily as a bird sings. There are three things he writes about superbly: the grace of young women (he had a dangerous faculty of being able to project himself into a young girl's mind); then there was the morning freshness of the world, and the vision of heaven that is like lightning. He was born with all the talents except one—he had no means to prevent his dangerous facility from overriding him. He could compose on anything. He could write about fairyland, a country he seems to have known well; he could write about the court beauties, the vanished glories of the past, the beauty of drunkenness, of his long journeys, his impassioned friendships; he wrote splendidly of dawn and flowers, and hardly less splendidly of night and the stars. His poetry is full of young girls, flowers, birds, stars, the plum blossoms in spring, and the chrysanthemums in autumn. All that was colored with life he celebrated, and death never enters his poems.

His greatest virtue was that he was equal to his boasts. When he said: "I am strong enough to meet ten thousand men," it was no more than an understatement. He insulted court officials whenever it pleased him, and nothing delighted him more than that the Emperor should order the powerful eunuch Kao Li-shih to pull off his shoes when he was in a state of drunkenness. He delighted in intrigue. He liked drowsing drunkenly in the market place. For a while he was almost ruler of the empire; the Emperor seasoned his soup for him with his own hands, and secretly ordered him to compose mandates and rescripts. But he seems to have preferred, rather than the highest honors of the state, the diploma he received from a Taoist archpriest that called him "the high heavenly priest of the White Lake." Once, traveling by river boat between Tsai-hi and Nanking, he robed himself in his palace robes of the finest silk, with girdle pendants clicking and pearls shading his eyes from his mortar-like hat, and suddenly and for no reason at all he burst out into the wildest laughter, rolling his eyes.

He was distantly related to Li Hua, who composed the saddest, though not the best, of the innumerable odes dedicated to battlefields; but no kinsmen could be more different. Li Hua composed deliberately—one can almost see him biting the hairs of his brush—but Li Po composed in a way that surprised even himself: "I compose verses without tiring, while in front of my house carts and horses go by." But if he composed effortlessly, he composed also with amazing strength. His strength is not so apparent in English, but Chinese scholars insist that his poetry has the quality of lightning, of sudden sharp illuminations and an endless sudden tearing down of veils. It is true that behind the veils he tears down, there are other veils—there is always fairyland, a landscape of an impossible flowering, but the fairyland is etched sharply with the dagger strokes of his calligraphy, which is supposed to have been as brilliantly haphazard as his poems.

Like Milton, Tu Fu rarely mentions colors; Li Po delights in them, runs after them, and sometimes runs them to earth. His flowers are so often like "blue smoke," his islands are so often "burning red with flowers," his skies are so often dark red or yellow or blazing blue that we tire of them, and there comes a time when even his remorseless vitality palls on jaded nerves. Nearly every poem seems to be written in the hard crystalline light of "The Phoenix and the Turtle":

GRIEF FOR THE JADE STAIRS

> A white dew grows on the jade stairs.
> When night comes it wets her silk shoes.
> She comes in, lets falls the crystal screen,
> And gazes through it at the autumn moon.

The translation, of course, is hopelessly inadequate, but we can at least follow the general movement of the poem. What is brilliant is the swiftness of the action, the evocation of mood, and the complete world enclosed within twenty words of Chinese. The dew "grows" like any flower, and the autumn moon brings no comfort. We can see the girl, but we cannot share her grief, for there is a crystal screen between—and how often do we feel when we are reading his poems that there is a crystal fountain separating him from the world, and he sees everything in the brightly colored refracted vision of someone looking at a landscape through a waterfall. The brilliance is there; there are more colors than we ever dreamed of; there is even more grief; but there is always the crystal screen.

Perhaps the screen was necessary. Sometimes he almost insists upon its necessity, and there is a mysterious poem, "To the Fisherman," in which he insists on hiding his purity:

> Do not shake your crown, if perfumed;
> Do not flap your skirts, if scented with orchids.
> It is better to hide the chaste soul's radiance.
> The world hates a thing too pure.

There was nothing original in this: the whole empire was full of carefree *Wandervogeln* who despised the towns and took refuge in the high cliffs or in the mountains. Tao Yuan-ming said that his greatest delight was to play with children; Li Po's heart's desire was "to go rowing in a boat with my hair down." He has all Shelley's delight in water and loneliness. He was never entirely human or at ease in the world. And though the story is almost certainly untrue, it is significant that for centuries men believed he died like Li Ho at the summons of the angelic hosts, who suddenly appeared to him on a moonlight night when he was supping in his boat. Dolphins came and stood on their tails and two children of immortality came carrying in their hands banners to lead him the way to the celestial palaces, which he reached riding on the back of dolphins. But it is more probable, as Liu Hsu relates in *The Old Book of T'ang,* that he died from overdrinking. And perhaps the two stories are not incompatible. He was buried near the river. Li Hua wrote the inscription on his tomb, and Po Chu-i visited the grave fifty years later, finding only a small mound in an endless plain of grass. He died in 762, at the age of about sixty.

After his death his works were collected together by his remote cousin Li Yang-pin under the significant title *The Thatched Roof.* Of the twenty thousand poems written in his lifetime, hardly a tenth remained. Li Yang-pin states categorically that nine out of ten of the poems written during the eight years following the rebellion of An Lu-shan (A.D. 755) are lost. These were the poems written in the full maturity of his genius, and those that we can least do without. Li Po had not arranged his poems, and seems to have taken no interest in their publication. It was not until 1080 that the canon of 1,800 poems was collected together by Sung Ming-chiu.

He was not perhaps the greatest of all Chinese poets, but

he remains the most celebrated, the most gifted, the most incorrigibly poetic. Like Hölderlin, he seems to have been almost a god. "He in his power," wrote Li Yang-pin, "may be said to rival Nature, the creator and transformer." It was no more than the truth.

―――――――∾―――――――

Song before Offering Wine

Do you not see the waters of the Yellow River flowing down
    from the sky?
The swift stream pours into the sea and never returns.
Do you not see the bright mirror in the high hall lamenting the
    silver hair,
Which in the morning was pure silk but in the evening has
    turned to snow?
You who are sated with life, come drink to the dregs.
Never let the gold cup lie empty by moonlight.

Since I am heaven-born, I must use my talents.
Though I spend ten thousand pieces of gold, they will be
    returned to me.
Kill the sheep! Slay the ox! Make merry!
In a single round I'll drink three hundred cups!

Come, Master Ch'in,
Come, Tan Chiu,
I offer you wine, don't refuse it.
I will sing you a song.
Pray, listen attentively.

The bells and the drums and the dainties are not to be prized.
I desire only to be drunk forever, and not to wake up.
The ancient saints and wiseacres have long ago been forgotten:
Only the great drinkers immortalized their fame.
Once Prince Ch'en gave a feast in Ping-yueh temple,
Gave ten thousand coins for a wine bucket, everyone feasting.
I am the host. Can I say I am lacking in money?
We will buy some wine and we'll drink together.
Though it cost my horse of five colors
Or my furs worth ten thousand gold,
I'll send the boy to barter them for excellent wine:
We'll drown the sorrows of a thousand generations together.

Conversation in the Mountains

If you were to ask me why I dwell among green mountains,
I should laugh silently; my soul is serene.
The peach blossom follows the moving water;
There is another heaven and earth beyond the world of men.

To a Beautiful Lady Encountered on the Road

Proudly, the sleek horseman tramples the fallen flowers.
With dangling crop he raps on the chariot of five-colored
clouds.[1]
The beautiful woman within smiles as she lifts the jeweled
curtain.
"There is my humble home," she says, pointing to a red house
beyond.

You Have a Yellow Horse[2]

You have a yellow horse,
Mine is white.
The colors are not the same,
But our hearts are united.

Together we wandered through the outskirts,
Two young blades of Loyang stepping side by side.
Our long jeweled swords dazzled in the sun,
Scarlet were our high headdresses.
Each wore furs worth a thousand pieces of gold.
Each was the guest of five orders of princes.[3]
You, the fierce tiger, have fallen into the trap.
The brave man submits to bitter fate,
But when you, my comrade, are in such distress,
What avails it if I alone am happy?

[1] No one appears to know what a "chariot of five-colored clouds" is. The
commentators refer the reader to the Taoist monk Chiu Yu-tzu, who was
summoned by Hsi Wang Mu, the Empress of the West, on the fifth day
of the eighth moon, and ascended to heaven in a five-colored cloud
chariot.

[2] The commentators refer to a song of the Han dynasty:
> You have a yellow horse,
> Mine is white:
> The horses do not go together.
> Mine is the better one.

[3] Refers to the five orders of nobility founded in the Chou dynasty: duke
(*kung*), marquis (*hou*), count (*po*), viscount (*tzu*) and baron (*nan*).

A Meeting

They met in the red dust.[4]
He raised his yellow-gold crop in salutation.
"There are ten thousand houses among the drooping willows:
O lady, where are you living?"

The Girl of Yueh

She is gathering lotos seed in the river of Yueh.
While singing, she sees a stranger and turns around;
Then she smiles and hides among the lotos leaves,
Pretending to be overcome by shyness.

A Song of Chang-kan[5]

My hair could hardly cover my forehead;
I was plucking flowers near the door.
Then you came riding a bamboo horse
And threw green plums near my bed.
A long while we lived together at Chang-kan village,
And we were innocent, without passion or desire.

At fourteen I became your wife.
I was so modest that I dared not smile.
I lowered my head into a dark corner.
Though you called me a thousand times, I would not look at
    you.
At fifteen I composed my eyebrows:
With you I was willing to be dust and ashes.
For your sake I would die on the pillar;[6]
Having you, why should I mount the watching tower?[7]

[4] Red dust means the world. The commentators refer to an earlier song,
called "West Capital":
            Red dust from the four corners of the world,
            Hidden in mist, mingling together. . . .
I do not know why they quote these lines, which entirely fail to illustrate
the poem; and suspect that the Chinese passion for commentaries and
footnotes must be as great as our own.

[5] Chang-kan, a village near Nanking.

[6] At some time in the sixth century B.C. a young scholar named Wei
Sheng arranged to meet a girl under a bridge in Ch'ang-an. He was
delayed, the river was rising, the girl remained and was drowned, holding
on to a pillar.

[7] A mound near the village from which wives looked for their absent
husbands.

At sixteen, you went on a journey.
The waves on Chu-tang gorge were crushed against Yen-yu
    rock.[8]
These rapids are not passable in rainy May—
Only the monkeys lamenting against the sky!

Before the door, where you went away,
Each footprint is overgrown with green moss—
So deep it is, none can sweep it away.
The first autumn wind added the falling leaves.

Then in September the yellow butterflies
Hovering in pairs over the grass in the west courtyard:
Seeing them, my heart aches.
Must I sit sorrowfully, seeing my red cheeks fading?

Someday, when you leave Three Pa district,[9]
Please write home a letter beforehand,
For though I cannot walk a long distance,
I will come to meet you in Long Wind Sands.

A Second Song of Chang-kan

I was a young girl hidden deep in her chamber;
I did not know the dust and smoke of the world.
Because I have married a man of Chang-kan,
Daily I go to the sands and look at the winds.

In May the south wind blows.
I think of you sailing down from Pa-ling.
In September the west wind whirls.
I dream of you coursing down the Yangtze River.

You came, you went away, and I shall always sorrow.
We were often parted, and rarely met.
When did you arrive at Hsiang-tan?
In wind and storm my dream follows you.

Last night the wind raged furiously,
And broke the trees on the riverbank.
The river flooded over, the waters were boundless and dark:
Where were you then, O my beloved?

[8] A dangerous gorge in eastern Szechuan. Yen-yu is the name of a great
rock that stands in the middle of the river, which floods in May.
[9] Three Pa is a place in Szechuan, where her husband was trading.

Your wife mounts the saddle of a flying cloud,
Desiring only to meet you east of the Orchid Island.
Then we shall be happy as mandarian ducks among green
    reeds,
Or as the sporting halcyons embroidered on a silk screen.

There was a time—I was just fifteen—
My face was as red as a peach flower.
Why should I be a river merchant's wife,
Thinking always of water and wind?

Verses

Clean is the autumn wind,
Splendid the autumn moon.
The blown leaves are heaped and scattered,
The ice-cold raven starts from its roost.
Dreaming of you—when shall I see you again?
On this night sorrow fills my heart.

The Moon over the Mountain Pass

The bright moon soars over the Mountain of Heaven,
Gliding over an ocean of clouds.
A shrill wind screaming ten thousand li away,
And a sound of whistling from Yu-men pass.
The imperial army marches down White Mound Road.
The Tartars search the bays of the Blue Sea.
The warriors look back to their distant homes:
Never yet has one been seen to return.
Tonight, on the high towers she is waiting.
There is only sorrow and unending grieving.

Fighting on the South Frontier

Last year we fought by the springs of San-kan River,
This year we fight on the Tsung-ho roads.
We have dipped our weapons in the waves of Chiao-chi Lake,
We have pastured our horses in the snows of the T'ien
    Mountains,
We have gone into battle ten thousand li away.
Our three armies are utterly exhausted.

The Huns think of slaughter as a kind of plowing.
From of old they have seen only white bones in the yellow
    sands.
Where the Ch'in emperors built walls against the Hu bar-
    barians,
The sons of Han burn beacon fires.
The beacons burn without ceasing.
There is no end to war!

On the field of battle men grapple each other and die,
The horses of the fallen utter lament to heaven,
Ravens and kites peck men's guts,
And flying away, hang them on the boughs of dead trees.
So men are smeared on the desert grass,
And the generals return empty-handed.
Know that weapons of war are utterly evil—
The virtuous man uses them only when he must.

Meditation on a Quiet Night

I see the moonlight shining on my couch.
Can it be that frost has fallen?
I lift my head and watch the mountain moon,
Then my head droops in meditation of earth.

Song of the Blue Water

The shining moon burns the blue water.
On the south lake he is gathering white lilies.
These lotoses are whispering tenderly.
Sorrowfully the boatman sighs.

In the Mountains on a Summer Day

Lazily I stir a white feather fan,
Lying naked within the green wood.
I hang my hat on a crag,
And bare my head to the wind of the pines.

To Tan Ch'iu

My friend is dwelling in the eastern mountain,
Delighting in the beauty of valleys and hills.
In the green spring he lies in deserted forests,
And he is fast asleep when the sun rises.

The wind of the pines ripples his skirts and sleeves.
The pebbled brook cleanses his heart and ears.
How I envy you, far from all striving,
Pillowed high in a mist of blue clouds!

A Girl of Yueh

The waters of Mirror Lake are white like the moon.
This girl in the stream of Yueh glitters like snow,
Her new dress dapples the waves,
An endless bright shining. . . .

On Hearing the Sound of Flutes at Loyang on a Spring Night

Whence comes the sound of the jade flute, flying through the dark,
Coming with the spring wind, hovering over Loyang?
On a night like this to hear the song of "Willow-breaking"—
What else can I do but think bitterly of my home?

The Girls of Yueh

The jade faces of the girls on Yueh Stream,
Their dusky brows, their red skirts,
Each wearing a pair of golden spiked sandals—
Oh, their feet are white like frost.

Leaving White Emperor City at Dawn[1]

At dawn amid colored clouds I left White Emperor City:
A thousand miles to Chiang-ling—I was there in a day!
Chattering monkeys on the cliffs, no end to their bawling.
So the light boat slipped past the ten thousand mountains.

A Poem for Wang Lung

Li Po was about to sail in his boat,
When suddenly he heard sounds of stamping and singing on shore.
The Peach Flower Lake is a thousand fathoms deep,
But it cannot compare with Wang Lung's love, bidding farewell.

[1] White Emperor City lies in Szechuan, Chiang-ling in Hopei. When he says he reached there in a day, Li Po is of course romancing.

Song for the Moon on Mount Omei

Like a crescent of autumn shines the moon of Omei:
The pale light floods the Ping-chiang River.
Tonight I shall leave Ching-chi for the Three Gorges—
Then down to Yochow, thinking of you whom I cannot see!

Boating Song

A boat of sandalwood and oars of magnolia:
At both ends sit "flutes of jade and pipes of gold."[2]
Pretty singing girls, countless flagons of sweet wine.
Oh, let me follow the waves, wherever they take me.
I am like the fairy who rode away on a yellow crane.
Aimlessly I wander, following the white gulls.
The songs of Chu-ping[3] still shine like the sun and moon:
Of the palaces and towers of the Ch'u kings no trace is left
    on the mountains.
With a single stroke of my pen I shake the five mountains.
The poem finished, I laugh—my delight is vaster than the
    oceans.
If riches and fame could last forever,
The Han River would flow northwestward to its source.

For the Dancer of the King of Wu, When She Is Half Drunk

The wind waves the lotoses in the scented palace by the water.
In the Ku-su Tower, the King of Wu is carousing.[4]
Hsi-shih, flushed with wine, dances coy and unresisting.
By the east window, laughing, she leans on a couch of white
    jade.

An Elegy for Yueh

The King of Yueh, K'u-chien, conquered the men of Wu.
These loyal servitors rode home, clad in brocade.
The court maidens were flowers filling the spring palace.
Where today only partridge are flying.

[2] I.e., the musicians are sitting at the prow and stern.
[3] Chu-ping is another name for Chu Yuan, who served in the state of
Ch'u.
[4] Hsi-shih, the most beautiful of all Chinese consorts, was discovered
washing her clothes by the side of a stream by K'u Chien, the King of
Yueh, who presented her to the King of Wu.

In deserted gardens wild terraces, the willows are green:
Once again they must sing "Gathering Chestnuts" because
    spring is here.
Now there is only the moon shining on the west river,
Which shone once on the fair girl in the palace of Wu.[5]

On Seeing Off Meng Hao-jan

Old friend, bidding farewell to Yellow Crane Tower from the
    west:
In march, among smoking flowers, making your way to Yang-
    chow.
From the tower I watched your solitary sail disappear among
    blue mountains.
There was only the immense river running to the edge of
    heaven.[6]

Saying Farewell to a Friend

The green mountain lies beyond the north wall of the city,
Where the white water winds in the east—
Here we part.
The solitary sail will attempt a flight of a thousand li,
The flowing clouds are the dreams of a wandering son,
The setting sun, the affection of an old friend.
So you go, waving your hands—
Only the bark of the deer.

Resentment

She has rolled up the beaded screen
And sits there deep in thought, her crescent eyebrows frown-
    ing.
I see in the corner of her eyes the tear stains still green.
I do not know why she is envious.

[5] King Fu-chai of Wu married Hsi-shih, who had been given to him as a
present by K'u-chien, King of Yueh. Twenty years later K'u-chien led his
army across the river and made the kingdom of Wu a big fishpond.
Li Po is here celebrating the vanished kingdom.
[6] Meng Hao-jan (689–740) was a friend of Li Po and Wang Wei, and a
considerable poet in his own right, ranking perhaps immediately after
Li Po and Tu Fu. He was a native of Hupeh, and is said to have been
responsible for a famous interview between Wang Wei and the emperor.
The Yellow Crane Tower overlooks the Yangtze at Wu-chang. It is here
that a dead man of Shuh, traveling on the back of the crane, stopped
to rest.

A Song of Ching-Ping

1

The glory of clouds in her raiment, the flowers shine like her
face.
The spring wind sweeps the balustrade, the dew lies heavy.
You will not see her on the Mountain of Many Jewels,
You will see her only in moonlight in the Palace of Crystal.[7]

2

She is a flowering peony, the dewdrops restraining the perfume.
Shall the King be ashamed of his dreams of cloud and rain?[8]
Pray, who in the palace of Han could be likened to her on
earth,
Save Lady Flying Swallow when newly dressed in her loveli-
ness?

3

The queen of flowers and the flowery queen rejoice together,
For the Emperor always deigns to watch over them with a
smile.
Vanquished the endless longings of love on the winds of spring,
While she leans against the balustrade north of the Chen-
hsiang pavilion.

To ———

When the fair one was here, the house was adorned with
flowers;
When the fair one was gone, only an empty couch remained.
On the couch the embroidered quilt is rolled up and no longer
used.
For three years since that day a perfume haunts the place.

The perfume stays forever,
But she is lost forever.
In deep anguish comes autumn, the yellow leaves fall.
White dewdrops wet the green glittering mosses.

[7] The first of three songs, set to music by Li Kuei-nien and played on a
jade flute by the Emperor, which were written in honor of the beauty of
Yang Kuei-fei during the royal feast in the Pavilion of Aloes.
[8] A euphemism for sexual intercourse.

The Summit Temple

Here it is night: I stay at the Summit Temple.
Here I can touch the stars with my hand.
I dare not speak aloud in the silence
For fear of disturbing the dwellers of Heaven.

Listening to the Monk of Szechuan Playing on His Lute

The monk of Szechuan on the heights of Mount Omei
Comes down westward, under his arms a Lu-yi lute.[9]
He plays for me, fingers brushing the strings,
And the sound is like the murmuring pine trees in ravines.
So with the "Flowing Spring" song he re-creates my soul.
For a long while the last echoes weave in the tolling of the
    frost bells.
In this entrancement the blue hills dim and darken.
Heavy are the autumn clouds sailing heavenward.

Translated by Chiang Shao-yi.

White Sun and Bright Moon

White sun and bright moon
Run their course day and night.
How could we humble mortals
Live on leisurely in the world?
I learn that in the sea
There is the fairy Peng-la hill
Where angels often climb over
To pick the green leaves of the jade tree,
Which, once being eaten, makes their heads too dark,
And they live in eternal youth.
I'll go there, I'll go there
To live and die in fairyland.

Translated by Nee Wen Yei.

Drinking Alone under Moonlight

Holding a jug of wine among the flowers,
And drinking alone, not a soul keeping me company,
I raise my cup and invite the moon to drink with me,
And together with my shadow we are three.
But the moon does not know the joy of drinking,
And my shadow only follows me about.

[9] Literally: a green silk lute.

Nevertheless I shall have them as my companions,
For one should enjoy life at such a time.
The moon loiters as I sing my songs,
My shadow looks confused as I dance.
I drink with them when I am awake
And part with them when I am drunk.
Henceforward may we always be feasting,
And may we meet in the Cloudy River of Heaven.[1]

Translated by Tsang Bing-ching.

The Song of the Four Seasons[2]

Spring

The lovely Lo-fu in the land of Chin
Gathers mulberry leaves by the clear water;
Her white hands rest on the green boughs.
The white sun shines on her red face.
"The silkworms are hungry, I must run away.
Your five horses should tarry here no more."

Summer

On Mirror Lake for three hundred li,
Gaily, gaily the lilies are blossoming.
In the fifth month Hsi-shih gathers them.
Multitudes are watching from the bank.
The boat does not wait the coming of the moon,
But slowly returns to the palace of the King of Yueh.

Autumn

A moon rises over Ch'ang-an,
From ten thousand doors comes the sound of pounding cloth.
The autumn wind blows sadly.
My thoughts mingle with yours at the Jade Pass.
When will the Tartars be put to flight?
When will my beloved be able to return from the battlefield?

[1] I.e., the Milky Way.
[2] The Han dynasty song of Lo-fu has been given earlier. A more exact
title for these four poems is: "Midnight Songs for the Seasons," a title
that was already old in the Han dynasty for four-line poems of five
syllables. Usually the songs celebrated the griefs of unmarried girls:
> The plum blossom has fallen and withered,
> The catkins are blown by the wind;
> My tender years are like the spring,
> And no man wants to live with me.
The midnight songs—*Tsu Yeh K'o*—owe their name not to late nights,
but to a maid known as "Midnight."

Winter

Tomorrow the courier leaves for the frontier.
All night she spends mending his coat,
Bravely her fingers ply the cold needle,
But the scissors are even colder,
Then at last it is over, and the coat is given away.
How many days will it take to reach Lin-tao?

Awakening from Drunkenness
on a Spring Day

Our life in the world is only a great dream.
Why should I toil my life away?
Let me be drunk all day,
Let me lie at the foot of the house gate.
When I wake up, I blink at the garden trees:
A lonely bird is singing amid the flowers.
I demand of the bird what season it is:
He answers: "The spring wind makes the mango bird sing."
Moved by his song, I sigh my heart away
And once more pour myself wine.
So I sing wildly till the bright moon shines.
The song over, all my sense are numb.

Drinking Alone in Moonlight

If Heaven had no love for wine,
There would be no Wine Star in Heaven;
If earth had no love for wine,
There would be no city called Wine Springs.
Since Heaven and Earth love wine
I can love wine without shaming Heaven.
They say that clear wine is a saint;
Thick wine follows the way of the sage.
I have drunk deep of saint and sage:
What need then to study the spirits and fairies?
With three cups I penetrate the Great Tao.
Take a whole jugful—I and the world are one.
Such things as I have dreamed in wine
Shall never be told to the sober.

On a Journey

The good wine of Lanling smells of apple seed:
Come, fill to the brim my jade bowl with glowing amber.
If only mine host can make me drunk,
I shall not worry if there is a strange country.

Looking toward Mount Wu

Mount Wu lies southeast of Lushan,
Chiseled against the blue sky, a gold hibiscus flower.
I twist the colors of Nine River Town into a knot.
Here I shall build my nest amid clouds and pines.

On Climbing the Phoenix Tower at Chin-Ling [8]

Once in the Phoenix Tower the phoenix made her nest.
Now the phoenix has gone, the tower empty, only the river
    flowing on.
There were flowers in the garden of Wu, but the paths are now
    hidden in deep grass.
Here the great lords of Chin are buried in grave mounds.
Half of these three mountains stretched into the blue sky.
The river's two streams wander round the White Heron Island.
Floating clouds forever are shading the rays of the sun.
And I am grief-stricken because I cannot see Ch'ang-an.

To My Wife from Yeh-lang, the Place of Exile [4]

Separated from you, I lament in Yeh-lang beyond the clouds.
To this moonlit house news seldom comes.
I see the wild geese go north in the spring;
Now they turn south—no letter from Yuchang!

To Tu Fu

On the Mountain of Boiled Rice I met Tu Fu,
Wearing a bamboo hat in the hot midday;
Pray, how is it that you have grown so thin?
Is it because you suffer from poetry?

Amusing Myself

With wine I did not notice the approach of evening.
All my clothes were covered with fallen petals.
Drunken I arose, and paced the stream by moonlight.
I saw few people or returning birds.

[8] Chin-Ling is the modern Nanking, once the capital of Wu, Chin, and many other states and dynasties.
[4] Li Po was banished to perpetual exile in Yeh-lang, roughly corresponding to modern Yunnan, in 758, but during the next year an amnesty was declared and the poet returned to Nanking.

Spring Dawn

I slept in spring not conscious of the dawn,
But heard the gay birds chattering all around,
I remember, there was a storm at night.
Pray, how many blossoms have fallen down?

A Song of War

Before the Peak of Returning Joy the sand was like snow.
Outside the surrendered city the moon was like frost.
I do not know who blew the horns at night,
But all night long the boys looked toward their homes.

A Few Words to Meng Hao-Jan

I like my friend Meng,
Whose art and fame are known to all under heaven.
Red-cheeked, he threw away carriage and cap.
White-haired, he lies among the pines and the clouds.
Like the ancients, he can get drunk on moonlight;
Preferring flowers, he has no desire to serve emperors.
How can one climb so high a mountain?
I can only breathe my admiration for his purity.

The Bravo of Chao

The bravo of Chao wears a cap with a Tartar cord.
His scimitar from Wu shines like the ice and snow.
His silver saddle glitters on a pure white horse.
He comes like the wind or like a shooting star.

At every ten steps he kills a man,
And goes ten thousand li without stopping.
The deed done, he shakes his garment and departs.
Who knows his name or whither he goes?

If he has time, he goes to drink with Hsin-ling,
Unbuckles his sword and lays it across his knee.
The prince does not disdain to share meat with Chou Hai
Or to offer a goblet of wine to Hou Ying.[5]

[5] Hou Ying was a recluse of Wei state in the third century B.C. Offered
a high position by Prince Hsin-ling, at the age of seventy, he refused and
recommended instead Chou Hai, who defeated the invaders.

Three cups is a sign of a bond unbroken.
His oath is heavier than the Five Mountains.
When his ears are hot and his eyes burn,
His spirit ventures forth like a rainbow.

Holding a hammer, he saved the kingdom of Chao.
The mere sound of his name was like shaking thunder.
For a thousand autumns three strong men
Have lived in the hearts of the people of Tai-liang.[6]

Sweet-scented be the bones of these dead heroes;
May the old scholar be put to shame
Who bent over his books near the window
With white hair compiling the *Tai-hsuan Ching*.[7]

Dreaming of Wandering through the Tien-Mu Mountain[8]

A Farewell Poem

The seafarers say there is an eastern land,
Lost in the misty sea waves and hard to reach.
The Yueh-landers say it is called Tien-mu.
Perhaps it can be seen among glimmering rainbows and
    clouds.
This land of the sky stretches over leagues of heaven;
It rises over Five Mountains, towers over Scarlet Battlement.[9]
The Tien-tai is forty-eight thousand feet high,
Staggering and leaning toward the southeast.
Dreaming of these lands of Wu and Yueh,
One moonlit night I flew across Mirror Lake.

[6] The capital of the state of Wei, of which Prince Hsin-ling was the ruler.
[7] Yang Hsiung (B.C. 53-A.D. 18) compiled the *Tai-hsuan Ching*, a commentary of the *I Ching*. He wrote voluminously on music, poetry, philology, acupuncture, received high appointments under Wang Mang, and is said to have studied by the window for so long that men had forgotten whether there was any other part to him except his white head. He was particularly despised by Li Po, who attacks him in several other poems.
[8] The commentators say that the Tien-Mu Mountain is 4,000 li square, and stands 700,000 li to the east. From a jade stone spring water tasting like wine flows. The island is full of immortals who resemble the people of Wu (Kiangsu).
[9] Mountains in Chekiang and Kiangsu.

The moon in the lake reflects my shadow
And follows me to the town of Yenchi,
Where stands the palace of Prince Hsieh.[1]

The green waters are quivering, the monkeys crying.
Putting on the sandals of the Prince,
I climb up the green cloud ladder.
Halfway, I see the sun rising from the sea
And in the sky I hear heaven's cock.

A thousand precipices and ten thousand turnings, the way not
    sure:
Flowers choking the path, I lean against the rocks, I swoon.
A bear roars, there are groaning dragons, roaring waters.
I tremble in the thick forest—oh, the overhanging rocks fall.
Blue, blue are the clouds threatening rain,
And the waters pour down and smoke pours from them.

Peal of thunder!
Mountains splitting asunder!
The stone gates of heaven opening wide,
And there between the hovering gates
Depth upon depth of blueness, no end visible,
Sun and moon shining together from their gold palaces!

In rainbow clothes, charioteering on the wind,
The lords of the clouds descend like spun silk,
Tigers beat on lyres, the phoenixes surround the chariots.
I was as one bewildered and filled with terror.
Suddenly there is an end to dreams;
I lift myself on my elbow and look around.
Waking, I see my bed and pillow.
Gone is the world of cloud dust!

The joys of the world do not last.
Of old all things have flown with the east-flowing river.
I leave you and go—when shall I return?
Let the white roe pasture among the green rocks,
Let me go and visit the delectable mountain.
How can I humble myself to serve the mighty ones?
To do so would make my heart small.

[1] Hsieh An (A.D. 320-388), the model of the refined scholar and ruler. At his last illness he dreamed of a cock, a presage of death, which is mentioned in the poem. When his nephew and brother won a resounding victory, he showed no emotion but continued to play the game of *wei-ch'i*.

TS'EN TS'AN

He was a devoted friend of Li Po and Tu Fu, who recommended him to the emperor Su Tsung, who gave him the high position of censor and later the governorship of Chia-chou. He wrote essays as well as poetry, and experimented with forms of poetry. He was younger than Tu Fu, who called him affectionately "younger brother," and in a famous but untranslatable poem Tu Fu describes a journey with him on the slopes of Mei Mountain. They were continually exchanging friendly poems with each other, but rarely are the poems more than occasional. He was a native of Ho-nei, and became *chin shih* at some time between 742 and 756.

Two Songs for General Chao

I

A coat of squirrel fur, many dancing girls,
Wines from the palace and silks belonging to the Black Khan,
But the old general on the east front fights keenly:
Though he is seventy he will fight to the death.

II

The wind on Tien Shan slashes the autumn like a knife.
South of the city their horses shiver, manes shrinking.
The old general rattles the dice,
And wins the coat of fur belonging to the Black Khan.

Horsemen on the Great Szechuan Road

Behold, the horsemen are galloping along the Szechuan road
    beside the snow-white sea!
Sand stretches like prairie grass, so vast, and the yellowness
    meets the sky.
Here in Lun-tai, in late autumn, the wind howls all night.
A river bed of broken stones as large as kettle drums
Is thrown up by the wind, and everywhere the air is full of
    stones.

The Huns pasture their fat horses on the yellow grass.
Westward among the gold hills, smoke and dust are flying.

The Han general collects his forces against the western enemy.
All night he has not removed his coat of mail.
All night the army marches, weapons touching,
And the wind's muzzle is a knife slashing the sky.

The manes of the horses are icicles, strings of cash turned
    to ice,
Five-petal flowers among the smoke clouds of sweat.
In the tent the general dips his pen in ice.
Ah, if the Huns heard of it would not their courage fail?
We—we know that they have no love for our short swords.
We—we know that the army awaits tidings of victory.

All translated by Wang Sheng-chih.

Farewell

The north wind sweeps over the land, twisting and breaking off
    the hoary grass.
The barbarian weather brings the fluttering snow of early
    August.
As though overnight a small wind came to make thousands of
    pear trees blossom.
These snowflakes slip through pearl curtains and wet the
    screens.
The fox fur no longer warm and the silk coverlet too thin,
Benumbed with cold, the general can hardly draw his horn
    bow.
But the border guards must still wear their freezing armor,
And icy pillars a thousand feet high pile high in the north
    ocean,
While overcast clouds hang curdled for ten thousand li.
Amid the booming of pipes and the squeaking of flutes,
The orderlies drink a toast in honor of the returning guest.
The evening snow whirls thick on the gates of the camp,
And the wind fails to move the frozen red flag.
Then, at the north gate of Lun-tai, I bid you farewell,
You who will go through the drifts of snow on Tien Shan.
I lost sight of you when you turned beyond the cliff,
Leaving only the footprints of your horse behind.

On Meeting a Messenger to the Capital

It is such a long way to the east, and my sleeves
Tremble. I am heavy with years and wet with tears.
Seeing you on horseback in this wilderness, without pen or
    paper,
I beg you to tell my people at home: I am safe and sound.

Ode to a Monk on the Tai-Pei Mountains

They say there is a monk on the Tai-pei Mountains,
Floating like scent, three hundred feet beneath the sky.
Once with his scriptures he hid himself in the middle peak,
And he has scarcely been seen by those who hear the ringing
  bell.

His metal stick once parted two tigers in a death struggle;
Now it lies against the window. Under his bed a jar contains
  a dragon.
His clothes were made of weeds and leaves; his ears
Touch his shoulders, and his brow hangs over his face.

No one knows his age. Only the green pines planted
By him cannot be ringed around by ten arms.
His mind is as clear as a flowing river.
His person, like clouds, knows neither right nor wrong.

Once an old man of Shang Shan met him,
But I can find no way through these untrodden heights.
Still in the mountains lives this unknown monk.
The townsmen do not know him: they look in vain to the
  melting blue sky.

All translated by Yuan Chia-hua.

TU FU (A.D. 713–770)

He is the greatest of Chinese poets without exception, and yet he is extraordinarily difficult to translate. No one has yet been able to convey in any European language the passion he commands, or the tremendous skill of his poetry. There is an immense calm and an immense irony in his work, and a terrible sympathy. He has little, or no, self-pity. Like Vergil, he looks at the earth calmly and dispassionately, having seen all evils, having shared all disasters, a man who is not unlike other men except in the range of his sensibility. One of his children starved to death. He was always wandering through wars. He held high positions, and ran away from them; he was loyal to the emperor, yet he knew that the empire was being wrecked on the policies of the emperor; he was irascible and ill-tempered; he was splendid in anger, and still more splendid in tenderness; but when he writes, he writes like the gods—calmly, almost efficiently, extracting from everything he contemplates the essence of its quivering life.

He came from generations of scholars. One of his ancestors, Tu Yuan-kai, wrote a famous commentary on the *Tso Chuan*. His grandfather, Yu Yen-yang, took part in the early days of the T'ang dynasty in the movement to reform poetry, insisting upon a far stricter antithetical versification than before. He was six years old when he first wrote poetry, and at fourteen was rivaling the minor poets of the time. He was brought up strictly, and attempted to obey the Confucian canons to the end of his life, but he was not a complete Confucian. He had little use for fantasy—though it appears here and there in his works, and notably in a surprising passage in "The Journey to the North"—and seems to have considered poetry as an art that must be fought for. Unlike Li Po, who wrote as a bird sings, he seems to have composed with difficulty.

At the age of twenty he went wandering; he was hardly ever to cease wandering as long as he lived. He failed in the imperial examinations, but the failure did not embitter him. It was the rebellion of An Lu-shan and the invasions of the Nan-chao (the half-Tibetan tribesmen from Yunnan who attacked from without almost at the moment when rebellion was being fomented within) that drove him to desperation, and made him write his greatest poetry. These are not Vergilian afterthoughts, portraits of wars when the wars were over. They were written by a man who felt the full force of the suffering around him, and shared it to a degree denied to Li Po, who would celebrate a defeat as easily as he celebrated

182

a victory. When the Nan-chao invaded Szechuan, conscription was imposed by the emperor. The results were disastrous: old men, and even women, were hauled off to the wars. There had been frontier wars from time everlasting, but this time the wars were infinitely more real, and conscription infinitely more terrible, because the times were desperate. But through all the failures of the reigning dynasty, Tu Fu retained his faith in the empire and in the common people who formed it.

He was twenty-five before he reached the capital, then known as Ch'ang-an, which means "eternal peace." After failing in the examination, he wandered over the provinces of Shantung, Shansi, and Honan. He met Li Po and Kao Shih, but produced no works of importance until he was thirty-five, and then the quality of his maturity was immediately visible. For ten years he wrote prodigiously. He returned to Ch'ang-an and received a minor official post, hardly sufficient to keep him alive. He celebrated the splendor of the court, the gaiety and beauty of the consort Yang Kuei-fei, but he knew the disastrous effect of the tyrannical abuses of power of her brother, the prime minister, Yang Kuo-chung:

Behind the red-painted doors wine and meat are stinking.
On the wild roads lie corpses of people frozen to death.
A hairbreadth divides wealth and utter poverty.
This strange contrast fills me with unappeasable anguish.

He enjoyed the ceremonials of the court, the great triangular banners with dragons embroidered on them flapping leisurely in the wind, the girdle pendants clicking on the grass as the officials knelt before the emperor, the smoke of the incense rising from the bronze *t'ings,* and all the elaborate ritual of court custom, but he knew the cruelties of the recruiting officers and the shoddiness upon which the dynasty was based. He lived in two worlds. There was still the world of his childhood, of the silver-crested phoenix and the Lady Kung-sun, who danced "the dance of the two-edged sword," which captivated him when young. He wrote three poems that pleased the emperor, but he was already forty years old and had no great achievements to his name. His worship of the dynasty remained, though corruption was increasing until nearly everyone in the empire was conscious that it could hardly survive much longer:

I shall transport the lord, my emperor, to the heights of the
    ideal rulers Yao and Shun;
I will cause the winds of instruction to reform and purify
    the customs of the land.

But it was easier said than done, and when the rebellion did break out at last, in December 754, he was as helpless as the rest. Worse still, there was famine. His child died. He was captured by the rebels, and it was ten months before he could make his way to the new imperial capital and pay his respects to the new emperor. Once again he received only a minor post. Later he was appointed Censor of the Left, a high position but an onerous one, which he exchanged as soon as possible for a sinecure in the east. He seems to have been always wandering during the years of war, but at last in 759 he retired from official life and settled down in Chengtu, where he stayed for five years. It was the longest time since his childhood that he had remained in a single place. He lived partly on the bounty of the governor of the city.

He was already a classic, and seems to have been conscious of his importance. There are legends of his quarrels with the governor, and of his intransigent arrogance, but the legends suggest no more than that Tu Fu was conscious of his fame and was determined to suffer no longer. He had been an old man for a very long time. He was tired. More than any other man he had celebrated the whole glory and decadence of the T'ang empire, and his poetical powers were still immeasurable. But the tone is quieter, he speaks of simple things, and there is less sign of suffering.

Once he had made a living as a wood cutter; now he lived in a small cottage outside Chengtu, watering the flowers, drinking tea, desultorily reading the Buddhist classics, without any cares in the world. But the governor died, there were revolts in Chengtu, and once more he went on his wanderings. For five years he wandered over the province, old and sick, weary of the interminable roads, the memory of the past dominating everything else. Yet even then, in these last days of his twilight, there is a swift tempo in his poetry, a grace and an unaccustomed lightness, as of a man who is about to lay down his burden forever.

In the last two years there is a decline of poetic power, but it is hardly noticeable—the poet's precision remains. No one knows exactly how he died, but it is recorded that he had been out alone on a boat that disappeared in the smoke of a storm, took refuge in an abandoned temple, and was half dead of hunger and cold when he was found and brought back to the town of Lung-yung. They feasted him, to honor his return; he drank copiously and ate copiously; and the next morning he was found dead in bed. He was fifty-nine.

If one could compare Tu Fu with anyone—though he is incomparable—it would be with Baudelaire, for his strange suggestive images derived from poverty and spiritual exhaustion. He has Baudelaire's power of evoking the real terrors, the long nights, the cruelties, the starvations, the miseries of the

common people; and there are lines of Baudelaire that read
like translations of Tu Fu:

> *Et les vagues terreurs de ces affreuses nuits*
> *Qui compriment le coeur comme un papier qu'on froisse . . .*

> *Mon coeur est un palais flétri par la cohue . . .*

> *Ainsi dans le forêt où mon esprit s'exile,*
> *Un vieux souvenir sonne à plein souffle du cor . . .*

Like Baudelaire, he was untamable and spoke of himself as:

> The sea gull who plays on the white waves,
> And flies to heaven, superb and tameless . . .

And like Baudelaire, too, he was possessed of an extraordinary
tenderness and sensitivity, especially toward suffering, while
at the same time and almost in the same breath he could evoke
a sense of majesty and dignity and regal splendor. There were
two worlds, and yet they were not incompatible: there was
splendor in poverty and in death, and there was misery enough
in the royal palaces during the wars. He described a princess:
"her dignity so flaming that it burned your finger," but almost
at the same time he wrote:

> Do not let your tears fall.
> Pick them up, drop by drop, from the floor.
> Even if all your tears are drained away,
> Neither heaven nor earth can help you.

The bald literal translation in English gives nothing of the
flavor of the original, whose sadness seems to reach out to the
extremities of all endurable suffering. Where he is supreme is
in the combination of a technical mastery of verse with the
deepest pathos. He exhausted the possible variation of the
"eight-line" poem. In his earliest days he imitated the poetry
of his grandfather, the flowery and euphuistic poems of the
earliest experiments of the T'ang dynasty, but as his own
sufferings increased, we become conscious of a somber power
and of a terrible expanding awareness. In this sense he is universal. No poet before or after him in Chinese history has been
so conscious of the human role that can be played by a poet,
and no one else would have dared to sum up all human history,
as he saw it, in six words so charged with meaning that they
burst out of the page with the effect of an explosion:

> *Blue* is the *smoke* of *war*, *white* the *bones* of *men*.

He remains to the end the eternal wanderer, complaining
against the cold, the poor profits of earth, the sorrows of death,

the ghastly (but splendid) rituals of empire. He cared for
nothing except the dignity and freedom of men to live their
own lives as they choose, and would have preferred to be
remembered, if he was remembered at all, as a man of simple
faith in simple things, as a poet and one who had wandered
over nearly all the provinces of his beloved China.

On a Historic Landmark

Where hills and valleys crowd toward Ching-men
Still prides a village on bearing the Bright Queen
Who left the palace as the desert's thrall—
Her mark this mound at sunset alone green.
From portraits recognize the face of spring?
Her pendants tinkle; she returns unseen
By moonlight, who taught mandolins to complain
These thousand years in Tartary of her wrong.

Prelude

This fugitive between the earth and sky,
From the northeast storm-tossed to the southwest,
Time has left stranded in Three Valleys where
Exotic costumes mixed with ours suggest
Alliance with Huns whose loyalty suspect
Adds cause for mourning by the enforced guest.
Most desolate was Yu Hsin's life who sang
Toward its end of northern valleys best.

Night in the Villa by the River

Twilight comes down the mountain to
The villa next the dike. By caves
On high the light clouds pitch their tents.
The moon turns over in the waves.
In silence left by flight of cranes
The wolves at feast howl while the fears
Of wartime prevent sleep from men
Powerless to adjust the spheres.

The Empty Purse

The bitter pine cone may be eaten,
The mist on high gives nourishment.
The whole world takes to go-and-getting;
My way alone is difficult.
My oven is cold as the well at morning,
And the bed wants warmth from coverlets;
My purse, ashamed to be found empty,
Still keeps on hand a single coin.

Song of the Vermeil Phoenix

See you not Heng Mountain towering over Hunan hills,
From its summit the vermeil phoenix murmuring leans
Over to gaze, forever seeking his comrades?
His wings are folded, his mouth is closed, but his mind is
  working
With pity for all the birds that are caught in nets,
From which even the tiny oriole hardly can escape.
He would dispense to them ants and fruit of bamboo,
Provoking hawk and vulture to scream their threats.

Lament for a Quince Tree Uprooted by the Storm

Claimed by our patriarchs to have survived
Two centuries, this quince tree by the river was
The reason that I cleared the weeds and built
My house behind to hear May cicadas.

The southeast wind arrived to shake the earth,
Overturn rivers, drive rocks and clouds uphill.
Still the quince grappled with the thunderstorm,
And if uprooted, was it heaven's will?

This old tree that my nature loved upheld
Above the river a green canopy.
Its shade forbidding, cold as frost and snow,
Its leafy music stayed the passer-by.

Tiger and dragon overborne are cast
To nettles; tears but conjure memories.
Where should I go to meditate new rhymes?
Henceforth my cottage must be colorless.

A Farewell to Ho Yung on His Leaving Min Valley for the Capital

Where life and death try friendships, here
I made a friend—beyond belief—
Whom petty duties shuttle back
And forth like swallows to my grief.
From hence Han River beds due north,
While the Tor stays in southern loam.
When flowers at Five Tombs fill your eyes,
Send tidings of the spring at home.

Autumn Countryside

Deficient in the polite studies,
My love for hills and woods enduring,
I nod my cap half off my head,
Back bare to sunlight through bamboo,
And gather wind-dropped pine cones up,
And bring in beehives during winter,
And where dispersed red and green
Emit a tenuous sweetness linger.

Quatrain

Before you praise spring's advent, note,
What capers the mad wind may cut:
To cast the flowers to the waves
And overturn the fishing boat.

All translated by Hsieh Wen Tung.

The Painting of an Eagle

From pure white silk winds and frost arise.
Look at the eagle painted with so great cunning.
His neck shoots out, he meditates on catching a hare
With the sidelong glance of some wild barbarian.
Those gleaming silk loops and gold rings can be grasped in
    the hand;
The roof beams are so clear drawn one could enter therein.
Oh, marvelous, if the eagle could strike down a bird,
On the grass a precipitation of feathers and blood!

Riding in a Boat on the Day before the Spring Festival

On this great day I must drink and eat; yet still I am frozen
    to death.
Like a stripped bough, I lean against the table and wear a
    feathered cap.
Gliding on this spring river is like having a place in heaven.
As if in a mist flowers appear to my old eyes,
Languidly the butterflies frolic over the parted curtains.
One by one the tame wild fowl slip down the quick stream.
The white clouds and green mountains are ten thousand li
    away.
In vain I look to the north in the hope of seeing Ch'ang-an.

Advent of Spring

The city has fallen; only the hills and rivers remain.
In spring the streets were green with grass and trees.
Sorrowing over the times, the flowers are weeping.
The birds startled my heart in fear of departing.
The beacon fires were burning for three months,
A letter from home was worth ten thousand pieces of gold.
I scratch the scant hairs on my white head,
And vainly attempt to secure them with a hairpin.

In My Late Age

In my late age I am compelled to live a stolen life.
When I came home, my spirits were drooping.
My darling children do not go away from my knees:
They are afraid I may run away again.
I remember in ancient times how I liked the shade,
And often walked beneath the trees near the pool
While the north wind screamed and chattered.
Now I embrace the past, burning with a thousand cares,
Consoled by the thought of the fat rice in harvest,
And the pure wine dripping through the wine press.
Now that there is enough wine to drink,
I can console the remaining days of my life.

The Return

Cliffs of scarlet cloud gleam in the west;
The sun's feet are sinking beneath the earth.
By the rustic gate sparrows are twittering.

The stranger returns to his home from a thousand li.
My wife is astonished that I still exist.
No longer bewildered, she wipes away her tears.
I was drifting sand in the wind of the world's anger.
It is just fate that has brought me back alive.
The fence gate is filled with neighbors' faces,
Sighing and shedding a few tears.
In the deep night we light a new candle
And see each other face to face as in a dream.

The Village and the River

My home is surrounded by a clear stream,
In the long summer days there is all the silence of a hermitage
Save where the swallows flit among the beams
Or where the wild sea gull plays fearless on a stream.
My wife rules the squares for a game of chess,*
My young son hammers a fishhook out of wire.
I, who am ill so often, want only to plant flowers—
My humble body desires nothing more.

To My Youngest Son

O Chu-tzu! Spring returns, and we are still separated.
A million golden orioles are singing in this warm weather.
We are apart, and yet I am startled by the change of season.
Who is as clever as you?
I know only the mountain streams and the hilly roads,
The grass gateway, the village surrounded by ancient trees.
Dreaming of you in my grief I think only of sleep.
There in the porch, bending toward the earth, I feel the hot
    sun on my back.

My Brother

My brother was a year older than I.
He was wise, and I was only a fool.
He despised vanity;
I was full of envy.
Chen-tzu was muddy in the autumn rain,
The horse was waiting for dawn, the first cockcrow,
The gate of the lord's house was still bolted.
When I arrived,
My brother awoke from sound sleep.
The cries of boys and girls were never unpleasing,
But clothes and food were always necessary.
The year I arrived in Chen-tzu

* Squares ruled on paper. Chinese chess is not the formal game it is in
the West; it can be played at any time on ruled or folded paper.

The whole town was filled with the fragrance of wine and
    flowers.
Upstairs we drank and downstairs we slept.
We sang each other's poems
And made calls,
And did not trouble to put on our caps and girdles.
The dust on our faces was never washed away,
So he lived in utter happiness,
Laughing and crying like a child,
Falling asleep at twilight.
Who was the man whispering in a soft voice?

Translated by Nee Wen-yei.

Song of Autumn

The Kunming Pool is the great glory of Han.
The banners of Wu Ti are there before my eyes.
By moonlight the Weaving Maid stands idle before her silk
    spools;
An autumn wind rattles the stone scales of a sea dragon.
Among heaving waves sink the dark clouds of the *kumi* seeds;
In the cold dew pink petals fall from the lotos pods.
The Sword Pass reaches the sky along the Bird Road.
An old fisherman wandering through all the lakes and rivers
    of earth.[1]

Cocks Are Crowing

Cocks are crowing, hens are cackling.
When the guests arrive, the cocks begin to fight,
So I drive them into the trees.
At first I hear only the knocking on the grass gate—
There are four or five neighbors of mine
Coming to console me after my long journey.
All of them bring gifts and presents.
Time after time we pour out food and wine.
They say: Do not complain if the wine is weak,
For there is no one to plow the millet field,
And the sound of battle drums has not yet ceased;
The boys have all gone to the eastern front.
Let me sing a song for you, old countrymen.

[1] During the time of Han emperor Wu Ti an expedition was sent to
Yunnan to conquer the barbarian tribes. The expedition failed in a sea
battle on Kunming Lake. Thereupon the Emperor decided to construct
near Ch'ang-an a large lake on which his troops could be trained; in the
center of the lake lay the stone dragon. The Sword Pass and Bird Road
refer to mountains in Szechuan connected with the flight of the emperor
Ming Huang; the fisherman is probably Tu Fu himself.

In these terrible times I am grateful for all your kindness.
After singing, I look up to heaven sighing.
Our eyes are bathed in tears.

All translated by Pu Hsiang-hsing.

The Roof Whirled Away by Winds

In the eighth moon of autumn, the wind howling viciously,
Three layers of thatch were whirled away from my roof.
The thatch flying over the river sprinkled the embankment
And some of it was entangled in the treetops,
And some whirled away and sank in the marshlands.
A swarm of small boys from South Village laughing at me
        because I am old and feeble.
They know they can rob me even in my face.
What effrontery! Stealing my thatch, taking it to the bamboo
        grove.
With parched lips and tongue I screamed at them—it was no
        use—
And so I came back sighing to my old place.
Then the wind fell and the clouds were inky black,
The autumn sky a web of darkness, stretching toward the dusk,
And my old cotton quilt was as cold as iron,
And my darling son tossed in his sleep, bare feet tearing
        through the blanket,
And the rain dripped through the roof, and there was no dry
        place on the bed.
Like strings of wax the rain fell, unending.
After all these disasters of war, I have had little sleep or rest.
When will this long night of drizzle come to an end?
Now I dream of an immense mansion, tens of thousands of
        rooms,
Where all the cold creatures can take shelter, their faces alight;
Not moved by the wind or the rain, a mansion as solid as a
        mountain—
Alas, when shall I see such a majestic house?
If I could see this, even though my poor house were torn down,
Even though I were frozen to death I would be content.[2]

[2] I have added "If I could see this." The last two lines form one line in
the original. Nearly all Chinese know this poem by heart. In it Tu Fu
expressed finally and perfectly the main impulse of his life—a desperate
and unavailing sympathy for all suffering things. It is important to realize
that this was something new in Chinese poetry, just as Vergil's insistence
on suffering was something new in Latin poetry. Vergil with his *pietas*
is at times extraordinarily similar to Tu Fu with his continual loyalty to
the throne and delight in the purely Confucian virtues.

Jade Flower Palace

Where the streams wind and the wind is always sighing,
Hoary gray mice scurry among abandoned roof tiles.
No one knows the name of the prince who once owned this
house.
Standing there, even now, under the hanging cliffs.
In dark rooms ghost-green fires are shining.[3]
Beside the ancient battered road a melancholy stream flows
downhill.
Then, from the flutes of the forest, come a thousand voices;
The colors of autumn are fresh in the wind and the rain.
Though the virgins have all gone their way to the yellow
graves,
Why is it that paintings still hang on the walls?
Charioteers of gold chariots—all have gone.
There remain of these ancient days only the stone horses.
Sorrow comes and sits on the spreading grass.
All the while singing, I am overwhelmed with lamentation.
Among these lanes of life disappearing in the distance,
Who can make himself eternal?

The Chariots Go Forth to War

Chariots rumble and roll; horses whinny and neigh;
Men are marching with bows and arrows at their hips.
Their parents and wives hurry to bid farewell,
Raising clouds of dust over Hsien-yang Bridge.
They pull at the soldiers' clothes, stamp their feet and cry out.
The sound of their crying soars to the clouds.

Some passers-by speak to the soldiers;
They shake their heads dumbly and say:
"Since the age of fifteen we have defended the northern rivers.
Till we are forty we shall serve on the western front.
We leave our homes as youths and return as gray-haired men.
Along the frontier there flows the sea of our blood.
The King hungers for territory—therefore we fight.

"Have you not heard, sir,
How through the two hundred countries east of the Tai-yeng
Mountains
Through thousands of villages and tens of thousands of hamlets

[3] In Chinese there are only five words. *Yin fang kuei ch'in huo*—dark
room ghost green fire. I know very few comparable lines that have such
power of evocation.

Thorns and nettles run wild?
Sturdy peasant women swing the hoe and drive the plow,
But neither in the east nor west is anything raised or sown.
The soldiers of Sh'ang will fight to the end,
But they cannot be slain like dogs or like hens.

"Oh, sir, it is kind of you to ask me,
But how dare we express our resentment?
Winter has come and the year is passing away;
The war on the western passes is still going on.
The magistrates are pressing us to pay our taxes,
But where shall we get the money?
If only I had known the fate in store for boys,
I would have had my children all girls,
For girls may be married to the neighbors,
But boys are born only to be cut down and buried beneath
    the grass.

"Do you not see, sir,
The long dead ancient bones near the Blue Sea⁴ bleached by
    the sun?
And now the lament of those who have just died
Mingles with the voices of those who died long ago,
And darkness falls, and the rain, and the ghostly whimpering
    of voices."

On Climbing the Heights on the Ninth Day of the Ninth Moon

The wind keen, the sky high, the gibbons wailing.
Blue islands, white sand, and sea birds flying,
And everywhere the leaves falling,
Then the immeasurable great river in torrent.
Ten thousand li from home, in such an autumn,
Wasted by sickness and years, alone, climbing the heights:
Sorrows and griefs and sufferings have given me new gray
    hairs.
Utterly cast down, I have just drunk a glass of wine.

A Meeting

We were often separated
Like the Dipper and the morning star.
What night is tonight?
We are together in the candlelight.

⁴ The Kokonor.

How long does youth last?
Now we are all gray-haired.
Half of our friends are dead,
And both of us were surprised when we met.

Who would know that after twenty years
I would call upon you in your hall?
You were not married when we last parted,
And now you have sons and daughters,
Who come courteously to greet their father's friend,
And ask me where I come from.

While we are thus greeting each other,
Your sons and daughters begin to prepare the wine.
They gather the spring spinach on this rainy night,
And prepare for the feast with new-made ale.

You said: It is a heavenly chance that we meet.
With a single breath we drank ten pots of wine.
I am not drunk, even though I have drunk all this wine.
I commend you for your courteous friendship.
Tomorrow there will be mountains between us,
Nor you nor I knows what will come.

The Rain at Night

The good rain knows when to fall,
Coming in this spring to help the seeds,
Choosing to fall by night with a friendly wind,
Silently moistening the whole earth.
Over this silent wilderness the clouds are dark.
The only light shines from a river boat.
Tomorrow morning everything will be red and wet,
And all Chengtu will be covered with blossoming flowers.

At the Frontier

In the morning we enter the barracks at the east gate.
In the evening we are sentries at Ho Yang Bridge.
The setting sun shines on our immense banners.
The horses neigh, a wind rustles the grass.
Tens of thousands of tents are spread on the sand.
Soldiers beckon to one another, whispering.
Bright is the moon shining in the sky,
Hard is discipline, silent is the night.
Mournful horns are sighing, sighing.
Even the knights are mournful, no longer proud.
"May we ask who the great general is?"
"Surely he is the famous Ho Piao Yao."

Spring

Mountains and rivers lie in the opening sun.
Spring winds freshen the flowers and herbs.
Swallows are flying to fill their nests with mud.
Doves spread themselves drowsily in hot sand.

The blue river reflects the white birds.
On the green mountains red flowers are burning.
Silently I watch the procession of spring.
Then I will return to my beloved home.

Parting from My Old Wife

The country is still at war; no safety yet.
Old as I am, I cannot retire and rest.
My sons and grandsons all died at the front.
What good is it to me to remain on earth alone?

I throw away my stick and go out of doors.
My heart aches, my spirit is dumfounded.
Fortunately my teeth are all sound—
But I am afraid my bones cannot stand it.
Do not worry—I am wearing my uniform,
I bow to the officer, I bid him farewell.

My old wife lies on the roadside weeping,
Her summer clothes pierced through by the winter wind.
Do I really know that we shall not meet again?
And yet I am afraid that she will catch cold.
I go on my way, I know I shall never return,
Yet she tells me: "Keep well, my love, keep well."

They say the citadel at Ti-men is formidable,
The ferry at Han-hsien is difficult to cross;
We lost the battle of Nu, but not the next one.
There are still months to live, though I shall die.

Death is there, before every mortal being,
And has very little to do with health or age.
I remember the happy days of my youth and middle age:
I sigh and meditate deeply for a while.
The whole world is in confusion of war;
The bale fire flares over the whole earth.
Corpses are piling on the grass, and the smell is terrible.
Blood runs like water, reddening the river and the plain.

There is no safe place on the earth.
How can I wander and not hesitate?
I must make up my mind without any pangs
To leave my pleasant home forever.

Summer Night

Cool perfume of bamboo pervades my room,
Wild moonlight fills the whole courtyard:
Drop by drop falls the crystal dew.
One by one the moving stars appear.
The fleeting glowworms sparkle in dark corners,
The waterfowl on the riverbank call to one another;
Everything in the world follows the path of war—
I sit on my bed, meditating through the long night.

Translated by Nee Wen-yei.

Chengtu

Now faintly the falling sun
Shines on my traveler's robes.
As I move onward, so does the scenery change.
Suddenly I feel as though under another sky.
I meet fresh people.
I do not know when I shall see my native home.
The Great River flows east,
As endlessly as are a wanderer's days.
Beautiful buildings fill the whole city;
The woods are dark in this late winter.
Noisily stands the famous city,
Full of the sound of flutes and reeds.
Marvelous, but I am still a stranger here.
Therefore I turn and look at the far mountains.
In the evening all birds return to their homes.
When shall I return to the center of China?
The moon is not very high;
All the stars are shining as in a contest.
Oh, from the ancient days always there have been travelers.
So why should I grieve?

The Recruiting Officer

When the sun set, I came to the village of Shi-kao.
At night the recruiting officer came to round up the men.
An old man took fright and escaped over a wall.
The old woman went forward and asked to be arrested—

How terribly the officer howled at her!
Then I heard the old woman saying through tears:
"My three sons have joined the camp at Yeh.
One of them sent me a letter, saying:
'Two of my brothers have died in the wars,
And the living one thinks he has not much longer to live.'
Oh, the dead, they go on their journey.
There are no more children in this house,
Except a grandson who is still suckling.
Even his mother cannot go with you—
She has not a whole skirt to go in.
Though I am old, and have little strength,
I beg you to let me go with you.
I will be some use—I can prepare food,
I can cook rice and prepare soldiers' meals."

The night was dead, the sounds of talking ceased.
I seemed to hear sobbing, and lamentations.
The next morning I continued on my way,
And said farewell to the old man of the house.

Translated by Chu Chun-i.

On Hearing That Our Arms Have Captured Honan and Hupeh

It is suddenly known that we have captured Chi-peh.
When I first heard it, I shed tears on my clothes.
I stare on my wife's face, and do not know where my sorrow is.
Then I gather up my poems and books in a wild pleasure.
We shall sing and drink wine,
We shall sing and return home together.
As soon as we have passed Wuchia and Pachia,
We shall return through Shanyang to Loyang!

On a Pine Tree Shown to Me by the Taoist Scholar Li

At clear dawn I comb my white hairs.
A Taoist priest from Yuan Tu temple comes to call on me.
Gathering up my hair, I call my son to invite him into the room,
In his hand holding a painting of green pines for a screen.
Mysterious, silent, and misty the fir forest on the screen;
For a moment, leaning on the balustrade, I see the red and blue colors disappearing.
Dark cliffs uphold the frosted stems of the pines,

Hanging canopies of pine needles, leaning back, like writhing
    dragons.
Oh, but from my earliest youth I have admired ancient things.
Gazing at this painting I am absorbed in contemplating divine
    spirits.
Already I know that the painting will always be dear to the
    celestial priest,
And now all the more I reverence the accomplishments of the
    artist's heart.
Under the pines are old men, with the same headcloths and
    shoes.
They sit together like the old hermits of Mount Shang.
Contemplating ancient times I sing the song of the "Purple
    Fungus."
The trials of the present time come with a sorrowing wind.

Translated by Pu Hsiang-hsing.

Staying at the Official Residence on a Spring Night

The flowers are hidden as the shade of twilight emerges;
Birds fly over the sky, twittering to their nests.
Over hundreds of homes move the stars in their courses.
On the heaven of Heaven the moon leans in brightness.
Sleepless now, I seem to hear the gold key stirring in the lock.
Early tomorrow I shall offer a memorial to the Emperor.
Many times I ask how the night is passing.

To Li Po on a Spring Day

Po, the unrivaled poet,
Who soars alone into the kingdom of imagination,
Yours is the delicacy of Yin,
Yours also Pao's rare freshness.
North of Wei River spring comes through the trees.
Meanwhile you wander beneath the sunset clouds of Chiang-
    tung.
When shall we buy a cask of wine once more
And argue minutely on versification?

To Li Po

When the cold wind visits you from the corners of the earth,
How are you, my beloved, what are you dreaming on?
When will the wild geese fly with your letter here?

The autumn rivers and lakes deepen and bring you my
    thoughts.
The god of poetry hates those whom fortune smiles upon;
The devil bursts into laughter when real men stand close to
    him.
The world is a desert! If only we could throw poems into the
    Milo River
And speak with the great soul who was sacrificed to loyalty
    and poetry.[5]

Thinking of Li Po

It is a long while since I have seen you, Li Po.
A pity that you have feigned madness—
The whole world would have you die,
But my heart dotes on your gifted soul,
For the thousand poems of your nimble wit,
For the wine-cup balm of such a wanderer.
Go to your old place of studying—Mount Kuang.[6]
Come back, O white-headed one! It is time!

Thinking of My Brothers on a Moonlit Night

No one walks when the guardian drum sounds;
The cry of the wild geese marks autumn on the frontier.
Now at night the dewdrops twinkle with a starry whiteness,
Yet how much brighter shines the moon on my home!
My brothers are separated and wanderers in the land,
And there is nowhere I can ask whether they have survived
    or are dead.
A letter takes so long upon the way.
Oh, but I know there is much more than war in this country.

Journey to the North

I

Autumn, in the second year of the Sovereign Land,
On the first day of the eighth intercalary moon,
I, Tu Fu, propose to journey to the north
In the hope of being able to call on my wife and family.
At this time of danger and anxiety
There are few days of leisure for officers and common people.
I am overcome with shame at the favors granted to me alone.

[5] Chu Yuan.
[6] Where they first met.

An edict permits my return to my "thistles and weeds."
So kneeling and bidding farewell to the throne,
For a long while I remain disconsolate and sad.
Though I lack the ability of a good censor,
Yet I am afraid my lord will neglect his duties.
Verily my lord has come to rule over a new age.
The complex strands will be planned with deliberation.
The rebellion of the east barbarians is not yet put down.
I, the humble Tu Fu, am filled with the gravest anger.
Shedding tears, reluctant to part from the exiled city,
I follow the road, sunk in deep reverie.
The whole nation has suffered such terrible wounds—
When will this sorrow and anxiety end?

II

Interminable are the pathways between the paddy fields;
Smoke from the cooking fires is rarely seen.
Occasionally I meet wounded soldiers,
Spilling out their blood, sobbing, moaning.
I turn my head toward Feng Hsiang.
Banners and pennants shine and disappear in the evening sky.
I climb wave after wave of ice-cold hills.
I pause and water my horse at wayside pools.
The land of P'in now lies deep in the valley.
The Ching River runs through it, shining.
Fierce tigers bar my way.
When they roar, the black precipice cracks.
Autumn chrysanthemums bend low their heads;
Rocks bear the scars of ancient cartwheels.
My spirits rise at the sight of blue clouds;
Yet this secluded landscape is still pleasing.
Multitudes of minute delicate hill haws
Grow like a net entangled with acorns and chestnuts,
Some red like cinnabar ore,
Some black like drops of lacquer.
Heaven's rain and dew nourish them;
Sweet and bitter alike they put forth fruit.
Dreaming of a distant peach-blossom land,[7]
Always I deride the senselessness of my wayward life.

III

From humpbacked paths I gaze on the temple of Fu;
Valleys and precipices appear and disappear in turn.
Already my path has reached the water's edge.
My serving man is still among the trees.
The horned owl hoots amid yellow mulberries,
The field mice run from their scattered holes.
In the depths of night we cross a battlefield;

[7] He is thinking of Tao Yuan-ming's "Peach-Blossom Fountain."

A cold moon shines on white bones.
I ponder the fate of a myriad soldiers speedily defeated
In days gone by on the fields of Tung-kuan,
When half the people of the province of Ch'ing
Fell dead, were wounded, were injured and slain!

IV

I, too, have fallen in the dust of the barbarians;
After I escaped my hair was streaked with white.
Nearly a whole year passed before I returned home.
There was my wife clothed in a hundred patches,
And our sobbing grief sounded like soughing pines,
And our lonely tears echoed like sad fountains.
That child whom I have adored from my youth,
Whose complexion was whiter than snow—
She saw her father turn back his face and whimper,
And there were no stockings on her dirty greasy feet.
In front of the bed stood two little girls,
Covered in patches, their clothes hardly reaching their knees;
From some embroidered sea their mother had cut the waves,[8]
But the ancient embroidery was stitched confusedly.
There was Tien Hu[9] and the Purple Phoenix
All turned upside down on their short clothes.
I, an old man, filled with resentment,
For some days lay on my bed, vomiting, purging.
Fortunately I have clothes somewhere in my baggage,
And perhaps this will save them from the shivering cold.
I take powder and black stones[1] from their wrappings;
Quilts and coverlets are soon folded and arranged.
Once again my poor wife's face is glowing,
And the silly girls comb their own hair,
Imitating their mother in everything—
So carelessly they paint their faces in the morning,
Absorbed in daubing themselves with rouge and white lead,
Scattering on their faces such widely spaced eyebrows.
Well, I have returned alive to play with my children,
And it is as though I had already forgotten hunger and thirst.
They ask questions, crowd round me, cling to my beard.
How can I be angry or drive them away?[2]
Meditating on my grief among the rebels,
I cheerfully listen to all their chattering.
So, newly returned, for a while I comfort my feelings,
But one thing remains—how shall I make a living?

[8] I.e., the waves on the embroidered dress had been cut off to clothe the children.
[9] Tien Hu is the god of the sea, with the face of a man and the body of a tiger.
[1] For eyebrows.
[2] Literally: to make a sound like "ha" at them.

V

The Sovereign Lord is still enveloped in the dust of war.
When will the training of the soldiers cease?
I gaze at heaven; soon there will be alterations.
Soon there will be an end to all these evil vapors.
A cold wind comes from the northwest.
Hardily the Uighurs will come to our rescue,
Their king obeying our command, offering help willingly.
Their custom is to master the cavalry and break through;
If they can send five thousand men,
They can drive ten thousand horse before them.
The youngest among them are most especially honored;
All men under heaven praise their great ardor,
And all such soldiers are as soaring falcons,
Who rise more swiftly than any arrow.
The imperial policy hesitantly welcomes them,
But now the courtiers strongly oppose them.[3]

VI

The two rivers I and Lo will easily be retaken,
The west capital is still more easily regained;
When the time comes the imperial army will go deeper,
The sharp edge of our reserves might perhaps accompany
    them.
So they will open a way into Ch'ing and Hsu,[4]
And wheel round to reach the foot of Mount Heng and
    Mount Ch'i.
The autumn heaven pours down dew and frost.
The True Spirit has the power of killing.
The turn of the year brings calamity on the Hu barbarians.
The moon has risen that determines their destiny,
And their fate cannot be delayed much longer.
Certainly the imperial government is not destined to end.

VII

I recall now that at the beginning of our retreat,[5]
All things were different from those in ancient times.
Vile courtiers at the end were executed by process of law;
All those concerned in crimes were swept away.
We have not heard that at the decline of Hsia and Yin[6]

[3] I.e., the Emperor desired to employ the Uighurs to safeguard the throne, but the court faction opposed him.
[4] Two provinces in what is now Shantung.
[5] Literally: jackals and lynxes, but the words in Chinese are customarily used to describe the terrors of a retreat.
[6] Both the Hsia (2205-1766 B.C.) and the Shang-Yin (1766-1122 B.C.) dynasties failed as a result of the intemperance of their kings.

The emperors themselves ordered the deaths of Mei and Tan.
In Chou and Han a new order was accomplished;
The emperors Hsuan and Kuan[7] were assuredly shining and
    wise.
The great commander Ch'en[8] was valorous indeed,
Who with his crescent halberd stirred the loyalty of the people.
Without him the people would certainly have failed.
But now the country is saved.

VIII

Oh, lonely is the audience hall of the palace,
Sorrowful is the Gate of the White Beast;
Men in the capital seek the Kingfisher Glory,[9]
Breath of good fortune falls on the gold-pillared gateway.
Already the imperial sepulchers demonstrate their divine
    influence.
The ceremonies of sweeping and sprinkling[1] have not been
    omitted.
Supreme are the auguries of T'ai Tsung,[2]
The empire is firmly established and reaches the skies!

Translated by Pu Hsiang-hsing.

---

[7] The emperors Hsuan of the Chou dynasty and Kuan of Han were
notoriously benevolent.

[8] Chen Huan-li, the great general of T'ang.

[9] The imperial chariot.

[1] Refers to the tending of the imperial graves.

[2] The second and greatest of the T'ang emperors (reigned 627-649).

PO CHU-I (A.D. 772–846)

Like Wang Wei, he was born in Tai-yuan in Shansi, and spent most of his poverty-stricken childhood in Honan. He was so precocious that he claimed later that at the age of seven months he knew a considerable number of characters after having them pointed out to him only once by his nurse. He graduated as *chin shih* at the age of seventeen, which even in those days of infant prodigies seems to have been remarkable; and thereafter he entered upon an official career, becoming a member of the Hanlin College and rising to high rank under the emperor Tsien Tsung. But more important to his poetry was the friendship he made early in life with Yuan Chen, with whom his name is inseparably connected. Yuan Chen was seven years younger, a poet whose verses were more often quoted at court than Po Chu-i's, for Po delighted from the beginning in making his verses as simple as possible. Both rose to high rank, both were regarded as among the greatest poets of their time; but though they admired and even loved each other, they were often separated, and so much of their poetry is concerned with their grief at separation. For the Chinese until recently this grief was deeper than any other grief: death comes as inevitably as birth and marriage, but there is a still greater inevitability in the constant separations of court officials from one another, since no official was allowed to serve for long in the same district. So the poetry of the T'ang dynasty is filled with the complaints of court officials, who lament their fleeting glimpses of their friends.

The friendship of Po Chu-i for Yuan Chen ran deeper than most, and throws a melancholy over his poetry from the very beginning. And they were strangely different. Yuan Chen was elegant, he possessed relations at court, and it is significant that he obtained the post of secretary in the Imperial Banqueting Chamber. Po Chu-i, more reserved, more Confucian, more deeply imbued with conceptions of morality, possessing a fundamental dislike for Taoism and a still more fundamental dislike for court displays, seems to have admired Yuan Chen more deeply because they were so dissimilar. Yuan was a braggart and a hero, with something of Li Po's temper. Once, when he was staying at an inn, he refused to leave when a court official arrived and was struck across the face for his impertinence. Po Chu-i would have left with good grace. He was humble in his youth, and once he complained that he possessed no skill in the accomplishments of calligraphy, painting, chess, or gambling, "which bring men together in a community of pleasure." Sad, silent, and solitary, he gazed on life

205

with unfailing good humor, as disinterested as Confucius in spirits and demon powers. He writes with something of Robert Frost's passion for exactness, and he is the easiest of all Chinese poets to translate into English.

He is not dull, but he sometimes verges on dullness. He occupied a succession of high posts, and was occasionally banished—it was comparatively easy to be banished in those days. On the accession of the emperor Mu Tsung, in 821, he was made governor of Hangchow, where he built one of the great embankments of the West Lake still known as Po's Embankment, a lake which was further embellished by Su T'ung-po 260 years later. In 829 he became governor of Honan, and finally in 841 became president of the Board of War. He died in 846, having compiled a complete edition of his works and presented them to deserving libraries and leaving a testament asking that he should not be buried in the family tomb, but beside the body of his favorite monk.

He is famous chiefly for "The Everlasting Sorrow," which gives a grandiloquent and not always historically accurate account of the death of Yang Kuei-fei at Ma-wei, but he preferred the poems in which some didactic element appears. He writes nearly always in a minor key, as of an old man recording a spiritual voyage. Significantly (and ironically) his *tzu,* or style name, was "Joyful Heaven," but he is more often known as P'o Hsiang-san, or P'o Scented Mountain, after the mountain near Loyang, where he retired during one of his longer periods of banishment, where he gathered round him eight others of a similar temperament who became known as the Nine Ancients of Hsiang-san. Yuan Chen had died. He was himself often ill, and one of his children had died; his only refuge lay in his poetry, in his daughter Golden Bells, who composed charming verses at the age of ten, and in memories of his friends. He enjoyed his fame with the passionate devotion to fame of a lonely man. He was proud that his verses were sung by plow boys and peasants, as well as by the emperor and the men of the court. "A certain Captain Kao Hsia-yu was courting a dancing girl. 'You must not think I am an ordinary dancing girl,' she said. 'I can recite Master Po's "The Everlasting Wrong."'" And she put up her price."

There were other consolations. He would find his poems written on the walls of lodging houses, temples, village schools, and ships' cabins. He was a classic before he died. In 824 he had taken two dancing girls, Fan-tzu and Man-tzu, into his household, and almost up to the end of his life he was engaged on platonic love affairs with young girls, whom he would accompany to the mountains and celebrate in his songs. The old man showed signs of youth in the last years of his life. Paralysis, arthritis, the losses of his friends—nothing could diminish his ardor for poetry and for picnics, and like Lu Yu of the Sung dynasty, he wrote far too many poems on subjects of no value at all. Most of his verse is, in the best sense, occasional, and it suffers precisely from his passion for the moment. There is nothing timeless or eternal; he never goes outside the gates of this world. In one of his latest poems, he is pleased at the thought of dividing his poems among his grandchildren—seventy whole volumes, and three thousand essays and poems altogether. But sometimes, and often it would seem by accident, he produces a magical phrase, an evocation of a mountain journey, some remark or description of one of his favorite dancing girls, a thought of Yuan Chen's, that is perfect in its absolute benediction.

The Everlasting Sorrow

The following poem, written in A.D. 806, when Po Chu-i was thirty-four, has been described by Mr. Waley as "a youthful bid for notoriety," but nothing could be further from the truth. Deliberately the poet is attempting to re-create the atmosphere of the tragic journey from Ch'ang-an during which the emperor Ming Huang saw his consort strangled and his empire threatened by treachery from all sides. The poem is hard and brilliant in the original, and sustained by the tragic force of the past; it is not the greatest poem he wrote, but it is certainly one of the most amazing efforts undertaken by any Chinese poet to describe the whole ethos of a departed civilization.

This Chinese emperor, loving beauty, longed for "the killer of
    Empires," [1]
Yet for many years of his reign he could never find one.
There was in the family of Yang a young girl grown to
    womanhood,
Reared in the inner apartments and scarcely known;
Nature had endowed her with beauty hard to conceal.
One day she was taken and presented to the Emperor.
When she turned and smiled, her hundred charms appeared,
Rendering colorless all the painted girls of the Six Palaces.
In the cold spring she was bathed in Hua Ch'ing Pool, [2]
In the caressing hot springs she was washed smooth as curd—
Enchanting her fragility when held up by the maidens.

[1] Refers to a beauty of the Han dynasty who with one glance could overthrow a city and with two glances an empire.
[2] Hua Ch'ing Kung, or Glory of Purity Palace, lay some miles southeast of Ch'ang-an and was famous for its warm springs. The place is now known as Lintung, and it was here that Chiang Kai-shek was arrested in 1936.

It was then that she began to receive the favors of the King.
Wearing flowering aigrettes and gold plumes,
In a warm bed netted with hibiscus she passed the spring
  nights.
O spring nights too short, O sun too early on high!
Henceforth the King never summoned his morning levees.
She shared his pleasures and feasts, was never at leisure,
Accomplice of his journeys in spring, companion of his nights.
There were three thousand beauties in the inner apartments,
But of all these three thousand he loved only one.
In a gold house she prepared herself for the night,[3]
In jade towers after feasting they surrendered to drunkenness.
Her sisters and brothers were honored with fiefs;
So bright a glory fell on the whole family
That all mothers and fathers in the empire
Thought it better to give birth to girls than to boys.
From the palace of the Dark Horse which pierces the blue
  clouds [4]
A fairy music, riding the winds, was heard throughout the
  land,
Of graceful singing and waving dances from zithers and
  flutes—
Rejoicing all day, the Emperor never tired.
Then the war drums were heard, shaking the earth, from
  Yu-yang,
Throwing into panic "The Song of the Rainbow Skirt and the
  Coat of Feathers." [5]
From the city of ninefold walls dust rose like smoke;
A thousand chariots, ten thousand horsemen rode southwest.
The Emperor's kingfisher pennon trembled and came to a
  halt
At a place a hundred li west of the imperial city.[6]
What could be done when the Six Hosts refused to march?[7]
Knitting her moth eyebrows, death caught her among the
  horses,
Her hairpins scattered over the earth, no one picking them
  up—

[3] Refers to A-chiao, a concubine of Wu Ti of the Han dynasty. When his aunt pointed to her daughter, the young princess A-chiao, the boy replied: "Ah, if I could have A-chiao, I would have a golden house to keep her in."
[4] Li Shan, or Dark Horse Mountains, lie twenty miles southeast of the capital, and Hua Ch'ing Kung lay in its shadow.
[5] The name of a song composed by Ming Huang after a visit to the Paradise of the Moon, or according to others on the basis of an Indian tune he received as an offering from the country of West Liang.
[6] Refers to Ma Wei P'o (Horse Ridge Slope) where the mutiny occurred.
[7] From the Chou dynasty onward the Emperor had been allowed six armies of 125,000 men each.

Kingfisher feathers, gold birds, combs of jade.
The Emperor hid his face, unable to save her;
At last he turned toward her, tears mingled with blood.
Yellow dust floating in space, winds whistling in the air—
Along winding bridges, over precipices, they climbed Sword
    Pass.[8]
On Mount Omei [9] few travelers pass.
In this dim sunlight how dull were their banners!
In Shu the rivers are green, the hills are blue.[1]
His Sacred Majesty sorrowed from dawn to dusk.
From the imperial palace the moon was seen to be grief-
    stricken;
The bells in the night rain twisted the entrails.
Heaven and earth revolved, the Dragon Chariot drove home;
Reaching the fatal place, he lingered and could not go on.
There in the dust and sand on the slope of Ma Wei,
He sees no more her jade face, only the empty death place.
The eyes of sovereign and minister meet, they wet their robes
    with tears,
Then look east to the capital and give rein to their horses.
There is the pool, there are the flowers as of old,
Hibiscus in the Sublime Lake, willows in the Palace of Endless
    Days—
Hibiscus like her face, willow twigs like her brows.
Seeing these things, how could he not shed tears
When plum trees and pear trees blossom in the spring winds,
When the leaves of the *wu-t'ung* tree fall in the autumn rain?
In the west and south palaces autumn grasses abound.
Unswept and red are the fallen leaves on the steps.
In the Pear Blossom Garden [2] the hair of the students is
    white,
The brows of the eunuchs of the Pepper Chamber [3] now are
    aged.
In the hall at night, where fireflies flit, he sinks in silence
Unable to sleep, though the oil in the lonely lamp has burned
    out—
So slow are the watchman's bells and the night so long.
Rivers of stars dimly scatter their light, pretending to be
    dawn,
The duck-and-drake tiles are cold, the frost sharp.
Who will share with him the kingfisher quilts of old?

[8] Sword Pass connects two great mountains in Szechuan.

[9] One of the five sacred mountains, not far from Chengtu.

[1] Shu is the ancient name for Szechuan; the implication is that the rivers
and mountains are both dark.

[2] An Imperial School founded by the Emperor where singing and dancing
were taught.

[3] The Queen's private apartment was painted with fragrant peppers in the
Han dynasty.

Oh, great is the distance separating the dead from the living!
Though a year had passed, her ghost had not visited him in
    dreams.
A Taoist monk from Lin-ch'ung, a guest from Hung-tu,[4]
Could by his faith summon the spirits from the dead.
Weighed down by the Emperor's mourning and perpetual
    torments,
The sorcerer was bidden to seek out the dead.
Borne on the air, charioting the winds, he flew like lightning,
Soaring to heaven, descending to earth, seeking everywhere,
Exploring the empyrean; below, the Yellow Springs;
But nowhere in these vast spaces did he discover anything.
He heard that on the sea lay a magic mountain,
A mountain engulfed among mysterious vacuities,
Where decorated palaces rose on five-colored clouds
And many divine creatures lived there delicately.
Among them was one called T'ai Chen,[5]
Whose snow-white skin and flowery face might be hers.
At the western wing of a gold house he knocked on a jade door
And bade Small Jade call on her mistress, Double Triumph,
To announce the presence of the Son of Heaven, Lord of Han.
Beneath the nine flower curtains the Queen awakened from
    dreams,
Put on her dress, pushed the pillows away, rose and hesitated,
Then slid the pearl curtains open with a silver hook—
The clouds of her hair awry as she awakened from slumber,
She stepped down into the hall with flowery headdress in
    disarray.
The sleeves of the goddess floated in the waving air.
Once more she seemed to be dancing "The Rainbow Skirt and
    Coat of Feathers,"
Her pure face sorrowing, slowly the tears falling—
O branch of pear blossom in the spring rain!
Subduing her emotion, with frozen tears, she thanked the
    Emperor:
"Since we parted, our voices and faces have been separated,
The passionate loves of Chao Yang[6] Hall have been cut short.
The days and months in Peng-lai[7] Palace were so long.

[4] Hung-tu is where the imperial archives were situated, not far from
Ch'ang-an. Taoist monks were traditionally archivists, since it was
recorded of Lao-tzu that he was archivist in the State Library of Chou.

[5] T'ai Chen, or Perfect Purity, the name by which Yang Kuei-fei was
known at court. Originally it appears to have been the name she received
when she was in a nunnery, during the short interval before she became
Ming Huang's consort.

[6] Intense Brilliance Palace, the Queen's apartments.

[7] Named after the mysterious fairy island, and situated in the center of
the great courtyard that included the Great Saliva Pool. Tu Fu speaks
of "the clouds of five colors that often float over the Peng-lai Palace."
It was the most ornate and the most beautiful of all.

Now I gaze down upon the world of men.
Never do I see Ch'ang-an—only the dust and the haze.
Only by these keepsakes can I show my undying love.
Through you I offer this gold hairpin and this inlaid case.
Tell him, if his heart endures as gold or metal,
In heaven or earth we shall one day meet again."
Then, as he went away, she confided an imploring message,
Speaking an oath known only to the two lovers,
Spoken in Eternal Life Hall on the seventh day of the seventh
      moon,
When they were secretly talking, no one present, at midnight:[8]
"In the skies we shall be twin birds that fly together,
On earth we shall be trees with branches intertwined.
Heaven is enduring, earth long living, but they will perish,
The everlasting sorrow will never come to an end."

Captives from the Western Tribes

The captives from the western tribes
Were driven into Ch'ing with ears pierced, faces broken.
The Son of Heaven had too much pity to kill them
And decreed them exiled to Wu and Yueh in the southeast.
A royal page dressed in yellow listed down their names,
And they were handed over at Ch'ang-an to go along the post
      road.
Bodies thick with wounds, faces bruised with sores,
Sick to death they traveled a post length [9] each day;
Hungry and thirsty in the morning, without any plates or cups,
At night sleeping on mattresses that were foul and smelled of
      blood.
Suddenly they came to a stream reminding them of the Chiao
      River;[1]
With hands hanging low they sobbed and chanted in unison.
Then one of the captives spoke to the rest of them:
"Your sufferings are not so heavy as mine."
One of them asked him what he was saying,
But he could hardly answer, his throat choking with anger.
He said: "My home town is Liang-yuan;[2]
I fell among the Tartars at the time of Ta-li.[8]
Forty whole years have passed since then.
Clothed with fur, belted with leather,

[8] See Li Shang-yin's poem "Ma Wei," which recounts the same tragedy
more briefly.
[9] About sixty li or twenty miles.
[1] In Turkestan.
[2] A village to the north of Ch'ang-an.
[8] The nin-hao or ruling date: 766-780.

Observing the Chinese rites only in levees,
Where always, setting my robe in order, I wept quietly;
I made a secret vow to return to my country,
While keeping it secret from my foreign wife.
And I was lucky that my limbs were still strong,
And feared that I would never return when I grew weaker
    and old.
The foreign lords were strict with their soldiers—a bird could
    not have fled,
But I escaped, risking my life, and returned toward my home.
By day I hid, at night I walked over vast deserts,
The clouds gray, the moon black, the winds and sands fierce;
In panic I hid among old tombs where the cold grasses were
    few,
And the ice was thin one night when I crossed the Yellow
    River.
Suddenly I heard the drumbeat of Chinese armies.
From the roadside I turned toward them and prostrated
    myself.
But the patrols found that I could not speak Chinese;
The general took me prisoner, thinking I was born in a foreign
    country.
Now I am exiled to the swamp country south of the Yangtze
    River,
Never looked after, nor provisioned, needlessly guarded.
Thinking of this I dumbly appeal to Heaven.
How shall I pass my life, how hard must I work?
Never again perhaps shall I see my home town of Liang-yuan;
Fruitlessly I have forsaken my wife and children in an alien
    land;
Captured by the Tartars, I pined for the Chinese earth;
Now that I have returned to China, they make me a Tartar
    prisoner.
Had I known this, I would never have returned.
Instead of suffering in two places, I would have suffered only
    in one.
O you prisoners from the west!
I am the most bitterly tormented of all—
Such an injustice cannot have occurred since ancient times;
A Chinese heart, a Chinese tongue speaking through the body
    of a foreigner!"

Sitting at Night

Against the lamp I sit by the south window,
Listening to the sleet and the wind in the dark.
Desolation deepens the night among the villages.
Through the snow I hear the lost wild goose calling. . . .

Seeing Hsia Chan Off by River

Because you are old and departing I have wetted my hand-
     kerchief,
You who are homeless at seventy, belonging to the wilderness.
Anxiously I watch the wind rising as the boat sails away,
A white-headed man amid white-headed waves.

Sleeping Alone at the Hsien-Yu Temple

The crane on the shore stood on a flight of stone steps;
The moon from the pool beamed through an open door.
I was charmed by this place and stayed there,
And could not leave for two nights.
Fortunate that I should have found so quiet a place;
Glad that no companion should drag me away.
Ever since I have tasted the loneliness,
I have decided never to come with companions.

Lonely Night in Early Autumn

Thin leaves wave on the *wu-t'ung* tree beside the well.
Through the pounding of the washerwomen, autumn begins
     to sing.
Under the eaves, I find a place and sleep alone,
And waking, I see the bed half filled with the moon.

The Harp

I lay my harp on the curved table,
Sitting there idly, filled only with emotions.
Why should I trouble to play?
A breeze will come and sweep the strings.

Song of the Pines

I like sitting alone when the moon is shining,
And there are two pines standing before the veranda;
A breeze comes from the southwest
Creeping into the branches and leaves.
Under the brilliant moon at midnight
It whistles a cool, distant music,
Like rustling rains in empty mountains.
When first I hear them, the heat of summer is washed away,

And this suffocating boredom comes to an end.
So I keep awake the whole night,
Both the heart and the body becoming clear.
Along the south street coaches and horses are stirring,
In the west city sounds of playing and singing.
Who knows that under the roof trees of this place
The ears are full, but not with noise?

On the Tower Overlooking the River

Beside the river stands the hundred-foot tower;
There a highway runs a thousand miles into the distance.
Looking at the far horizon from this height
Suffices to comfort my mind and heart.
Couriers bustle along the road,
Soldiers hurry to their garrisons.
In such troubled times
Especially I feel it good to be idle.
Now that I am past forty,
It is really not too early to retire.
Let me now clean my dust-stained garments.
It will not be too late to return to the hills.

On an Ancient Tomb East of the Village

Among the ancient tombs both high and low,
There is a path for cattle and sheep.
As I stand alone on the highest of them,
How carefree is my heart!
Turning to look at the village,
I see nothing but weeds in deserted fields—
The villagers are not fond of flowers,
And have planted only chestnuts and dates.
Ever since I came to live here,
I have never been delighted with the scenery.
The flowers are few, the orioles are scarce,
And when spring comes it can hardly be seen.

Visiting the Hermit Cheng

I hear you have gone to live among the village mounds
By the lonely gate where the bamboo groves abound.
I have come now only to beg you:
Lend me your south garden that I may look at the hills.

The Heart in Autumn

Few visitors come through this gate.
Many pines and bamboos grow in front of the steps;
The autumn air does not enter through the east wall;
The cool wind blows into the west courtyard.
I have a harp. I am too lazy to play.
I have books. I have no leisure to read.
All day long in this land of a square inch,[4]
There is only quietude and no desires.
Why should I make this house larger?
There is no use to say too much.
A room of ten square feet is enough for the body,
A peck of rice is sufficient for the belly.
Besides, without any ability in managing affairs,
I idle and receive the emperor's salary.
I neither plant a single mulberry tree
Nor hoe a single furrow for rice,
Yet I feed well all day,
And all the year round I am well clothed.
With such a conscience, knowing my shame,
Why should I be discontented?

Woodpeckers' Song

Do not buy precious scissors—
A thousand dollars will bring no return.
I have sorrow in my heart,
But you cannot cut it.
Do not sharpen the knot-breaking awl—
Your labors will be of no avail.
I have a knot in my guts:
You cannot disentangle it.
Do not dye the silk thread red—
The lovely color would be proud, yet helpless.
My tears are two strings of beads,
But I know you cannot gather them.
Do not ask me to approach the fire in the red stove.
The heat would oppress me; there would be no result.
I have frost on my temples,
But I know it cannot be thawed.
Scissors cannot cut the sorrows in the heart,
Awls cannot disentangle knots in guts,
Threads cannot string the beads of tears,
Fire cannot thaw the snow on hairs.
Let us drink the heavenly cup—
All cares and worries cease at once!

[4] I.e., the heart.

Buying Flowers

In the capital spring comes late.
The noisy chariots and horses are passing.
They say, "It is the time of the peonies."
So they come together to buy flowers.
Prices, high and low, may change,
But also it depends on how much you buy.
Hundreds shine bright red,
There is a bouquet white as crystal,
Sheltered by curtains overhead
And constructed on a bamboo framework,
Watered and set in mud.
These are the old colors, but changed.
Every house buys them according to custom,
And nobody thinks wrong of it.
Only an old man from the farm
Coming by chance to the flower market
Lowers his head, deeply sighs—
A sigh that no one understands.
Over a single posy of deep-colored flowers
Ten common families might sing!

On the Fasting Monk Chu Chuan

For thirty years you sat facing the wall,
Exchanging nothingness for life in this world.
At mealtimes you now and then laugh at the bells.
How could you be so free to eat as not to eat?

Sauntering through Chao Village at Apricot-Blossoming Time

Sauntering through the village where red apricots blossom each
    year—
For fifteen years I have been here several times.
I am seventy-three; it will be difficult to come again.
Now in spring I come to say farewell to the flowers.

The Charcoal-Burner

On the hill to the south of the city
The old charcoal-burner burns the wood.
His face is dusty and covered with smoke,
His hair is gray at the temples, his fingers black.
What would he desire from the money he gains

Except garments to wear and food to eat?
Yet frozen to the marrow in his thin coat
He prays for a colder day,
Lest the price of charcoal should drop.

During the night a foot of snow fell,
Whitening the world outside the town;
Breaking the ice, the old man
In the early morning takes his charcoal cart along;
But the beast is exhausted, the man hungry.
While the sun is riding high and the cart is standing
In the mud and refuse outside the south gate,
Who should he see coming gracefully on two horses
But royal messengers in their white and yellow livery,
Shouting aloud with papers in their hands.
He guides the cart north, lashing at the animal,
With cargo weighing a thousand catty.
Twenty yards of gauze and eight of sarcenet
Are tied to the head of the ox to pay for the fuel.

The Sand and the Waves

The sand comes and goes, wave after wave.
The surge dies, another rises.
Stirring and re-forming endlessly,
They level the mountains and seas in time.

The white waves go out into the vast ocean.
The smooth sand stretches away into boundless distance.
Ceaselessly, day and night, never ending
They will make the east ocean into a land of fields.

To journey ten thousand miles over a green grass lake,
I set sail alone in monsoon rains,
Continually perturbed at the thought of a harbor at night,
Where the winds whistle and somber waves are lapping.

Tell me why the river and the sea
Resemble so much your love and my heart.
What disturbs me is that you are not so faithful as the waves;
To be without you is to see the depths of the seas.

There will be a day when dust will fly over this sea.
One day, too, the mountains will turn into sand.
Who had thought my love would abandon me here,
Or that the prow of the ship is never turned back?

Following the tides, riding the waves to the horizon,
How many travelers ever returned?
You may search in the city for wealth and power,
But remember always what happens to sand and waves.

Looking in the Lake

I look at my shadow over and over in the lake;
I see no white face, only the white hair.
I have lost my youth, and shall never find it again.
Useless to stir the lake water!

A Flower?

It seems a flower, but not a flower;
It seems a mist, but not a mist.
It comes at midnight,
It goes away in the morning.

Its coming is like a spring dream that does not last long,
And its going is like the morning cloud. You will find it
    nowhere.

Myself

White beard and pink face,
Happy in my half-drunkenness.
A hundred years pass in an instant;
All becomes vague as I turn my head.
I am a hermit lying sick and lean,
A crazy old drunkard walking and singing.

At I-Ye Temple

I play with stones and sit beside the stream,
I search for flowers and walk around the temple.
Sometimes I listen to the songs of birds;
The sounds of spring are everywhere.

The Mirror

The brightness of a bronze mirror,
The whiteness of silken thread.
How can I prevent people knowing my age?
Surely you do not believe I have grown old?

To the Distant One

I try to forget, but it is in vain.
I try to go, but I have no way.
There are no wings on my axles;
My head is covered with white hairs.
I sit and watch the leaves falling,
Or go up to the top of the tower.
Shades hover in boundless twilight.
A vast sadness comes to my eyes.

Heavy Taxes

Yesterday I went to the yamen to pay my taxes,
And peeped through the storehouse gates.
The cloth and silk were piled as high as hills,
And gauzes and cotton mounted up like clouds.
They were fine tributes
To be offered to the sovereign,
But they were really the warmth stripped from my back
To buy them temporal favors,
That they might enter the golden royal house
And become dust through the ages.

The North Garden

The east wind is blowing in the north garden.
Flowers of all kinds blossom one after another,
Well aware that they will fall in a little while.
I come to gaze on them three or four times a day.
It is not that there is no wine among the flowers—
Wine enough; I pour it out and hesitate.
I am thinking about things thousands of miles away.
Oh, who will pour the wine for me?

Grass

How luxuriant the grass in the meadow!
Flourishing and decaying in a single year.
Even fire will not burn it up,
For the spring breeze will blow it to life again.
A distant fragrance invades the ancient road;
Its deep green color adjoins the ruined town.
In bidding farewell to the departing lords,
How tender its affection!

All translated by Ching Ti.

LI HUA (ninth century)

The Old Battlefield

So infinitely vast,
The level sands without end,
Ringed round by rivers and waters,
Hummocky with hills,
In such a dark twilight,
The wind moans at sunset.
Grasses and herbs have perished;
In the early morning a chill hoarfrost.
The birds flying up and down,
The beasts having no place there.
The keeper said to me:
"Here was an old battlefield,
Again and again there were wars.
Here the dead weep
Under heaven's darkness."

O heart of darkness!
The Ch'ins and the Hans passed away,
All these dynasties passed away.
I heard when the Ch'ins and the Weis gathered on the border,
The Hans and the Chings made their levies;
Ten thousand li they marched
Through many years of misery.
They gazed on the sands by day,
Forded the rivers by night,
The earth endless, the sky eternal,
Not knowing when they would return,
Bodies exposed to knives.
Endless their misery and woes!

Since the Ch'ins and the Hans have passed,
Many events have occurred in the four corners.
The middle empire has been ravaged,
No generation has remained unharmed.
In ancient times the Chinese and the Huns
Did not protest against the imperial rule.
The place of right was surrendered to power.
The rough soldier cast aside benevolence and duty.
The rule of the Tao was sacrificed!

Now once again I see these things;
I see the north wind shrouding them in dust,
The Tartar soldiers caught in ambuscades,
The general hardly fighting,
Preferring to wage war at the camp gates.
Banners wave over the plain,
The river surrounds the combatants.
Order is enforced on beating hearts.
Commands are uttered; life is valueless!

The harsh spear penetrates flesh,
The frightened sand enters their eyes,
The armies are locked together.
Mountains and streams cry aloud,
The rivers scream
Under the thunder of arms.
Then the cold night falls.
They are knee-deep in snow,
Their beards are stiff with ice.
The screaming vulture flies to its nest,
The huge war horses are broken.
Garments do not protect from the cold,
Arms are frostbitten and the flesh torn.
Heaven helps the Tartars,
Sending a deadly wind,
Working with them to bring death.
Ambulance carts block the way,
Our flanks are pierced,
Our officers surrender,
Our general lies dead.
The river is swollen with corpses;
Blood streams along the ditches of the Great Wall.
Nothing of worth, nothing of value remains.
All, all are the same—
A heap of rotting bones.

Softly and more softly beat the drums,[1]
Strength made small, all arrows spent,
Bowstrings snapped, swords smashed to pieces.
The two armies wage mortal combat.
Should we yield,
We shall become the slaves of the barbarians.
To fight against the Tartars
Is to mingle our bones with the desert sand.

No bird sings on the hushed hills,
A long night, the wind whistling.
Ghosts of the dead wandering under dark heavens,
The spirits gather under the menacing clouds.

[1] Here and elsewhere Li Hua introduces the musical sobbing vowel that Ch'u Yuan had used throughout the *Li Sao*.

The sun shines its cold light on the trampled grasses,
The fading moon glitters on the white frost.
The heart bleeds, seeing these things,
In the knowledge that such things have happened!

    I have heard say
That Li Mu led the soldiers of Chao[2]
And gained victory over the Tartars.
For ten thousand li the earth was swept clean.
The Hsiung-nu were erased from the land.
But the empire was exhausted.
They had neither the strength nor the men;
Their numbers availed them nothing.

    So did the Chous also
Drive the barbarians north.
They occupied the land,
And at last returned to their homes.
Then they gave thanks to heaven,
And gave themselves up to enjoyment,
To feasting and dancing,
The pleasures of peace.

    The Ch'ins built the Great Wall
That stretched down to the sea.
But war breathed its vapors;
For ten thousand li there were only corpses.
The Hans seized the territory of the Hsiung-nu,
They laid siege to Yin Mountain.
Their bodies lay on the plains;
The gain was smaller than the loss.

    O High Heaven, I beseech you!
Those who are fathers and mothers
Who raise their children
Fear to bring them to maturity.
Those who have brothers
Love them as much as themselves.
Those who have wives, so close and dear to them—
None owe their thanks to life,
None deserve death.
Whether they are alive or dead,
Their family knows nothing of it.
If a man should bring them news,
They will be half trusting, half doubtful,
Hearts overflowing with grief.
Sleeping or waking they see him.

[2] Li Mu, died 229 B.C., was a great general of the Chao state who inflicted so great a defeat on the Hsiung-nu that they did not venture to make war for ten years.

They prepare sacrifices and libations;
They look toward distant heaven;
Heaven and earth sorrow,
So too do the trees and herbs.
And when the spirits fail to return,
Where shall they find peace?
There will be disasters for years;
The people will be scattered in the winds.
Such is the command of life,
Such it has been from the beginning.
There is nothing left to us
But to remain within four corners.[3]

[3] The poem is generally written in four-syllable lines, which give it an overwhelming sense of *solid* desolation in the original, but the poet occasionally and quite deliberately introduces lines of seven or even eight syllables to break the monotony, and to rend the heartstrings. Though he accomplishes this purpose perfectly, the poem remains an academy piece, too generalized to have sprung from deeply felt emotions.

WANG TS'ANG-LING

A native of Chiang-ning, he graduated as *chin shih*, entered the capital, and became for a while archivist in the secret archives of the emperor, but fell into disfavor and suffered banishment. When An Lu-shan's rebellion broke out, he returned to Chiang-ning, where he was murdered by the censor Lu Ch'iu-hsiao.

―――――――⌒⌒――――――――

The Young Wife

The young wife, upon whom grief has not yet come,
On a spring day paints her face and climbs the emerald tower.
Suddenly she sees the willow buds bursting along the path,
And sorrows that she has sent her husband to the wars.

Recruiting Song

Over the Kokonor the long clouds darken the snow mountains.
The lonely city in the distance looks toward the Yumen pass.
There in the yellow sand of a hundred battles, armor was
   pierced through.
We swear we shall defeat the tribesmen before we return.

In the great desert wind and dust darken the sun.[1]
A half-furled crimson flag stands at the barrack door.
At night our vanguards fought north of the Tiao River.
They say: We have captured alive the enemy tribesmen.

It is still the moon of the Ch'ins, the frontier of the Hans.
The expedition went ten thousand li away and may never
   return.
If only the flying general of Lung-chen were still here,
Never would the Hsiung-nu pass over the Yin Mountains.[2]
Astride a roan mare with a white jade saddle,
In the cold moonlight the fighting has ceased in the desert.
From the heights of the city the rumbling of drums can be
   heard.
The sword with the undried blood is laid in the metal sheath.

Translated by Wang Sheng-chih.

[1] Literally: Great desert wind dust sun color dim.
[2] The Yin Mountains, which are continually referred to in connection with the border warfare of the poems, are a range of mountains running across Shansi, Hopei, and the Jehol border. The wars mentioned in this poem were the wars of the Han dynasty, not of T'ang.

CHANG HSU (eighth century)

The Ravine of the Flowering Peach Tree

The hanging bridge is lost in wandering mist.
There in some far and distant region,
Beneath high rocks, close to the western shore,
A fisherman's boat is drifting.
Who alone can tell, since all the long day
Peach blossoms follow the moving water,
If this may be the crystal mountain stream
That leads into the empire of the immortals?

CHIEN HSU (ninth century)

The Stone Well

A piece of colored cloud shines on the stone well,
And colors the peach flowers under the spring.
Who knows that under this delicate stone
There may not be a road to fairyland?

CHU WAN (ninth century)

A Retreat in the Mountains

At last I have found the spring where everything is hidden;
I have gone through a desert country where there are no ways.
Riding my horse through clumps of wild bamboos,
I have come to the flowering peach trees and the men here.

Mountains crowned with snow surround the lost valley.
Smoke rises from a few cottages spread thinly on the plain.
The woodcutters greet me. "Old men, I have nothing to say
Except that the empire of Ch'in has passed away."

LIU TEH-JEN (ninth century)

Strolling in a Village

Leisurely with some rustic fellow beside the wild river,
In early spring high trees in the blue moonlight.
Oblivious to the endless events in the dusty world
The two white birds fade into the jade forest.

WEI YING-WU (C. A.D. 735–830)

A native of Ch'ang-an, he was for a while a soldier in the bodyguard of the emperor Ming Huang, but later he entered a civil career and rose to be governor of Suchow.

The Cuckoo Sings

In the high forest dew drips this clear summer night.
On the South Mountain the cuckoo sings one song.
Near by, a widow holding her child is weeping.
Alone I toss in the bed. When will the dawn come?

WEN T'ING-YUN (A.D. 830–880)

He is famous for his own lovesick poetry and for his friendship with Li Shang-yin.

Beyond the Tower

Beyond the tower lies the river,
The moon is low over the sea,
The horns sob on the walls,
The willows wave in the dike;
Gray is the mist on the island.
Now two columns of geese are flying away
Along the road to Chin-kou:
The sails of ships passing.
Now that the fragrance of spring is vanishing,
The silver candle burns down.
The stars in the Jade Ring are sinking.
A cock crows in the village.

YANG CH'U-YUAN

He became *chin shih* in 789, and in 830 is known to have been superintendent of instruction at Ho-chung in Shansi.

East of the City, Early Spring

Far the best time for the poet is early spring,
The willow leaves greening and yellowing.
If you wait till the leaves in the park are of full brocade,
There will always be too many people looking at flowers.

LIU TSUNG-YUAN (A.D. 773–819)

Famous as calligraphist and essayist, he rose to be secretary to the board of rites. He was a friend of the distinguished poet Han Yu, but disagreed with his interpretations of Buddhism, and remained himself a Buddhist to the end of his life. In 815 he was banished to Liuchow in Kwangsi, where he retained the title of governor. Here he died, and Han Yu wrote the memorial that was read and later burned over his grave.

Ice in a Stream

Across thousands of mountains no birds fly,
Across thousands of paths there are no footprints.
On a lonely boat lies an old fisherman
Fishing solitarily in the ice of a frozen stream.

CHIA TAO (A.D. 777–841)

Like Liu Tsung-yuan, he was a friend of Han Yu, whom he is supposed to have met first when absent-mindedly knocking against him in the street while composing a poem. He was banished to Szechuan for composing lampoons, and died shortly after he was restored to favor.

Searching for the Hermit in Vain

Under the pines I asked the boy.
"My master has gone gathering herbs," he said.
"He is somewhere in the mountain,
Deep in the clouds where no one knows."

WANG HAN (ninth century)

The Song of Liangchow

The beautiful grape wine, the night-glittering cups;
Drinking or not drinking, the horns summon you to mount.
Do not laugh if I am drunk on the sandy battlefields.
From ancient times, how many warriors ever returned?

CHANG CHI (eighth and ninth centuries)

The date of his birth is uncertain, but it is known that he was born in Niao-chiang in Kiangnan of one of the most illustrious families in the empire. He, too, was a friend of Han Yu. He was first attached to the imperial archives, but in 815 he became a tutor on Han Yu's recommendation in the Imperial Academy. He died with the rank of president of the academy at the age of eighty.

Song of a Modest Woman[1]

My lord, you know that I am married and have a husband,
Yet you still give me this pair of crystal pearls.
I am moved by your lingering passion;
I conceal the pearls in my coat of red silk.
There in the high towers adjoining the palace,
My husband holds the gold sword of a king's guard;
I know your heart shines like the sun and moon,
But you must know that I have sworn constancy whether I
    live or die.
I return your crystal pearls, while tears fall from my eyes,
Regretting that we did not meet when I was unmarried.

[1] The poem is said to have been written to a rebel, who had made overtures to him.

LU LUN (ninth century)

On Meeting a Sick Soldier

The way is long, the body overburdened;
Foodless, he journeys the thousand li to his home,
Tearing his hair and sobbing before the old city walls,
While the autumn wind pierces his golden scars.

On Seeing Ch'ang-an in Spring

The east wind blows over the green rain mountains.
I see a thousand green houses in my dreams.
When shall I arrive at my homestead?
Spring falls on the river. How many ever return?
Over rivers and plains float the curling clouds.
Palaces and castles stand in the setting sun.
Who remembers the scholar in a world at war?
Gray-haired, I stand alone at the pass of Ch'in.

Dark Night, the Wild Geese Fly High

The arrows of Chimpoko are tipped with hawks' feathers;
Our pennons gleam with swallowtails.
They wave alone, proclaiming the new order.
A thousand companies raise a single shout.

In the dark forest the grass is frightened by the wind.
At night the general stretches his bow.
In the early morning he finds the white feather
Hidden amid white stones.

Dark night; the wild geese fly high.
The Hsiung-nu are fleeing, fleeing.
We pray for daylight and a cavalry charge.
A great snowfall conceals our bows and knives.

In the desert our broad tents filled with food.
The western tribesmen praise the victory.
We drink and dance together in iron mail.
The thunder of drums moves the mountain rivers.

LI I (died 827?)

At one time he was probably the most popular poet in the whole T'ang empire. He was an official who later took to wandering, but returned to the capital to become a sublibrarian in the Imperial Library. He retired as president of the Board of Rites.

———————❧———————

Following the Army to the Northern Expedition

The Tien Shan snowed soon after the cold sea wind came;
The flutes blew all the time, and the roads were hard.
There were three hundred thousand soldiers on the desert.
Suddenly they all turned and looked at the moon.

HSU HUN (ninth century)

Song at the Frontier

All night they fought north of Hsiangkiang;
Half of our soldiers of Ch'in have not returned.
But when morning dawned, letters arrived from home,
The folks at home were sending them winter clothes.

CHANG CH'IEN (eighth century)

He is known to have graduated in 727, in the reign of Ming Huang. For some time he occupied an official position, but later becoming a Taoist, he became a wanderer and henceforward all trace of him is lost, except for the poems he left behind him.

———————❧———————

Sanctuary in Po-Shan Temple

I entered an ancient temple at the dawn.
Already the early sun was shining on the forest.
Through winding paths I came to this solitary place,
There where the cells of monks were heaped high with flowers.
The mountain colors have made the birds sing.

The shadows in the pool empty the hearts of men.
The ten thousand sounds of the world are hushed in this spell.
All is still, but the resounding bells.

WANG CHI-WEN (ninth century)

Going beyond the Jade Gate Pass

The Yellow River climbs amid the white clouds;
A lonely city stands and heaven-piercing peaks.
Why should the Tartars complain of the willows?
The wind of spring never crosses the Jade Gate Pass.

LI HO (A.D. 791–817)

He was a descendant of royal princes—in the early years of the T'ang dynasty, somewhere about the year 630, his ancestor had been ennobled under the title of Prince Ch'un—and there is in his poetry, as in the poetry of Li Ho Chou, the last of the southern T'ang emperors, an extraordinary nobility and consciousness of power. Li Ho was born when his family was in decay, poverty-stricken, genteel, and not altogether respected. He was born in Ch'un Ku, a small town in Honan, where according to his own description three rivers ran near his home, and there were mountains thickly covered with junipers and bamboos, and somewhere in the neighboring forest lay a ruined temple dedicated to a virgin goddess; but the temple was ruined and worm-eaten, with spiderwebs hanging on the pillars and fireflies swarming in the sacred chamber of the goddess. Thither he rode on horseback alone, or accompanied by a page, a silk bag attached to the saddle into which he threw his poems, completely cut off from the world, living in dreams, possessing a deep attachment to the royal house, and, like many lonely people, strangely brutal at times.

In person he was handsome, with thick eyebrows, a narrow waist, long fingernails, and a detached aristocratic expression. He had something of Baudelaire's satanism and talked to ghosts. When he was still young, his beard turned white. When he was eighteen, the great poet and scholar Han Yu visited him, and he wrote one of his greatest poems in honor of the occasion. Han Yu managed to obtain for him a small official position, and he spent three years away from home. When he returned, the poverty continued. He pledged his clothes for wine, his hair grew whiter, a deeper melancholy settled on him. He still hoped the emperor would pour favor on him and even wrote for the emperor's eyes: "When will the eye of heaven open, and when will my old sword roar?" But he was fated to remain impoverished to the end, having succumbed to the disease of poetry, for he was writing endlessly and with tremendous concentration—Li Shang-yin, who wrote a short biography of him, records that when he returned to the house one day, his mother looked into the bag, and seeing that there were many more poems there, exclaimed: "My son wants to vomit his heart." He died at the age of twenty-seven. Li Shang-yin records also the circumstances of his death:

When Li Ho was dying, he saw in daylight a man wearing red garments, riding on a red dragon and holding in his hands a wooden tablet on which ancient characters were engraved. He said:

"We have come to summon Li Ho." Li Ho could not read the ancient characters on the tablet, but left the bed and knelt down saying: "My mother is old and sick, and I do not want to leave her." The man in the red garments smiled and said: "The King has just built a white jade palace and desires you to write about it. Heaven has sent me to accompany you—the journey will not be painful." Li Ho wept. All the men and women near his deathbed saw the miracle. After a while, there was no breath left in him. Mist rose from the window, and there was the sound of chariots and music. His mother bade the people to stop crying; they waited for a few moments, and then he died.

His poetry was hard and metallic, and is almost untranslatable—so great is the compression of images and the leap of his verse. Fragments are often more revealing than his finished poems. Images are struck off, like sparks from flint, and the sparks turn into fireflies and will-o'-the-wisps. Chinese critics are fond of comparing him with Keats, but he is entirely himself, one of the greatest of Chinese poets and one of the most difficult. Li Shang-yin insists on his complete dedication to poetry: "He passed his days writing, except when he was absolutely drunk or going to a funeral." One suspects that Li Ho enjoyed funerals as much as Shelley enjoyed cavorting round graveyards at night.

Something of the spirit of his dedication to poetry can be seen from the lines:

> Li Ho of West Shansi is a dejected guest;
> After drinking, he feels a constriction on his heart.
> Flax clothes are in tatters in this autumn in the north city.
> All night I write poetry until the east grows pale white.

Tu Mu said in a preface to Li Ho's collected work that he was following the tradition of the *Li Sao* of Chu Yuan, which is translated in this book. Like Chu Yuan, he bitterly attacked the court, but for different reasons, and these reasons were not always commendable. He wanted power and position, but more than anything he wanted to shine in the brilliance of the T'ang court. He failed, and resumed his interminable pilgrimage in search of the vanished kings of the past. In one of his poems Li Ho said: "Chu Yuan was foolish to drown himself in the Hsiang River," but Li Ho seems to have been less foolish in his own death—there was never in Chinese history so great a dedication to poetry.

He has Marlowe's power; in three words he can summon up vanished glories, and make them sing:

> Nine pillars stand in rows on the marble; flower-painted square stones.
> Blood from a stabbed leopard flows down to fill a silver cup.
> Trumpets and drums attend the fruitful banquet—no strings, no lutes . . .

I have not translated this poem, which refers to the great hero Chu P'a-wang, because it is almost impossible to translate, but few other poems have so much power. Yet he could sing of his poverty as gracefully and as angrily as Tu Fu:

> I live in my home among mountains;
> I have one acre of lean weedy land.
> In the night and the rain the tax collector cries.
>
> My family prays for my success in earnest,
> So that I can stuff my hungry stomach.
> Oh, my mind is in turmoil;
> The flowers of the lamp shine on my tearful eyes. . . .

He was tender toward his younger brother, Shu-tzu:

> The little swan is soaring over the highest mountain,
> And its shadow falls deep on the Great River. . . .

and though there is a kind of implied satanism in nearly everything he wrote, there were times when a pure tenderness of lyric feeling comes to him. Working in the capital, he thinks of home:

> In the wind and rain of night in the capital,
> I, a guest of books, dream of Ch'un-ku.
> My mother is laughing in the center of the hall,
> My little brother is planting a green bamboo. . . .

He liked riding on horseback over dangerous mountains, he liked all that was ancient, and he hated the deterioration in the empire. The critic Sun Wan-chan has pointed out that "because he was a descendant of the royal house, he grieved for the country founded by his ancestors, he hated the marriage policy by which the barbarians were married into the imperial family, he objected to the emperor's addiction to Taoist magic and to the independence of many of the generals in the great towns; he objected to the military possessed by the eunuchs, to the quarrels at court, and to the invasions of wild tribes. He was a subordinate officer, and therefore could not reach the emperor. So he rode on his lean ass over wild precipitous mountains, and embodied his poetry in melancholy, peculiarity, a wild temper, and figurative speeches."

We do not know how many poems Li Ho wrote—probably many hundreds more than have been preserved. Shortly after his death the poems were collected together. The poet Tu Mu received a letter from a certain Sun Tze-ming who said: "My dead friend Li Ho was my friend. Day and night, we rose and slept together, we drank and ate together. When he was dying, he gave me all the poems he wrote during his life. He divided them into four volumes, altogether 233 poems." Li Shang-yin suggests that many more were written. Some were thrown carelessly away, others according to a legend were destroyed by the poet's cousins, still others probably disappeared in the continual upheavals that rocked the kingdom. The poems that remain may, however, have been the best and those that he wanted preserved.

After Li Ho's death Li Shang-yin wrote a fragment that may be considered as his epitaph: "Alas, for heaven is great and high, and is there really a king of the gods above, and does he entertain himself with palaces and gardens and colonnades? If this is true, then the far and high heaven and the grand and solemn king himself should possess writers of their own—why do they love Li Ho so much and make him die young? Is it because earth has few poets of genius that heaven also has very few?"

And even though there are comparatively few Chinese poems, there is no doubt that Li Ho wrote some of the greatest. He was singularly gifted; he possessed an eye for color that no one has ever equaled, and sometimes in the poems you can feel the physical power of the poet, and you can almost see him as he walks toward the abandoned temple, stoop-shouldered, with a short white beard, followed by a lean ass on which there rests a silk pannier full of poems.

HO CHIH-YUAN

Song of Ch'un K'u

Today, the fifth moon, there are rice shoots at Chun-k'u.
Slender and green are the smooth flooded fields,
And on the far mountains the peaks press down.
I grieve for the jagged green rocks, afraid they will fall.

Pure brightness of air where no autumn is;
Cool winds drifting through enchanted green lands.

There is a sad loneliness among the scented bamboos;
White powdered gnarls, leaves freshly green,
Furry grass drooping sorrowful hairs,
Glistening dew shedding faint tears,
A road winding to a green cavern among dense leaves
Where the flowers in the pathway are faded, drunken, and red.
There, swarms of wood lice bore into ancient willows
And the cicadas cry shrilly from the highest and deepest leaves.

The huge scarves of yellow vines weave down;
Crisscrossed over slender streams are the purple flag leaves.
Thick moss like pennies clings to the stones
And there are succulent clusters of hanging leaves.

Oh, white and smooth is the washed sand
Where green emblems are printed by horses' hoofs.
In the evening fishes swim freely along.
In the dusk the lone lean stork stands.
Liao-liao, sing the damp frogs,
And a slow surprised stream dashes against the rock.

Crooked and winding is True Jade Road.
A virgin goddess lies in a violet flower.

Willow-sedge coils over pebbles and streams;
Mountain fruits hang scarlet and red.
Sapling cypresses shake like waved fans,
And plump pines ooze out crimson juices.

A singing stream utters resonant songs.
Glowing corn ears droop from the autumn slopes,
While orioles mimic the song of a bird-throated girl.
Like a white satin dress hangs the waterfall;
The spray is filled with laughing eyes.
The cave-crannied cliffs are about to fall.
Tangled bamboo shoots sprout from the highest rocks,
And the slender-necked bird clamors from the fountains'
     stones.

The sunrays sweep up the dun mist;
New clouds rise with transparent depths of color.
Silent and clear is this hateful summer night;
A west wind pours through the crystal air.

She sleeps in her shrine; her jade face is at peace.
Incense of burnt cinnamon adores her heavenly throne.
In this dark night she lies clothed in veils of scent.
Deep in meditation she dreams on her sleeping altar.
Waiting for the king, the ancient roosting birds of bronze.
The walls in the old palace are broken and yellow like pepper.
Ting-ling, sound the few remnants of bells.
The wandering courtier listens, filled with his icy thoughts.

Cool ivy binds the red door springs.
There are evil spirits dwelling in the dragon-painted curtains.
Flowering willows pierce through the green blinds.
The scented bedsheets once served the fallen dukes.
Dust of singing maidens lies on the worm-eaten floor
And the skirts of dancers are curled up like tenuous clouds.

The tithes of earth are stripped into lengths of satin.
Once did the peasants cherish their virtuous ancestral customs;
Once at funerals no one beat time with pestles,
Nor was there evil witchcraft concerning plagues and disease.
Then old men with fish-scale skins were generous and kind
And children with horn-braided hair knew shame and modesty.
There was no need to have judges at court
And no one thought of scolding tax collectors.

Bamboo clusters add to lost bamboo leaves.[1]
The stone banks tempt the fishermen with hook and line.
The streams wind liquid scarves,
Banana trees incline their papery leaves.

Gleams from high peaks dazzle like shot gauze.
I see the lonely moon sweeps away sorrows.
The spring stream flows like a beaker of Tao-ch'ien's[2] wine.
Ting-ling, ring the distant bells.
Chiao-chiao, echoes the lonely bird.
High soaring porphyry rocks shine black and purple.
Dangerous explosions of spring rival the fountain's uproar.

The moon floating in a smooth cobalt sky
Lies dim, the invader, among haggard clouds.
A cool light overflows the banks and streams,
Dissolving all outlines of the mountain.

The fisherman's boy lowers his net at night.
The frost bird claps smoke-gray wings.
In the mirror-clear pool glides the crocodile's saliva.
Fish spit floating bubbles of pearl.

The plane tree in the wind soughs like a harp encased in jade.
The fireflies are messengers coming to the embroidered city.[3]
Branches of willow weave out long streamers.
A bamboo grove, quivering, rustles with the sound of small
    flutes.
Green moss creeps among pebbles.
The reed shoots peer through the muddy water.
The sky is reflected in drifting whirlpools.
Old junipers seize the hands of a cloud.
In the somber moonlight shine the red curtains of eglantine.
The scented thorn grasses lie under overhanging clouds.
The beards of wheat stretch for a hundred miles.
Thousands of empty carts lie idle in the market place.
I, a descendant of the royal house, now a servant of others
With the deepest pleasure bow low to the earth.

[1] As in English, there is a pun on the two senses of "leaves."
[2] Tao Yuan-ming, one of the greatest of Chinese poets, known for his
love of wine.
[3] A common sobriquet for Ch'ang-an, the capital of many of the T'ang
emperors, now known as Sian.

Journey among Ruins

The sun has returned to the west mountains.
Deep and far rises the blue night sky.
Where do the past and the present end?
Thousands of years have been blown away by the wind.
The sands of the sea bed are fused into rock.
Fish are still breathing bubbles under the emperor's bridge.
Time has wandered its long road,
And the bronze pillars were long ago destroyed.

Song of the Arrowhead

The arrowhead mingled with black ash, brown powdered
    bones, watery-reddish stains,
And cold is the ancient blood that resembles green flowers.
The white feather on the rigid stem has rotted in the rain.
There is only the wedge-shaped arrowhead like a wolf's tooth.

I was wandering along the plain, my two horses with me,
East of the traveling post, among stony rice fields, beneath
    weed-ridden hills;
A wild wind, a short day, the stars few and solitary,
Damp clouds in the night sky hung like black flags.
The hungry ghosts on the left, the lean spirits on the right
    cried out aloud.
I poured out a bottle of wine, dedicated a roasted sheep.
The insects were silent, the wild geese lamenting, the red reeds
    shone.
A whirlwind came to blow the will-o'-the-wisps, bidding the
    guest farewell.

A long while ago I held up the iron arrowhead with tears.
The once-red broken head had once pierced someone's flesh.
In the south village east of the city a boy on horseback
Begged me to buy fresh bamboos and furnish him with this
    arrowhead.

A Lady's Sepulcher

I rode on a painted chariot.
My beloved rode on a blue horse.
When shall we become true lovers
Under the pines and cypresses beneath the West Hill?
               —Old Song

Dewdrops of shaded orchids
Gaze as the eyes weep;
They shall never be true lovers;
The dancing girl will never enter her lover's home.

The grass shall be my carpet,
The pine trees my cloak,
The wind my embroidered dress,
Streams shall be my blue jewels.
Within my painted chariot
I have lingered all night.
Cold are the green candles of the will-o'-the-wisps.
Ever flickering, ever glowing.
Beneath the Western Hill
The wind blows cold rain.

Departure of Autumn

The wind in the plane trees shakes my heart, alas!
In the weak lamplight the cold crickets cry like the reeling of
  silk.
How may I look on a green bamboo leaf
Without first driving away the worms eating at the holes?
Thinking of my helpless works, I must make my heart stead-
  fast.[4]
What scented souls in these cold rains will share my grief?
On autumn graves the ghosts are singing Pao's[5] poems.
After thousands of years in the earth the hateful blood turns
  green.

Meditation

Woe to the South Mountain!
The rain mist showers on the dead grasses.
In this midnight in the capital
How many will turn old in the wind?

I am lost in the evening pathways,
Winding dimly among dim oak groves.
The moon at the pole drives away the vast shadows of the
  forest,
And the mountain glares in a gray-white dawn.

The green torches jump to welcome new ghosts;
The gleam of fireflies sparkles among the new-dug graves.

[4] Literally: "pull my intestines straight."
[5] An unknown poet, perhaps of the Han dynasty.

A Long Song after Short Songs

Long songs wore out my garments,
Short songs broke my white hair.
The Emperor does not allow himself to be seen.
Internal fevers shake my body morning and evening.

Thirsty, I drink wine.
Hungry, I take corn.
This melancholy-cool April will soon end,
And then there will be a thousand miles of green.

Look, how each mountain peak at night stands alone.
The moonlight falls on each rounded stone.
Lingering, I search among them.
The moon shines above the high battlements.
I cannot wander about when the moon is there.
The song over, my hairs have changed color.

Plant No Trees

Plant no trees in the garden.
Trees only worry you throughout the year.
Sleep alone under the moon at the south window.
One autumn resembles another.

Song of Returning to Kwei-chi[6]

In the Liang dynasty, the poet Yu Chien-wu wrote gallant songs echoing those by the emperor's son. When the state was destroyed, Chien-wu took refuge in Kwei-chi before returning home. I feel sure that he left some works behind, but of them no trace has been found. And so I have written a Song of Returning to Kwei-chi, to mend his grief.[7]

The peppered mud walls are yellow,
Damp fireflies swarm over the palaces of the Liangs.
Once a tutor in the court of princes,
He dreams in his autumn bed of regal chariots of bronze.

The frost of Kwei-chi falls on my hair as I return.
I shall grow old with the flag leaves in the pond.
Speechless, I have departed from all the world's glory.
The wandering courtier, even in poverty, remains loyal to the throne.

[6] A town in Chekiang.
[7] Written by Li Ho as his own introduction.

Song for the Bronze God

During the Wei dynasty, the emperor Ming[8] sent his palace officials westward with their chariots in order to bring back the Bronze God, who held a dew plate[9] in his hands and who had been made by the emperor Shao* of Han to be placed before his palace. When these palace officials removed the dew plate, the Bronze God, whose spirit was appointed from Heaven, burst into tears. Li Ho, the descendant of the royal house of the T'ang dynasty, therefore writes a Song for the Bronze God in bidding farewell to the Han dynasty.[1]

Within the grave lies the king whom autumn winds have swept away;
At night his horse whinnies, but it vanishes again at dawn.
Beyond the painted galleries fragrance lingers round branches of cassia.
Within the thirty-six halls of the palace climbs the green moss.

An officer of the new empire turned his chariots here from afar.
When the sour melancholy wind from the east gate struck my eyes,
I, whom the ancient moon escorted, removed from the palace gate,
Thinking of the wild emperor, let fall tears of pure lead.

Withered orchids scatter the highroad as the officer rides away.
Heaven itself will wither in pity.
Alone beneath the desolate moon I depart with my dew plate.
Listen to the soft waves, and the faraway city near a river.

"Die for His Majesty"

Black clouds press on the city; the city would seem to be destroyed.
Like golden scales our bright armor glitters in the sun.
The throbbing of horns spreads over the autumn-colored sky.
At night the rain clouds grow thick and purple on the frontier.
We reef up the scarlet flag before reaching the Yi River.

[8] The second Emperor of the Wei dynasty (A.D. 227-239).
[9] A plate which received the dew at dawn and sunset: those who bathed in the dew were believed to become immortals.
* One of the last emperors of the Han dynasty (reigned A.D. 189).
[1] Written by Li Ho as his own introduction.

The frost so heavy, the cold drum can hardly be heard.
On a gold altar we will reward the Emperor for his confidence
    in us.
Holding jade-dragon swords, we shall die for His Majesty.

To the Harp Player

On the taut silk-spun strings of high autumn
Clouds resound against the empty mountains.
Like the daughters of Shao² who wept among bamboos
Or like the sad white girl who plucked the strings,
So does Li P'ing play his harp through the country,
Clean as split jade, soft as the bluebird's song,
Sad as dewdrops on lotos leaves, happy as fragrant orchids.
His song melts the ice on the twelve imperial gates.
His twenty-three strings move the heart of the purple-robed
    king.
Listen, from the stone-mended cliffs of Heaven that the god-
    dess restored,³
The stone broke again, the sky shuddered, autumn rains fell,
But the harper walked in a dream to teach the old goddess on
    the mountain
Near the abyss where ancient fish leap and gaunt dragons
    dance.
The unsleeping listener leaned on a cinnamon bough
And saw the feet of the dew climbing up the shivering Hare.⁴

I Pass the Great Hall

The courtiers Han Yu and Huang Pu-tzu came to my house
and commanded me to write poetry.

The bright silk trappings are onion-green,
Gold rings hold down the saddle, shaking with sweet music;
The sound of the horses' hoofs thunders in my ears.
They enter the gate with the glory of a rainbow.
People say: Here comes the genius and the great writer from
    the east capital,

² The emperor Shao (B.C. 2357-2258) had two daughters, Wu Huang and
Nu Ying, and both at the same time became empress and consort of the
second emperor Shun (B.C. 2258-2206). Their teardrops falling on his
grave on the island of Hsiang-shan on the Tung-t'ing Lake left speckled
marks on the leaves of the bamboos growing there.
³ In the beginning of the world the rebel prince Kung Kung struck his
head against the sky, breaking it. The empress Nu Kua, who had the
body of a serpent and the head of an ox, thereupon replaced the hole in
the sky by melting stones of five colors. A fuller account of her success
is given in the prologue of *The Dream of the Red Chamber*.
⁴ I.e., the moon.

And their breasts contain the twenty-eight stars of heaven.
Such honorable loyalty pierces the center of their hearts.
Their poetry written at court sounds their names to the highest
    skies.
With their pens they can mend the forgotten works of the
    Creator: heaven's labor in vain!
The student with the large eyebrows feels like a dry autumn
    reed.
But who knows, the dead grasses might meet a warm wind?
Dropping my own wings, I climb on those of the great swans.
Though I am a serpent, I will not be ashamed of becoming a
    dragon.

Below the City of P'ing

Hungry and cold we stand below the city.
We watch the moon every night.
The swords we have brought from home do not shine like jade.
The sea winds break our hair.

Long, long is the desert stretching to the edge of a white sky.
A splash of red—the flags of the Hans far away!

In the blue tents we play on the slender flutes.
Fog and mist moisten our dragon flags.
At sunset we stand on the city wall
Looking down toward the dim gate of the city.
The wind blows and shakes the withered grasses.
Within the city the lean horses whinny.

Let us ask the officer who built the city
How many thousands of miles we are from home.
We grieve only when our hungry corpses are sent home.
We do not regret falling by the sword.

A King Drinks Wine

Riding a tiger, this king rode through the eight poles of heaven.
The light of his sword lay on the sky; the sky grew more deeply
    blue.
He heard the tinkle of the glass as a god knocked on the sun.
Misfortunes fell away. History came to peace again.

Now from the dragon head wine flows for the wine guests.
Like a lyre in a golden case playing all night,
So do the flutes seem to be blown by the falling rain of the
    Tung-t'ing Lake.

In their drunkenness they call the moon to move away.
Mountains of silver clouds shine on the glowing palace of jade.

Now the gatekeeper says: "The first watch has come."
In painted galleries flutes sound like the tender voices of birds.
The delicate sea yarn[5] is scented, is luminous and crystalline.
The girls dance "The Yellow Goose Is Falling" and offer the
      King the wine of longevity.
Fairy candles puff up little bright vapors.
The lyres sing sadly. From the drunken eyes of the girls flow
      hot tears.

A Sword in the Spring Office

In the ancestral chest lies a watery sword, three feet long.
Once it followed and killed a dragon in the chasm of Wu.
Like a slanting crescent moon seen from a cave, the moon
      shaving the chill dews,
Or like a stretched strip of satin, smooth, unruffled by the wind,
The sheath like an old dragon's skin bristling with thorns.
The blade has absorbed sea birds' oil, shines like a white bird's
      tail.
This sword contains the whole heart of the hero.
Do not let its light be reflected on the print in the Spring Office.
Let there be tasseled silk twists and bright metals hanging from
      it.
Just the heavenly light from the sword can cut jade to pieces.
When it was drawn, the White King of the West shuddered;[6]
On the autumn pathways his ghostly mother wept at midnight.

A Song of Heaven

The Milky Way revolves at night among the floating stars;
The clouds wander by the Silver River and imitate the murmur
      of water.
Within the moon lies the Jade Palace, unfading flowers and
      cinnamon trees.
The goddess with her headdress of silk plucks the fragrant
      grasses.
The queen pulls up her curtains; in the north window it is
      dawn.
There is a bluebird on the tree in the small window.
The prince blows the long pipe of his flute,

[5] An exceedingly delicate silk that resembles the skin of the smallest
fishes.
[6] The commentators refer to the White King who transformed himself
into a snake, but was killed by the Red King.

Then calls the Dragon to plow the earth and plant holy grasses.
She wears a red gown; underneath there is a purple skirt.
She gathers the flowers along green beaches,
She points to the God of the Sun careering like a charger.
The sea dust below the Stone Mountain has only just been
  born.

A Great Song

The south wind blows the mountains; the mountains become
  plains.
The king of the gods sends his servant to sweep up the sea.
When the peach blossoms of the fairy queen have reddened
  a thousand times,
How many deaths have the long-lived men died?

The blue manes of the piebald horses are mottled with coins.
Willows this sweet spring wave among whirling vapors.
The flute-player persuades me to drink wine from the gold
  beaker.
Unless I calm my blood and soul, how shall I live?

I say to the general: It is not necessary to drink too much;
For naturally the hero cannot find his master in this world.
Buy silk to embroider the clothes of Pin-yuan-chuan.[7]
All the wine we have, we can only sprinkle it on his earth.

From the mouth of the Jade Toad[8] the water clock hurries
  time.
The hair of the young dancer is too frail for the comb.
I see the brow of autumn changing into the freshest green.
Why should the young man of twenty be always a slave?

The Twelve Moons

First Moon

I mount the turret steps to welcome spring. New spring returns.
Dark yellow the willow buds; the water clock in the palace is
  slow.
Faint spirals of mist sport and creep over the fields.
In this cold green a dark wind settles on the grass beards.

Asleep at dawn on the embroidered bed, cool is her amber skin.
Her dewy face, not open, faces the morning dusk.

[7] A famous hero.
[8] A fountain called the Jade Toad, which was used as a water clock.

In the highroad the scarves of the willows may not yet be
    plucked.
Soon the knotted cord of the flag leaves will fade.

Second Moon

Drink wine by the stream where you gather mulberries,
Where dandelions grow and orchids are smiling.
Flag leaves like crossed swords wave in the scented air.
Restlessly singing swallows complain of the intoxication of
    spring.
Green specks are seen in the lingering mist of grass curtains.
With high-pillowed hair and a bird tail of gold, she grieves for
    the evening clouds.
On the swift steps of the wind she dances in her skirts of pearl.
At the ferry she bids farewell and sings the "Flowing River
    Song."
The spines of the wine guests grow cold. The South Mountain
    is dead.

Third Moon

The east wind comes and spring fills up our eyes.
In the city of flowers the shaded willows grieve in earnest.
In the deepest hall of the palace the wind sports among bam-
    boos.
The new green dancing skirts are clear as water.
The bright wind stirs the grass for a thousand miles.
A warm mist flaps the clouds from heaven to earth.
The slave girls dressed for war[9] carelessly pencil their eye-
    brows.
Waving embroidered banners[1] warm the imperial city.
The floating scents of the winding river never return.
Pear blossoms fade. Autumn comes to the emperor's garden.

Fourth Moon

Cool at dusk and dawn are the trees on the earth.
In depths of green a thousand mountains hover beneath the
    clouds.
The faint-scented rain falls among evil mists.
Teeming leaves and round flowers shine on the curved garden
    gates.
In the stone ponds the water shakes off leisurely green ripples.
So heavy is this summer the blossoms are not surprised to fall.
Faded red flowers on the earth glow in the shade of the trees.

[9] Camp followers.
[1] Red was a predominant color in the T'ang dynasty. The horses' manes
were dyed red, and so were many flags—hence the banners warming the
city.

Fifth Moon

Engravings of jade decorate the lintel over the curtain.
Thin gauze curtains fill the empty door.
We draw from the well water bright as lead.
Fans are decorated with ducks and drakes.
Snowy skirts dance through the cool palace halls.
Sweet dews wash the blue sky.
Silk sleeves hover in the wind.
The precious corn smells sweet as sweat.

Sixth Moon

Now the people cut the unbaked silks,
Now they split the speckled bamboos:
Wearing frost-colored silks, we lie on bamboo mats cool as
    autumn jade.

A flame-red mirror opens on the east,
A vertiginous cartwheel forever climbing upward,
Comes the Red Emperor riding on a humming dragon.[2]

Seventh Moon

The stars near the Milky Way grow cold.
The bubbles of dew on the dew plate are round.
Pretty flowers shoot from the ends of twigs,
Fading grasses grieve in the empty garden.
The night sky is paved with jade.
The leaves in the lotos pond are like green coins.

She only regrets because her dancing skirt is too thin.
She feels faintly cold on her bamboo mat woven with flowers.
How swiftly the morning wind sweeps away!
The Great Bear glitters and curves down the sky.

Eighth Moon

All through the long night the young widow mourns.
The lonely wanderer dreams of returning home.
The spider in the eaves spins out its silk.
Near the wall the hanging lamp bursts into flower.
Beyond the curtain the moon shines to brightness.
Easily now fall the flying dews,
Making more lovely the lotos petals in the pool.

Ninth Moon

In the summer palace the fireflies have lost their way. The sky
    is like water.
The bamboos are yellow, the pond cold, the water lilies dead.

[2] The first verse describes the people; the second contains three apostro-
phes to the sun.

Speechless the moon shines on the gold rings of the gate.
Beyond the cool courtyard and the empty hall lies a white sky.
A hurrying wind has strewn the frost flowers.
Brocades of dappled emerald are piled on the road.
The cock herald crows[3] no more, dawn flows like diamonds and jade.
Above the gold well croaks a raven. The leaves of the plane tree fall.

Tenth Moon

It is difficult to pour from the silver arrow mouth of the jade beaker.[4]
The flowers of the lamp laugh at the gathering darkness.
Broken slivers of frost slant down the silk curtains.
A pair of dragon-painted candles lights up the lady's high chamber.
Beneath a curtain of pearls she sleeps, grieves, unable to sleep.
Beneath a dress embroidered with gold phoenixes her body feels chill.
Her long curved brows vie with the crescent moon.

Eleventh Moon

The walls of the palace city lie chill in the winter light.
The white and broken sky drips in snowflakes.
Ring the bells! Drink to the fill wine reserved for a thousand days!
Wine will conquer the cold! A cup for the king's longevity!
Royal moats and fountains are frozen with white rings.
Oh, where is the well of fire, where are the warm springs?

Twelfth Moon

A faint red glow is shed by the feet of the sun.
The rime no longer melts under the branches of cinnamon.
Rare warm airs try to drive away the winter.
The long nights will end, the long days begin.

All translated by Ho Chih-yuan.

[3] The cock herald was a palace servant who announced the coming of dawn.
[4] The commentators explain that the mouth of the beaker was shaped to resemble an arrowhead.

TU MU (A.D. 803–852)

He was a native of Loyang, who graduated around 830 and rose to be secretary of the Grand Council. He is sometimes called "Little Tu" to distinguish him from Tu Fu.

―――――❦―――――

Separation

Love assumes the color of unlove,
But at a farewell feast our smiles fail.
Even the wax candle feels our sorrow,
And at night sheds tears in honor of our separation.

The Silk Curtain

On the silk curtain the slanting sun suggests approaching
    evening.
Companionless in the royal chamber, I shed tears.
In the solitude of the empty courtyard spring comes to an end.
The doors are closed. There are pear blossoms scattered over
    the earth.

Gold Rivers and Jade Gates

Year after year I linger round gold rivers and jade gates,
Morning after morning I set off with hooked knife and horse
    crop.
The whiteness of midspring snow melts in the greenness of wild
    graves,
And the long stretched Yellow River flows eternally round the
    black mountain.

The Red Bridge

By Red Bridge grass and flowers overgrow a wilderness,
At the entrance of Black Cloth Lane the sun is slanting again.
Once the swallows nested in the houses of the Wang and Hsieh
    nobles,
Which nowadays fly to the houses of ordinary people.

Happy Regret

I roamed with wine along the lakes and rivers.
There was always the slim waist of a Hunan girl in my arms.
From this dream of ten years' wastefulness in Yangchow,
I awake, and there is nothing but regret for my unfaithfulness.

The Garden of the Gold Valley

The splendid glories of the past
Have been scattered in fragrant dust.
The stream flows unconsciously,
The grass of spring flourishes.

At sunset blows the east wind,
And the birds are lamenting,
While the falling petals recall
A girl throwing herself from a tower.

The Nightingales

For thousands of miles the nightingale sings.
The green mirror turns red.
Villages by the river, city walls on the hills—
Comes the clatter of the wineshop boards.
In the south dynasty there are four hundred and eighty temples.
So many balconies lurking in the smoky rain!

Morning at Chien-wei River

Smoke-veiled chill waters, moon veiling the sands,
We anchored at Chien-wei River hard by some wineshops.
The dancing girls did not know the bitterness of our defeats.
They were singing "The Flower in the Garden" on the further
   bank.

To Hen Chu, Magistrate of Yangchow

Dim the mountains, far away the waters.
Autumn came stealing without withering the south grasses.
The moon shored up the twenty-four bridges.
Where is the sweet girl who taught me to play the flute?

The last three poems translated by Yuan K'o-chia.

LI SHANG-YIN (A.D. 813-858)

He was born in Honei in Honan, the son of a distinguished scholar, and became a *chin shih* in 837. His fame as a scholar preceded his fame as a poet, which explains perhaps his constant obsession with classical allusions. There was a time when his fame was so great that the daughter of a high state official was given to him in marriage simply in honor of his scholarship.

He occupied many important official posts, and was governor of many towns, and reader in the Hanlin College. He wrote funeral elegies, was a friend of Wen T'ing-yun, and seems to have been the first to develop the style that was associated with his name—a fantastically accurate and evocative use of mythology and a strange sensuousness.

———————⚘———————

A Letter Home

You ask when I shall return; there is no knowing.
Night rain on Pa-shan floods the autumn pools.
Someday we shall trim the wick beneath the west window.
I'll tell you what it was like—the night rain falling.

No Title

So difficult the meeting, so difficult the parting;
When the east wind dies, all the flowers wither.
The silkworm dies because she is spinning,
The candle's tears are dry only when she is ashes.
Looking in the morning mirror, I am afraid of the changing
    color of my hair.
The voice in the night feels cool moonlight.
The way is not far to Peng-lai.[1]
O bluebird, visit her oftener for my sake!

The Inlaid Psaltery

I wonder why the inlaid psaltery has fifty strings.
Every string and peg evokes the beautiful years,
Dawn-dreaming Chuang-tzu, the hovering butterfly;
In spring the Emperor's heart haunting the cuckoos,

[1] The fairy mountain in the eastern seas, the home of the immortals.

Moonlight in the blue sea, pearls shedding tears,
In the warm sun the jade in the blue fields engendering smoke—
So should our loves endure, being filled with memory;
But already these days are fading into the years.[2]

Ma Wei

Beyond the seas they say there is another earth.
Is there only one life? Only this one exists.
Will the tiger guards be heard, beating their bamboo rods?
Will they return—those watchers of the palace water clocks?
On the day when six regiments mutinied, their horses pawing
    the earth,
Did the Herd Boy smile at their seventh-night vows?
The emperor who reigned for half a century
Could not, like the Lu boy, have his darling Mo-tzu.[3]

Fallen Flowers

From their high pillared halls the guests have flown.
In the small garden the leaves are whirling,
Thick-falling on the winding paths,
In long parade making bright the sun.
I cannot sweep these petals—my heart is broken—
The fewer flowers remain the more I see them.
Have their fragrant souls surrendered to the spring?
Nothing remains. Tears fall on my garment.

Coming and Going

Coming is an empty word, going leaves no trace.
The moon hangs aslant over the roof beams—oh, the evening
    bells!

[2] Li Shang-yin is tenuous and recondite; nearly every poem needs a long commentary. Chuang-tzu is, of course, the famous philosopher who dreamed he was a butterfly. The soul of the emperor Wu returned in the shape of a cuckoo. The "pearls shedding tears" may refer to mermaids—"in the outer southern seas there are mermaids who can weave under the sea and whose tears are pearls." Huai Nan-tzu claimed that pearls wax and wane with the moon. The legend of the blue fields may refer to the poor man who planted jade that flowered, ate the fruit, and with it won the beautiful lady; it probably has an evasive sexual meaning. No one quite knows what the poem is about, and what the inlaid psaltery represents, but there is, at least in the original, an extraordinary effect of a stream of images that dissolve into one another and gain brightness from their dissolution. In Chinese the poem is sharp-edged as well as pleasantly obscure.

[3] Ma Wei was the scene of the murder of Yang Kuei-fei, to whom previously on the seventh night of the seventh moon the emperor Ming Huang had vowed eternal devotion. The Herd Boy is a star. Lu and Mo-tzu were the types of devoted lovers.

A dream has difficult names for a long departure:
The letters are hurried though the ink is not black enough.
Candles shine over a half niche of gold emeralds,
And embalmed incense steals over the embroidered rose.
The lovelorn knight hates the long journeys of fairyland,
Yet how much farther away with each step he goes!

The Lo-yu Tombs

Feeling fretful toward evening,
I drove my chariot to the Lo-yu tombs.
How infinitely lovely was the setting sun—
Only it is so near the yellow dusk!

LI YU (A.D. 936–978)

He was the last of the emperors of the southern T'ang dynasty, and easily the greatest of the imperial poets. In 961 he succeeded his father, Li Ching, but the Sung empire was already established and he reigned with the greatest difficulty. In 975 the Sung emperor sent an embassy to demand his subjection, which he offered with good grace, resigning from the throne and living for the rest of his life imprisoned in his palace. He had sent his favorite minister, Hsu Hsuan, to explain his conduct to the Emperor. "He really regards Your Majesty as a father," Hsu Hsuan explained, "and Your Majesty may well therefore leave him in peace." "Sons do not separate from their fathers," the Emperor answered, "and do you think I shall allow another man to snore alongside my bed?"

He complains bitterly against his imprisonment and the loss of his imperial titles in his poems, which found their way to all corners of China; but the complaints were hardly more than personal; he had few followers, and he preferred the company of Buddhist monks, painters, and musicians to the company of courtiers. He had extraordinarily handsome features; he was elegant and suffered from the disease so common in China— that of living in a remote golden past. By the Sung emperor he was given the title of Fate Resisting Marquis, but when one line of one of his short poems was thought to be a demand for assistance from the loyal followers of the T'ang dynasty, the Emperor had no hesitation in having him poisoned. He died on the seventh day of the seventh moon, at the age of forty-two.

Known sometimes as Li Chou, and Prince of Wu, he typifies the end of the T'ang dynasty in his poetry as Liu Pang typifies the beginning of the Han dynasty. He was an accomplished scholar, musician, and painter as well as a poet. There are moments when he seems to share the emotions of Nalan Hsinteh, the Manchu whose poetry breathes the same atmosphere of remoteness and decadence; but Li Yu is infinitely more profound, and uses words with a more subtle evocative cunning. He will use the simplest words and charge them with tremendous emotional effect. Only about thirty of his poems have been handed down, but each of them is masterly. His tragic death and the faint hysteria of his poetry have given him a place in poetry far higher than any he reached in history.

To the Tune of "The South River Song"

Oh, what sadness!
Last night in my dreams,
Once again I was roaming in the royal park;
My chariots were streaming like rivers, my horses like dragons.
There were flowers shining in the moon, and the spring winds!

To the Tune of "Crows Crying by Night"

Silent and alone I climb the west tower.
The moon is like a hook.
Desolate *wu-t'ung* trees in the shady courtyard imprison clear
      autumn.
Cut, and not severed,
Disentangled, not unraveled;
The sorrow of parting
Is a strange and unknown flavor in the heart.

To the Tune of "Meeting Happiness"

The flowers of the wood have lost their spring redness
In too great haste;
How can they endure cold morning, evening winds?
Tears of rouge,
So many drinking companions,
When will they return?
Interminable sorrow like a river flowing east.

Meditation

One range of mountains,
Two ranges of mountains,
The mountains far, the sky high, the misty water cold.
My deepest thoughts have reddened the maple leaves.

Chrysanthemums blossom.
Chrysanthemums fade,
The wild geese fly high, the traveler has not returned.
The wind and moon hover on the bamboo screen.

To the Tune of "Mountain Flowers"[1]

The fragrance fades from the lotoses, emerald leaves wither,
The sorrows of the west wind are scattered among green
    ripples.
The light of all things fades with the passing of years.
I cannot endure to see it.
With silk rain my dreams hover on the border of cockcrow;
Cold in this small tower playing through a jade flute.[2]
Endless sorrow flows down with pearl tears.
Silently I lean on my balcony.

To the Tune of "A Clear Calm Music"

Since we parted, spring is half over.
Everything I see is filled with sorrow.
Below the steps plum blossoms whirl in the snowflakes;
No sooner brushed away, then I am buried again.

The wild geese have brought no news of home.
The roads are long, my dreams are thinning out.
Sickness for home is like the grass in spring:
The farther you travel, the thicker it grows.

Native Land

South of the river, north of the river, lies my native land.
For thirty years my life passed in a dream.
Henceforward the palaces and pleasances of Wu shall be
    desolate,
Terraces and halls of Kuang-ling shall be wild and forlorn.
Clouds enshroud the distant summits like a thousand toils of
    sorrow;
The rain beats on the boat like a myriad filaments of tears.
There are left only my three brothers and I and three hundred
    kinsmen.
Unbearable to sit here, brooding over such small things!

[1] Sometimes attributed to the emperor Li Chin (916-961), the second
sovereign of the southern T'ang dynasty, who in 958 surrendered all his
territory north of the Yangtze River and in 960 transferred his allegiance
to Chao Kuang-yin, the founder of the Sung dynasty.

[2] In the original: *Little tower played through jade flute cold.* No one has
ever been able to make sure whether the jade flute is playing through
the little tower or whether the little tower is playing through the jade
flute. Nor has anyone ever been able to discover what is cold—the flute,
the tower, the poet, the autumn, or the courtyard with the lotos pond.

Before the Pavilion

Before the pavilion spring hastens the red flowers;
Delicately they dance to and fro.
The small rain gently falls.
So for a while I relax my knitted brows.
The green leafy window is forlorn of her sweet voice;
Her fragrant body has become slime and ashes.
My heart is full of irremediable thoughts.
Drowsily I fall in a dream.

Melancholy

Weariness has aggravated since the year;
Desolation has augmented my despair.
A ruthless wind cuts my ailing bones,
The misty rain chokes my melancholy heart.
At night the incense tripod is used to simmer herbs.
In the morning I find there is frost on half my beard.
Where are the affinities of old?
Who would ask now about the dethroned king?

Spring Blossoms

Spring blossoms, autumn moons, will you never cease to come?
Oh, what immeasurable memories!
Last night when the east wind again blew through my towered
    chamber,
How unbearable to see the ghosts of lost kingdoms in the
    moon!

The carved balustrades, the marble steps must still be there.
What has changed only is their delightful youth!
Tell me, has anyone suffered such vast woes as mine,
Endless as a river in spring that forever flows to the east?

An Angel Enclosed

An angel enclosed in paradise,
There in her room, hushed with silence, she sleeps at noon,
With jade trinket and cloudy hair flung over the pillow,
Her embroidered gown suffusing exotic fragrance.
I enter stealthily, but the tinkling of my jade ornaments
Awakens her from her dream of two lovebirds.
Slowly her face becomes gracious with smiles.
She gazes in my eyes with infinite gentleness.

The Past

The past only to be lamented,
The present so hard to expel!
Autumn winds crowding the courtyard and porches,
Lichens invading the stone steps.
As usual the pearly screen remains unrolled—
All through the day will anyone come?

The gold sword is buried deep in the earth,
The dauntless spirit quails like the fields of autumn.
Cold night, the moon blossoming in the clear sky;
I dream of how the Ching Huai River reflects in vain
Shadows of marble towers and jasper palaces! [3]

To the Tune of "Breaking through Battle"

For forty years my country and my home—
Three thousand li of mountains and rivers.
The Phoenix Pavilion and Dragon Tower reaching up to the
    Milky Way,
Jade trees and jasper branches forming a cloudy net—
Not once did I touch sword or spear!

Suddenly I became a captive slave.
Frail my waist, gray my temples, grinding away.
Never shall I forget the day when I bade hasty farewell at the
    ancestral temple.
The court musicians played the farewell songs.
My tears streamed as I gazed at the court maidens.

Fisherman's Song

Foam resembling a thousand drifts of snow.
Soundless, the peach and pear trees form their battalions of
    spring.
With one jug of wine
And a fishing line,
On this earth how many are as happy as I?

[3] Li Yu is lamenting his own palaces and lost kingdoms, but inevitably he
is also lamenting the palaces of others; there is a terrible melancholy in
the original, but the melancholy is not necessarily directed to himself.
One line in "Spring Blossoms" may have caused his death—"Last night
when the east wind again blew through my towered chamber" was
thought by Chao Kuang-yin to be a presage of rebellion, the east wind a
messenger or a spy.

I dip the oar—in the spring winds the boat drifts like a leaf.
A delicate hook on the end of a silk tassel,
An island covered with flowers,
A jugful of wine.
Among the ten thousand waves I wander in freedom!

All translated by Hsiung Ting.

THE SUNG DYNASTY

(A.D. *960–1278*)

SU T'UNG-PO (A.D. 1036–1101)

Like Wang Wei and a host of other poets, he was a painter as well as a poet. His paintings of bamboos have a studied precision and an almost Buddhist immersion into the spirit of the leaves, which seem to stir and tremble as we look at them. So, too, in his poetry there is a curious conformity (which comes from his Confucian ancestry) and a breathless depth (which comes from his understanding of Taoism and Buddhism). He was the complete scholar and the perfect dilettante, the most amazing of all the Sung poets in his efforts to probe the secrets of the universe. The Sung dynasty showed a tougher metal than the T'ang. The age of glory and glittering color had passed; all poets were philosophers now. And Su T'ung-po, who probed everything with a keen analytic mind and at the same time, and by some miracle of accomplished purpose, entered into the heart of things, was a philosopher even before he was a poet.

He was born in Meichou in Szechuan, the son of a scholarly father who rose to high office in the state, and of a mother who trained him early in an understanding of the classics. The whole family was bewilderingly brilliant; both his brother and sister attained considerable literary fame. He was taught by a Taoist priest. He came under the influence of Ou-yang Hsiu, who later brought him to the attention of the emperor. From the very beginning he was marked out for important posts. He was appointed to the commission that examined the innovations of Wang An-shih, on whom he reported unfavorably, with the result that he was compelled to withdraw to Hangchow. In 1074 he took Chao Yun as his mistress, and lived with her contentedly until her death twenty years later. He celebrated her in many of his poems. In 1080, after being imprisoned on trumped-up charges, he was banished to Huang-chou, in Hopei; he built himself a hut on the *T'ung-po* or eastern slope of a hill, and afterward assumed these two words as his *hao* or fancy name. Here he lived placidly and quietly, almost forgotten by the world, until the death of Wang An-shih in 1086 brought about his return to the capital, a favorite of the Empress Dowager, who had always admired his genius since the day of his appointment to the Hanlin College more than thirty years before. With her own hands the Empress served him with tea and ordered him to be escorted home at night by ladies of the palace with flaming torches.

Two years later he went to live at Hangchow, where he built dikes and pagodas and planted trees around the West Lake, which has ever since been inseparably connected with his name. For a while he returned to the capital, and for a few months he occupied the supremely important post of president of the Board of Rites; but his irony, and sometimes his sarcasm, made him enemies, and once again he was banished—this time to the relatively unimportant post of magistrate at Ting-chou in Chihli.

In 1094 he was banished again to Kwangtung, and three years later he was banished still farther from the capital to the island of Hainan. Then gradually, and step by step, he was allowed to proceed closer to the center of things. In 1100 he was pardoned and allowed to return to Kwangtung; shortly afterward he was allowed to enter Hunan, and then once again he was appointed to high position by the emperor Hui Tsung, but died shortly afterward at Ch'ang-chou in Kiangsu. In 1235 his tablet was placed in the Confucian temple, but for some odd reason it was removed in 1845, apparently on the grounds that "he had never advanced Confucianism in the sense necessary to merit this honor."

It was, of course, partly true. He was far too intelligent, and far too great a poet, to surrender entirely to the inflexible rules of the Confucian canon. Once he said: "The fullness of the moon and the calmness of the river are reflected in me." But the river and the moon are continually changing, and he was plagued with a feeling for the impermanence of life. When his mistress died, he recorded that her last words were taken from the *Diamond Sutra:*

> Like a dream, like a vision, like a bubble,
> Like a shadow, like dew, like lightning,

and they may well have been his own. Chao Yun died in the Buddhist faith, but his own faith was too complex; he was a Taoist as well as a Buddhist, and above all he retained a half-amused allegiance to Confucian doctrine. He liked watching others drink, but drank himself only in moderation, explaining that "the attributes of drunkenness are not in keeping with a gentleman." He had something of Po Chu-i's sense of morality, and something of Tao Yuan-ming's delight in a country hermitage, but he admitted that "wine is the law of man's life."

As a poet he stands in the very first rank, and nothing could be more erroneous than Mr. Arthur Waley's statement that his poetry is "almost wholly a patchwork of earlier poems." His poetry, according to the Chinese, is marked by the qualities of the poet, and those qualities were wholly singular and could have come from no one else. His greatness lies where the greatness of the Sung dynasty poetry lies—in a deeper penetration, a more sufficient philosophy, a calmer and more inquiring passion. Where T'ang rises, Sung probes deep. Where T'ang is all color and vigor—so much so that there are moments when the whole T'ang dynasty seems to be reflected in the famous

chargers ridden by T'ai Tsung, the founder of the dynasty—
Sung is as resilient and meditative as Su T'ung-po's own paintings of bamboos, which have their roots in the earth. It would
be a mistake to underestimate Su's poetry. He has a considered gravity and a depth of feeling that are foreign to his T'ang
predecessors, but there are times when he rises above them,
forms new worlds of the imagination, and wanders through
entirely new landscapes.

Meditation at Red Cliff [1]

Eastward runs the Great River
Whose waves have washed away
All the talented and courteous men in history.
West of the old fort, they say, there lies Red Cliff,
Where Chou, the young general in the time of the Three
    Kingdoms,
Defeated the enemy.
Broken rocks pierce the clouds,
Thundering billows dash on the shore,
Rolling up thousands of flakes of snow.
What a picture of rivers and mountains!
How many heroes there were at that time!

I cannot help thinking of the day
When Kung-ch'in first married Hsiao Ch'iao,
And with a bright warlike air,
A feather fan in his hand, a blue turban on his head,
Annihilated in the midst of his talk and laughter
The strong enemy who vanished like smoke and dust.
Traveling through this ancient kingdom in my imagination,

[1] In 208 A.D. a famous battle was fought at Red Cliff, near Hsia-k'ou in
Hupeh. The battle is recounted at length in the famous novel *San kuo
chih yen i*, known familiarly as *The Three Kingdoms*. Here Chou Yu,
"the young general" of the poem—he was only thirty-four—inflicted a
disastrous defeat on the navy of Ts'ao Ts'ao, whose war vessels were said
to stretch for a thousand li and whose forces were said to number more
than 800,000. Against these Chou Yu possessed only 30,000 men.

The defeat was inflicted by a stratagem. A great number of war vessels
covered with black oiled cloth were collected together, filled with dry
reeds and fuel, and covered with sulphur, saltpeter, and whatever else
inflammable was obtainable. In the prows were hoisted "fang-shaped"
dragon flags. A letter was thereupon sent to Ts'ao Ts'ao offering to surrender, and saying that the embassies would travel on grain ships due to
sail downriver. Ts'ao Ts'ao promised to accept the embassies, and shortly
afterward the grain ships sailed downriver. When they reached Ts'ao
Ts'ao's navy, they began to burn, setting fire to all his ships, burning to
death every man on them, and all the horses, and leaving a red mark on
the cliffs from the smoke and burning that was visible eight hundred
years later when Su T'ung-po visited the place.

I should be laughed at for such sentiments,
Turning my hair gray so early.
Life is a dream. Therefore to the river and the moon,
I sprinkle this bottle of wine!

Leaving Ching-K'ou

Soft are the clouds, and the moon is weak.
At the second watch I wake up from my drunken stupor—
It was the moment when the boat was cast off.
Looking back, I see only the lonely city
Buried in gray mist.
I can remember the time of singing,
But of the time of returning I can remember nothing at all.

My hat is askew, my fan fallen from my hands;
Slippery is this couch of creepers.
There is no one to whom I can tell
My solitary dream.
When shall I cease floating?
My home is in the southwest—
But I am always journeying to the northeast!

On the Tower of Gathering Remoteness

The endless blue mountains disperse,
Nor can they assemble together;
The waves roll, the clouds continually running
Huddle into this screen beside the window.

Therefore pour out your eyes,
Define the limits of your vision;
Having this, you will not be poorer
Than a man who rules a dukedom.

Seeking Spring beyond the City

The wild birds on the roof are bitterly complaining to man;
Suddenly ripples appear in the ice pool in front of the balus-
    trade.
I am becoming old, and increasingly more tired
Of getting drunk in the company of those with red skirts.
Rising from my sickbed, in vain I am surprised
That all my hair has freshly turned white.
Lying on this couch, I hear the drum and horn of His Highness.
Therefore I bid my boys prepare my hat and my dress.

Passing through the winding veranda and coming out in the
     arbor,
And leaving behind me this terribly pressing cold,
I find, ah, what a boundless spring in the savage plain!

Spring Scene

The flowers have lost their withered red,
Small are the green apricots.
When the swallows come and fly,
The cottages are ringed round by blue streams.
Blown by the wind, the catkins are made small.
Oh, where can I not find fragrant grass
In this boundless earth!

There is a swing within the walls,
And beyond there is a path.
Someone is walking outside,
And inside a lovely girl is laughing.
Gradually the sound of laughter is no more,
And the lover is vexed by the cold!

Midautumn at Huang-Chou

Human affairs are dreams.
Mortal life endures but a few autumns.
When the night falls on the veranda,
Leaves are already rustling in the wind.
Gaze at my eyebrows and my hair.

When wine is cheap, I am always sorry
That my guests are too few.
When the moon is full I regret
That she is often hidden by clouds.

Who will enjoy with me
The solitary night of midautumn?
Holding up my cup to heaven,
I look grievously toward the north.

Tien-Ho Temple

Here are green tiles and scarlet balustrades;
From a distance a temple that looks adorable.
Then pause for a moment and gaze earnestly upon it—
It will save you the trouble of looking back,
Turning and twisting your head a hundred times.

The river sinks low, rocks emerge;
Dust whirls high, the towers are hidden.
Do not roar, do not roar against the wind.
The echo will be dispersed in the faraway distance,
Beyond your power to recall.

Sitting at Night with My Nephew Who Has Just Come from Afar

My mind is worn out, my features grown sharp and gaunt.
You would hardly recognize me but for my old accent.
Where is our home? I am thinking about it all night.
In my declining age I know why you have come.

Afraid of strangers, I would sit in idiot silence.
Then, inquiring about old friends, I cry in surprise
That since half of them are dead, only half survive.

The dream vanishes. The rain no longer falls.
I am awake now from my drunken stupor.
I look with a smile at a hungry mouse
Climbing up the stand of my oil lamp.

Boiling Tea

Living water should be cooked
With living fire.
I go to the rock where once I fished,
Myself drawing up the limpidity of the pool.
I keep a gourd vessel in the store;
The moon is kept in a jar.
I slice the river with a ladle;
The river is kept in a jug.

The snowy milk has risen
From the bottom, where it was boiled;
Suddenly the wind is heard
Pouring through the pine forest.
It is hard to prevent my withered tongue
From draining three full cups.
Sitting idly, I listen to the watches
Beating in the deserted town.

Echoing Chang Tzu-Yeh's "Spring Daylight"

Reaching home, having retired from official service,
You have shed all your old burdens from your shoulders.
What you once possessed has mostly worn away,
What remains is merely your refined gaiety.

Once you asked long leave to eat the water plant *shun,*
Not long ago you composed a poem in praise of your mistress.
You do not pray, but you are always sane and comfortable,
For you were born healthy, predestined to a long life.
You have tried to hide your writings from the world,
Yet your fame in poetry can hardly be concealed.
You fill your cup, roses grow on your cheeks.
You carve your verse. It acquires a perfect harmony.
As you choose to live in a snail's shell,
Your mind is easy, your heart released.
Despite your age, your eyes are keen and bright;
So you can write characters as small as a fly's head.

Oh, you ought to smile that you
Have passed so successfully through all these ups and downs.
As for me, I, too, am calm
Whether in favor or disgrace.
Counting the days on my fingers, I am afraid
That the east wind will not linger long.
The cuckoo is about to sing the spring away.

Verses

I am old, sick, and lonely.
I make my home on East Slope.
White, sparse, and unkempt,
My beard mingles with the wind.
Often my little boy is delightfully astonished
To find roses on my cheeks.
How should he know, I smile,
That they are the redness of wine?

Listening to the River

Drinking on East Slope at night,
I am tipsy and sober.
It must be the third watch
When I reach home.
My boy snores like thunder;

No one answers my knock.
Leaning on my staff,
I listen to the river.

Always do I regret
That my being is not mine.
When shall I not remember
To hurry about after nothing?
In deep night the wind slumbers.
The white silk lies flat.
Soon the little boat will float away,
The rest of its life spent in rivers and seas.

Dreaming of My Dead Wife

Away and away,
We have been sundered for ten years.
There is one living and one dead.
Even if I try,
I cannot forget her,
Her lonely grave a thousand miles away.
Where shall I find her
And tell her of my solitude?
Oh, but she would not recognize me
Even if we met,
For my hair is covered with frost
And my face with dust.

Tonight when I came home,
In my melancholy dream
I saw her dressing her hair
Under the small window.
We looked at each other in silence.
Tears overflowed down our cheeks.
It seems to me that the place
Where my heart breaks each year
Is the pine ridge
On a moonlight night.

The Fisherman

So the fisherman goes to his drink
And enters the wineshop,
And at the same time orders
Fish and crabs.
As for wine, he asks only enough
To intoxicate himself.
He does not inquire of the cost.

The fisherman gets drunk,
Dances in his grass coat,
Tries to find his way home.
He allows the short oars to cross,
And the boat to float.
And when he wakes up
Has no idea where he is.

He wakes up at noon,
And there on the river his dream
Breaks to pieces in this spring
Among falling blossoms
And flying catkins.
Sober yet drunk, drunk yet sober,
He laughs at mortality—
All that is ancient and new.

Thinking of My Brother

When will the bright moon come?
I ask the blue sky,
With a wine cup held in my hand.
I do not know
What year this is,
According to the calendar of those who live
In the Palace of Heaven.
In spite of my desire to return
By riding the wind,
I fear I shall never be able to bear
The cold in those high jade towers.
So I rise to dance
With my light shadow.
Am I living in this mortal world?

Stepping round the red pavilion,
Stooping to peer through the embroidered door,
The moon shines on the one
Who cannot fall asleep.
There should not be any worries.
Why is she always full
When men are separated from one another?
Men have sorrows and joys, partings and meetings,
But the moon may be dull or clear, or full or on the wane.
There has never been constancy in this.
I only wish that men might live long,
That they might enjoy the same milky color of the moon,
Even though separated by a thousand miles.

A Poem Written on a Painting Called "The Smoky River and the Folding Peaks" Possessed by Wang Ting-Kuo

Over the melancholy river thousands of peaks are folded.
The emerald stored in the empty sky resembles clouds and
    smoke.
How far away is the smoke? How far the clouds?
We know nothing but that the peaks remain
When the smoke vanishes and the clouds disperse.
The valley is darkened by the rich leaves on the cliffs.
Out of the valley there come down a hundred streams—
They ring round the wood, twining the rocks together,
And after incessantly being lost and coming to light again,
Finally flow into a single torrent at the gorge.

Then the water is quiet; the mountains stand apart.
At the foot of a broken hill covered with briers
A peasant wineshop looks out over a tiny bridge.
A wanderer is slowly pacing among the stately trees,
A little fishing boat is bobbing on the river,
Which has swallowed up the whole sky.

Ah, where did you get that painting
Decorated with splashes and stipples,
Shot with such rich, bright colors?
I want to know where this place is,
For I have the greatest desire to go there
And buy two acres of land.

Do you not know, at a quiet place in Fan-k'ou,
I, Su T'ung-po, lived for five years?
Spring winds were swinging the river under a silent sky,
Evening clouds rolled up the rain among desirable mountains,
The crows fluttered amid scarlet maples or slept by the water,
And the snow falling on tall pines awakened me from a noon
    drowse.

The stream loaded with peach blossoms was of this world,
But why are all these people fairies—the people
Discovered by the Wu-ling fisherman on leaving his boat?[2]

In spite of the river, the mountains, the blue sky,
I after all live on this secular earth.

[2] See the prose fragment by Tao Yuan-ming: "The Peach-Blossom Fountain."

I am prevented by my fate to find out
The way leading into that fairyland.
I return you this painting with a deep sigh,
But I expect my old acquaintance in the mountains
To write me a poem calling me to return.

All translated by Yu Min-chuan.

Rowing at Night on the West Lake

Endlessly, endlessly on the vast lake grow the water cresses.
Night winds and dews are scented with the perfume of lotoses.
Gradually a lantern light in a distant temple comes into view.
Let us wait and watch the lake's glimmer when the moon is
  down.

For My Brother[3]

By the love of the heavenly emperor all things grow as in
  spring,
But I, a small official, have invited ruin through my ignorance.
I will be free of a great debt before I am a hundred years old;
The ten helpless ones surviving in my family will be a burden
  to others.
Good only are the green hills here for burying my bones.
There will be sad memories on rainy nights to come.
Would that you and I could be brothers for all ages,
Continuing our broken brotherhood in a life to come!

Translated by Yang Chi-sing.

CH'EN SHIH-TAO

He was a poet of the southern Sung dynasty remembered
for his striving after the perfect line. A contemporary poet,
Huang T'ing-chien (A.D. 1050-1110), said of him: "In order
to obtain a good line, he will shut himself up in a room."

Books

It is when we are near the end of a book that we enjoy it.
Guests whom we anxiously expect often fail to come.
So the world runs always contrary to our wishes.
How rarely in a hundred years do we open our hearts!

[3] Written for his brother Su Che (A.D. 1039-1112), who was serving a
sentence in jail because he opposed the innovations of Wang An-shih.
Su T'ung-po was afraid that his younger brother, who was also a poet of
considerable accomplishment, would die as a result of his hardships.

LI CH'ING-CHAO
(A.D. 1081–c. 1140)

The most famous and the most accomplished of Chinese women poets. Her father was a lifelong friend of Su T'ung-po. The greater part of her poetry was written after the death of her husband.

———————

To the Tune of "Like a Dream"

Who sits alone by the bright window?
My shadow and I, only we two.
But the lamp burns out; there is darkness.
Even my shadow forsakes me.
Alas, alas!
I am forlorn!

To the Tune of "A Sprig of Plum Blossom"

The fragrance of the pink lotos fails, the jade mat hints of autumn.
Softly I unfasten my silk cloak
And enter the boat alone.
Who is sending a letter from among the clouds?
When the swan message returns, the balcony is flooded with moonlight.

The blossoms drift on, the water flows.
There is the same yearning of the heart,
But it abides in two places.
There is no way to drive away this yearning.
Driven from the eyebrows,[1]
It enters the heart.

The Midautumn Festival
To the Tune of "Intoxicated by the Shadow of Flowers"

Thin mist, dense clouds sorrow over the whole day.
The incense is burning in the Gold Animal.[2]
Once again the happy festival of Midautumn!
Early coolness at midnight
Creeps through the jade pillow and silk screen.

[1] The eyebrows knit together in sorrow. The poem refers, like so many of her poems, to the death of her husband.

[2] A *ting* or tripod used for incense burning, the two handles being usually formed of animals.

275

When wine has been poured through the east hedge at twilight,[3]
The sleeves are flooded with a secret fragrance.
Do not say it is not enchantment!
The curtain rises with the west wind,
And I am thinner than a yellow flower.[4]

Mounting the High Balcony

Mounting the high balcony, I see
The rugged mountains, the rolling plain, the thin mist—
A mist so thin!
When the crows return to rest,

It is dusk; bugles blow.
How weary is my heart, the wine not finished yet.
The west wind hastens the fall of the *wu-t'ung* leaves—
The *wu-t'ung* leaves fall!
It is autumn,
Oh, so lonely!

Spring Returns

Winter is gone, and spring returns.
The early plum blossoms of Kiang-nan have betrayed the
news!
Last night, among the deep snows of the village,
One blossom opened.

How delicate and refined the jade petals appear!
How fragrant the scent that comes softly with the wind,
Breaking the traveler's heart in vain
As he halts the horse, wondering, wandering.

All translated by Sophia H. Chen.

[3] From a line by Tao Yuan-ming (A.D. 365-427):
        Gathering chrysanthemums by the east hedge,
        Leisurely I gaze up at the south mountain.
[4] Refers to the small yellow chrysanthemum beloved by Tao Yuan-ming.
These are the most celebrated of all her lines.

CHU TUN-RU (c. A.D. 1080–1175)

A native of Honan province, he produced poetry when he was hardly out of the cradle. He refused a high appointment at court, believing that he would lose his freedom if he ventured far from the wine pot. His earliest poetry celebrates wine and his own love affairs, but there is a progressive mellowness in his verses: toward the end, he surrendered entirely to philosophy.

Traveling

The red has parted from the green.
I'm half sober from my drink last night.
The horse in harness waits outside the door.
Fading bells without the house,
Fading candles before the curtains,
Fading moon beside the window.

She must be sleepless on her embroidered pillows,
Remembering that now the traveler has departed.
So hard to dismiss it from the heart,
So hard to see it,
So hard to speak it.

Translated by Ching Ti.

HSIN CH'I-cHI (A.D. 1140–1207)

Hsin Ch'i-chi was born in Li-cheng in Shantung, and rose to distinction as a warrior and statesman under the emperors Kao Tsung and Ning Tsung of the Sung dynasty. He delighted in wine, and in one of his poems declared there were only three things worth doing: to get drunk, to travel, and to sleep.

———— ∽ ————

Drinking

Let me enjoy myself in drunkenness.
How can I spare a moment for my troubles?
Now I find there is not a single drop of truth
In all those books written by the ancients.

Last night I reeled against a pine tree.
I asked the tree how sober I was.
I thought the tree moved to offer me help;
Pushing against it, I said: "Go away!"

Translated by Ching Ti.

To the Tune of "The Ugly Slave"

Young, I was unacquainted with sorrow,
Loving to climb the high places,
Loving to climb the high places,
Composing poems compelling myself to sorrow.

Now that I have drained sorrow to the dregs,
I am loath to talk of it,
I am loath to talk of it,
I say instead: "How nice is the cool autumn."

Translated by Hsiung Ting.

YO FEI (A.D. 1102–1141)

Advancing from the north, the Golden Horde kidnaped two Sung emperors and imposed conditions on the government that would have been unacceptable to all patriots. Unfortunately for China, the prime minister of the time, Ch'in Kuei, was prepared to buy a delusory peace at the price of surrendering Chinese territory. Yo Fei, one of the greatest Chinese generals, attempted to continue the fight but was recalled by the prime minister, imprisoned and sentenced to death at a time when the government was prepared to abandon all the territory north of the Huai River. The conquests in Honan by Yo Fei were forgotten, and the Sung dynasty fell from this moment into a state of intolerable weakness and decline.

More famous even than his loyalty was the inscription that, according to legend, was inscribed with hot irons on the boy's back by his mother, an inscription that may now be read on a million walls of China—*tsin chung pao kuo,* meaning: With the utmost loyalty save the state. He was put to death in 1141 and canonized in 1174.

———❧———

Full River Red

My hair bristles in my helmet.
Standing in the porch I see that the pattering rain has ceased.
I raise my eyes to the skies and shout with the vigor of my ambitions.
At the age of thirty fame and brave deeds are nothing but earth and dust.
Eight thousand li away lie the clouds and the moon.
Do not tarry. The hair of young men grows white with empty sorrows;
The same heaped on us in the year of Ch'ing Kung is not yet wiped away.[1]
When will the sorrows of the Emperor's subjects come to an end?
Oh, let us drive endless chariots through the Ho Lan Pass.
Now our sweet ambitions are directed upon the flesh of the Huns,
And laughing we thirst for the blood of the Hsiung-nu.[2]

[1] The forces of the Sung dynasty were defeated and the emperor was captured in the year 1126, known as the year Ch'ing Kung.
[2] Barbarian tribes.

Oh, let everything begin afresh.
Let all the rivers and mountains return to us,
Before we pay our respects once more to the Emperor.

Translated by Wang Sheng-chih.

YANG W'AN-LI (A.D. 1124–1206)

He was a native of Chi-sui in Shansi and graduated as *chin shih* in 1154, rising to be keeper of the Imperial Library. Eventually, like so many others, he lost favor at court and was exiled to a provincial post, where he composed a commentary on the *I Ching*.

Sleeping on a Summer Day

The sour taste of strawberries lingers in my mouth and teeth;
The *pa-chiao* tree shares its green with my window curtain.
Waking from a nap on a long day, I feel listless.
The hours are consumed in watching children catch willow
    blossoms.

Lines Written in a Small Inn While Staying in the Capital in the Late Spring

My eyes are sick, I dare not open books.
With spring mud on the road visitors are detained.
What shall I do through this long day,
But keep on pacing the veranda a hundred times?

Translated by Yang Chi-sing.

LU YU (A.D. 1125–1209)

He was born in Shanyang, Chekiang, and outlived six emperors, and in sixty-seven years wrote eleven thousand poems. He seems to have been prematurely old from birth. The only exciting event in his life was his continual affection for the girl whom he was compelled to divorce on his mother's orders. He was thirty-four when Chin Kuei, the prime minister who was responsible for the death of Yo Fei, died, and then he received a small clerkship in the provincial government of Fukien. The place did not suit him, and he was glad to remove to the more romantic atmosphere of Szechuan. Thereafter the scenery of Szechuan, the flowers and the sacred mountains, became the themes of his poetry. After his term of office expired, he enlisted in the army—it had been the dream of his youth to fight against the Golden Tartars—and he was distressed when he discovered that the frontiers were safe, there was no fighting, only an endless boredom. At fifty-four he left Szechuan and returned to his native village, distressed by the luxury and incontinence of the government, and by his own failure to obtain high office at the court.

In his old age he was extremely poor, and lived chiefly on his memories of the past. He grew more and more enamored with nature, and found his companionship in mountains, flowers, birds, children, and trees. The slightest event in the village was recorded in his poetry. In 1205 the Mongols became increasingly powerful, and began to attack the Golden Horde from the rear. Although he was eighty-one, he applied for enlistment in the army, hoping that before he died he would see himself in battle. But the armies of the Sung emperors continued to be defeated by the Tartars, especially in Szechuan, and he retired once again in disgust to his native village, where after a few years of peaceful village life he died at the age of eighty-five.

He was not, perhaps, a great poet. He had none of Tu Fu's passion, or Tu Fu's sympathy. A Chinese critic wrote: "His poetry is as simple as daily speech, in its simplicity there is depth, in its tranquillity there is such wonder that we are compelled to think again and again." Nothing could be more inaccurate than Lu Yu's own description of himself when he gave himself the name of Lu Feng-on—Lu the wild, irascible old man. He was placidity personified, and he seems to have regarded the cultivation of poetry as a kind of drug to make himself still more placid. At the age of seventy-seven, while drinking under a flowering plum tree, he wrote in a prefatory note: "Behold, in the last sixty years I have written exactly ten thousand poems." He was more just to himself when he said he was "a scholar without a scrap of use."

But he remains an important poet—not only because he was the most voluminous. He possessed a deeply patriotic spirit, a calmness of mind that might under different circumstances have made him as great a poet as Tao Yuan-ming, and he was utterly sincere in his love of beauty. The passion breaks through, the thing seen is placed on paper so that we see it again, and sometimes he will fill the poem with overbrimming life. But he did not experiment in verse forms, and he added little that was new to the outworn tradition, and when he confessed that he was writing poetry because he was lazy and wanted something to occupy his time, he was telling no more than the truth.

In the year of his death he still wandered round the country-side, his long legs straddling the back of a small pony. He would pick flowers, recite poems to himself, contemplate the ambiguity of fame, drink wine by a wayside inn, and talk to whoever would listen to him. He was famous in his village, but he knew the end could not be long delayed. Early one morning he fell sick. Everything was ready—the thin coffin, the two thick quilts to cover his hands and feet, the money for the monks, and the site of the grave already prepared. But even then, on the very next day, he wrote some verses in regular seven-syllable lines, saying that he would have one more drink in the market place. It was that kind of life—humorous, scholarly, dispassionate, graceful, and calm. But he would have been happier if it had been less calm, and if he had really seen in the smoking dust he described in one of his poems "the tremendous dust of chariot racing."

PAI CHWEN-YU

The Moon over the Pass

It is fifteen years since peace was declared with the Tartars;
When there are no wars, the generals guard the frontiers in
　　vain.
In huge mansions dances and songs go ceaselessly on.
Horses die fat in their stables; bows lie with their strings
　　snapped.
The horn at the frontier post hastens the dropping moon.
At thirty I enlisted; now my hair is white as snow.
Who can know their loyal hearts by listening to flutes?
In vain you shine on the unburied warriors' bones in the sand.
Once in the ancient times wars were common on the central
　　plain,[1]

[1] The central plain corresponds to modern Honan.

But now we never hear of any barbarians left alive.
The northerners defied death in the hope of salvation,
But tell me, how many folk tonight are shedding tears?

The Night Rain

The pattering rain on the empty steps quickens at night.
Frost breaks through the thin walls and the broken window.
The flying wind trembles on the slender lamp flame.
I, the old man, stand alone by a shelf of books.

Often I take books to read, and then put them back
And walk away from my room, scratching my snow-thatched
    head.
Daily the town inn sells a thousand gallons of wine.
The people are happy; then why should you be sad?

The Wind and the Rain

Though I am seventy, I do not want to leave my books;
I fear that only death will be able to snatch me away from
    them.
I wake and poke at the lamp beneath my window,
And so I pass through this night of wind and rain.

Gazing after Her Husband

I saw you go beyond the river to guard over the frontier,
For men ought to dedicate their bodies to the country.
I can neither bend the bow nor ride untamed horses.
Therefore, my lover, how could I follow your example?

I climb the hill with my head raised, gazing at the northwest
    clouds.
Though my features have changed, still my heart is constant.
All night the winter moon shines on my tear-marked face,
But to you, my lover, I send my heart of iron.

Autumn

Like a fairy spirit I leave the gate of the city.
I am rapt when I cross the streams and climb snow mountains.
I am afraid that not much time is left to me.
Thirteen more years have slipped away unawares.

The Flower-Seller

Do you not see the old flower-seller at the south gate of Huei-
chi,
Who feeds on flowers like a bee?
In the morning he sells a purple blossom,
In the evening a red flower.
Through the broken rafters of his house blue sky can be seen;
His rice jar is always empty.
The coins he receives he gives to the wine seller,
And only goes to work when his wine jug is empty.
Every year in spring the flowers blossom;
Every day he is continually drunk.
An appointment at court would be unthinkable to him;
So too would be the embankment at the chief minister's
home.[2]
He cannot greet the guest who calls on him—
Only hides his face with his drunken hairs.

The Yellow River

I live in poverty; day by day,
Year by year I have been growing old like this.
Even the Yellow River will be clear some day,[3]
But never will gray hairs turn black again.

Dying Spring

Since I returned from garrison in the west, my hairs have
turned gray,
And my son has grown taller than his father.
I would be content with old age if I had clear eyes and health;
I would throw the world away for soft rice and sweet tea.
I have avoided my studies except to write my name;
I do not even dress properly to receive my guests.
The country is peaceful and calm; spring is dying.
I am madly in love with honey-sweet lonely flowers.

Death

Old Chang died after three years' sickness;
Old Wu suddenly went out one night.[4]
My body is hard like steel.
I lean on the door, gazing at the green hill.

[2] There was a custom, when a chief minister was appointed, to sprinkle
sand on the road leading from his house to his office—this, for some
reason, was called "making an embankment."
[3] There was a legend that the muddy Yellow River grows clear once
every thousand years.
[4] Close neighbors of Lu Yu.

The Old Apothecary

He is as old as I.
Sells drugs to replace husbandry.
The coins he receives he gives to the wine seller,
And leaves not one for himself.

He accompanies old neighbors in singing,
And teaches the young when it is raining hard.
I would like to write his life,
But no one knows his name.

To His Sons

I know that to die is to be dead to the world.
I bitterly regret I shall not see the Nine States united.
Do not forget to tell your father at the family temple
When the royal troops march northward into the central plain.

Returning at Night

The soft sound of bells floats over the river;
The shining moon leans on the forests.
I recognize my cottage from the plume of smoke.
I lean on the ship's screen and gaze upon it.

A Roadside Song

Cold rice mingled with sand—
A short coarse coat to keep off the frost and dew,
Dry leaves heaped up near the small house on the hill,
And the people going past, on the backs of donkeys.

South and north run the straight highways,
The wheels of vehicles rolling on forever.
Are they in any way more talented than I?
And must I starve alone from morning till night?

Such is my melancholy roadside song.
None of the wealthy are aware of it.
In autumn locust leaves fall on the roads—
Oh, how terrible this time of heartbreaking sadness!

The Cries of Birds

The peasants in the fields have no calendar;
They know the seasons through the cries of birds.
In February they hear the cuckoos;
Then they know it is time for the spring plowing.
In March they hear the nightingale's song;
Then the young maids pity the hunger of silkworms.
In April they hear the turtledoves;
Then the household silkworms put on straw arrowheads.[5]
In May the crows begin to crow;
Then it is time to remove the weeds near the young seeds.
Men say a peasant's life is hard and cruel,
Forever craving for rain and for fair weather.
But who knows the joy that lies among these peasants?
For in their lives they know no officials,
They are content with their coarse cloth, wheat, and rice;
Among these lakes and bridges wine flows like oil.
Each night they return home drunk, leaning on one another,
And they have no fear of meeting the sentinel of Pa-ling.[6]

Prune Flowers

All day long I lean on the pavilion balustrade;
I gaze at the prune trees until they fade.
No wonder I have no desire to welcome guests;
It is not that I fear the cold coming of spring.

The Guest Goes on His Way

Facing each other in drowsiness on the straw stool,
The host and the guest forget each other's company.
Suddenly the host starts up, and sees no guest is there.
One half of the west window is not lit by the setting sun.

Drinking at the Village

When I am fed, with no occupation or care, I am glad.
Old people indeed are like children in swaddling bands—
To fall asleep before the evening bell has rung,
And wake up when the sun has reached the zenith.

[5] The silkworms are placed on small bundles of straw shaped like arrowheads (*ts'u*) to await the formation of the cocoons.
[6] Li Kuang, a famous general and archer during the Han dynasty, returned one night and was detained by the sentinel at Pa-ling.

Old Age

Unbearable is the sickness that invades old age.
Often I hold up the mirror and sorrow over myself.
The west wind blows away the wine I drank in the morning,
And restores me to my withered leaf of a fading face.

Autumn

The village wine is sweet and sour, the town wine rotten,
But better than staring at an empty cup all day.
My cottage cannot stand the autumn's loneliness,
And so I tramp in the rain and knock at the inn door.

Prune Trees

Prune trees begin to stir before and after the snow.
North and south of the street wine can be bought on credit.
While I am healthy, let me be drunk wherever I go.
To have a home is not always better than none.

On Hearing the Flute

The weather is fair after the fall of a few snowflakes.
Bright tile-piercing frosts accompany the shining moon.
Suddenly I hear a hermit piping on his flute,
And turning to the window I join him, reading aloud.

Old Age

Irrigate the high wasteland and the slopes for plowing.
I did nothing praiseworthy in life; after death no fame.
Do not ask why I have become more and more useless.
It was thirty years ago when the snow hairs descended on me.

The Evening Wind

The evening wind begins its whistling sound;
The waning moon pours out shining beams.
I love to open the door and gaze idly—
I can stroll slowly if I have a stick.

Little frost, the trees mostly green,
The spring water is flowing through the field ditches.
I remember the days of my childhood,
Playing chess, with a board scrabbled on the ground.

August

In August the cool wind blows to drive the heat away;
From all the courtyards comes the sound of threshing.
The harvest is threefold, the ears many and full of grain—
Enough to break carriage axles and redden men's shoulders.

In former days government sent summonses like rain,
But now no officials walk along the road.
At the cottage doors the old and the young are eternally
    dancing,
And the pots in the kitchens are tired of stewing pigs and
    sheep.

Strolling under the Moon

It is midnight, yet sleep will not come to me,
So I rise and stroll beneath the dim moon.
The wind starts to blow and the frightened leaves fall,
And the lotus bends under the thick dew.

The pleasure found in wine is rough and harsh.
How stupid to me appears posthumous fame!
The fever still continues. I close the door,
I sit down and wait for sunrise.

The Clouds

Above us the clouds are weaving and unweaving,
The breeze in the courtyard goes and returns.
Take life easily—it will always be the same.
Who can prevent us from being convivial?

Autobiography

I have a new vegetable garden, about two acres,
And three shabby and ancient straw cottages.
My health has improved a bit since my sickness has gone.
Cool and gentle are the nights of early autumn.
Sometimes mild wine makes me sober, sometimes drunk.
Only one half of the torn book remains.
I often smile, advising my poor lonely self
Not to sorrow unnecessarily.

                        All translated by Pai Chwen-yu.

THE CH'ING DYNASTY

(A.D. *1644–1911*)

NALAN HSINTEH (A.D. 1655–85)

Song of the Golden Pavilion for Liang Fen

I am just a mad scholar.
By mere chance I came from a family stained with the dust of
    the court.
If I had wine, I would only sprinkle it on the tombs of the
    heroes of Chao.
O Cheng Sheng, who understands my intentions in life?
Unbelievable that at last I have met my bosom friend—
Pure eyes, high-spirited, both of us young.
Wine cups before us, we wiped away heroic tears.
Look, the moon is like water!

With you tonight I shall be drowned in wine.
Let the silly women gossip—in ancient times it was permissible
    to revile them.
No, no, the red dust of the world is not worth our trouble!
Cast a cold eye on them!
When I dream of the past, I would have everything blotted out!

To the Tune of "Pusa Barbarian"

A heaven-shrieking gale harries the earth this depth of winter.
Ungirthing the saddle strings, I see the ravens hurrying across
    the sky by twilight.
The ice has blocked up the Great River.
Oh, terrible immensity of sorrow!
Scars of the burned earth eternally meet my gaze;
Drums and horns sound from the high walls.
Tomorrow I shall arrive in Ch'ang-an.
In the heart of this wanderer there are unending sorrows.

To the Tune of "Gathering Mulberry Seeds"

The bright moon in love must surely laugh at me,
Mocking at my stupidity.
I have been unfaithful to the heart of spring,
Wandering all alone, humming songs to myself.

Of late I have been afraid to talk of past events.
I have sought solace in the orchid dress.[1]
The moon wanes, the lamp burns in its socket.
Within the dream where is the vanished cloud?

All translated by Hsiung Ting.

[1] I.e., male companionship. The Chinese *lan* or orchid is the same color
as its leaves, and does not suggest effeminacy.

THE REPUBLIC OF CHINA

(A.D. *1911–*)

MODERN CHINESE POETRY

A tradition had grown up effortlessly through the years, but like all traditions it was the result of constant change, of constant forces working from outside and inside on the texture of the civilization. The songs of the state of Chu, written originally in a language akin to Tai, altered the shape of the poetry; the five- and seven-syllable lines were introduced during the Han dynasty from the barbarian tribes. These, until recently, were the greatest foreign influences on Chinese poetry. Then there came the invasions of the west, and a knowledge of the verse forms of a hundred other nations came at a time when Chinese versification was suffering from an excessive crystallization. When in 1917 Dr. Hu Shih began a campaign for introducing the vernacular language, he was doing no more than setting the seal on a movement that had begun long previously. The novel that we know as *The Dream of the Red Chamber* was written in *pei-hua;* so were countless other novels, and countless poems. But the official language was still *wen-li,* that delicate and deliberate monosyllabic language that had hardly changed since the time of Confucius. Only officials could read it; hardly anyone could understand it when it was read aloud. But the language of the people was there, it had force and vigor and luxuriance and resilience, all of which were lacking in the more ornate official language, and the time had come for a swift change and an abrupt break with the past. But it came slowly. It was difficult even for the scholars who insisted most on the change to accustom themselves to the new atmosphere.

Dr. Hu Shih's "Experiments," published early in 1920, still celebrated "the wind, the flowers, the snow, and the moon." The themes were hackneyed and threadbare, but at least the versification was revolutionary. The interminable parallel versification was abandoned. There were to be no more verses like:

> Two piece yellow oriole sing emerald willow
> One row white egret soar azure sky.

Instead there were to be attempts to reflect the life of the people, using the words of the people, their emotions and present sufferings. There was Hsu Chih-mo, the brilliant expounder of a culture he had derived from Cambridge; there were a host of young poets, like Chu Hsiung, Liu Meng-wei, and Wen Yi-tuo, who were determined to take the new fortress by storm. They only half succeeded in the beginning. Even Hu

294

Shih, the most revolutionary of all, wrote in a mood derived from the past:

Again the thin clouds,
Again the brilliant moonlight after the clouds,
But no more the traveling companion of last year,
And no more the youthful feelings of that time.
Not willing to be reminded of love lost,
I dared not go outdoors to look at the moon;
But the mischievous moon came in by the open window,
And made me sleepless the whole night.

This was not revolutionary poetry, but it was revolutionary verse. Hu Shih seems to have withdrawn from the movement shortly afterward, and it was left to Wen Yi-tuo to insist that free verse was not the necessary concomitant of the new poetry. He developed the theory that poetry should possess the qualities of architecture and music; the poets should obey definite laws; they should root poetry in the earth; they should give it the appearance of form, and the utmost of their art. He failed to start any movement, but something of his insistence on an almost classical foundation to Chinese poetry remains even in the poems of Tien Ch'ien and Ai Ching.

The war, more than the literary coteries of Peking in 1917, changed the course of Chinese poetry. Mayakovsky's influence was more lasting, and more effective, than Shelley's. The rigors of the war, the desperate weariness, the vast travels of armies brought about a mood that had something in common with the mood of the Han dynasty—a hardness of fiber and of imagination that disappeared in Chinese poetry on the death of Su T'ung-po. The poets, who were often young students, were not dilettante revolutionaries; they had seen the country blazing with Japanese fire, and they had suffered unendurably. There is an end to their dreams of peach-blossom fountains—or almost an end. The world is seen in the revealing light of war to be a thing that can be trodden on, shaped, tortured, made hideous with cries. They had seen these things before. There had been almost uninterrupted civil war since the birth of the Republic; but this war came from abroad, and it was more terrible than any wars of the past, and more revealing of their own weaknesses. The river changed course. The past was jettisoned. Out of these hard sufferings they made hard poetry.

But the past remained. We see it occasionally in the poems of Pien Chih-lin, whose translations of Mallarmé and Valéry were among the first to appear in China. We see it more clearly in the poetry of Feng Chih, who learned from Rilke and Goethe almost the same lessons that he learned from Chuang-tzu. We see it in the poems of Ai Ching, who follows the patterns of Whitman but describes the bustling sand-bitten life of north China, with a desperate joy in the land. And though it is deliberately absent in Tien Ch'ien, who lives in a moment of time, there are indications that even in his poetry it will return. The poetry of Mao Tse-tung follows the patterns of T'ang dynasty poetry, but twists these patterns into modern shape. And there are countless others.

As in the old days, nearly everyone in China writes poetry. It is scribbled on walls, pasted on wall newspapers, printed—usually at tremendous cost to the poets themselves—on ragged brown or yellow paper in type that was almost indecipherable. It flourished in the universities of the southwest and all over the northwest, and though much of it was sentimental, there was more poetic vigor during the years of war than in all the previous years of civil war. And though the Chinese poets themselves insist that they have cut themselves adrift from the past, the past is always returning, the peach-blossom fountain is always flowering, and we see the same melancholy in these poems of war against the Japanese as we see in the poems written about the Hsiung-nu and the barbarians who held their forts beyond the Yu Men Kuan. But though the melancholy is the same, there is a new strength, a new vitality in these poems that more than anything else reveal the minds of the Chinese of the present—their sapling vigor, their love for life, and their amazing strength in spite of all weariness and all defeats.

The new poetry has come to stay. It is too early to say whether it will follow the direction of Tien Ch'ien or of Pien Chih-lin, the two outstanding poets of the new age. What is certain is that though the figures of the great poets of the past loom hard behind them, they are determined to make a poetry of their own. The wheel seems to have turned full circle, and once more, as in the days when unknown poets were singing *The Book of Songs,* they go out in search of an undiscovered world.

So I wrote some fifteen years ago, and I see no reason to change what is said here. The coming of the Chinese Communist revolution seems to have had very little effect on Chinese poetry. Immense quantities of propaganda verses have been written—there are accounts of some forty million verses written in the province of Szechuan alone—but the main stream of Chinese poetry continues as before. So far the Chinese Communists have produced few important poets, and it is still too early to measure the significance of the young poets who have arisen in the last ten years.

THE MONK OF EIGHT FINGERS
(1841–1921)

He was known as the Monk of Eight Fingers because he dedicated two to Buddha by holding them in a flame. He reached high rank in the Buddhist hierarchy of China, but his poems remain entirely traditional. The following poem might just possibly have been written a thousand years previously.

———————❧———————

Song of a Soldier

At thirteen I followed the army and garrisoned a border town.
Five thousand iron horses marched together.
At the Great Wall we fought; all perished.
I have no desire to have my portrait in the Hall of Clouds.

With broken banners in my hands the setting sun:
"Heroic souls, follow me back to your village homes."
Suddenly a skeleton arose and talked like a man:
"Honorable Sir, take this letter to my mother and father.

"Tell them I am in exile, a ghost among new ghosts;
Tell them I am far from home, a wanderer—
They do not know whether I am alive or dead,
And tell my wife not to suffer for my sake."

Translated by Wang Sheng-chih.

WEN YI-TUO

He was born in 1898 in the province of Hupeh, studied painting in New York, and on his return to China threw himself into a tremendous and necessary reinterpretation of the ancient Chinese classical writings in the light of recent research. He published only two books of poetry: *The Red Candle* (1922) and *The Dead Water* 1928), but they have exercised an influence on the poetry of the younger writers far in excess of their size. He remained essentially the scholar, occasionally writing critical articles, but more often devoted to pure scholarship and the illumination of present political problems by the examination of the past. He was murdered by Kuomintang soldiers on July 15, 1946.

The Dead Water

Here is a ditch of dead and hopeless water;
No breeze can raise a ripple on it.
Best to throw in it scraps of rusty iron and copper,
Pour out in it all the refuse of meat and soup.

Perhaps the copper will turn green like emeralds,
Perhaps the rusty iron will assume the shape of peach
    blossoms;
Let grass weave a layer of silky gauze
And bacteria puff up patches of cloud and haze.

So let the dead water ferment into green wine,
Littered with floating pearls of white foam.
Small pearls cackle aloud and become big pearls,
Only to be burst like gnats and to rob the vintage.

So this ditch of dead and hopeless water
May boast a touch of brightness.
If the toads cannot endure the deathly silence,
The water may burst out singing.

Here is a ditch of dead and hopeless water,
A region where beauty can never stay.
Better abandon it to evil—
Then, perhaps, some beauty will come of it.

The God of Love

How beautiful are those eyes!
The god of love, two calm ponds of clear water.
O you poor weak swimmers,
I would advise you to return to the shore.

There are hazel bushes by the waterside.
How charming those black jade eyebrows!
The nose sloping down like a pyramid
May perhaps be some lover's grave.

And there are the two red door leaves,
Red as the mellowest cherries.
And inside there is a screen of cowries.
Who knows what kind of snare he is setting?

This may be the paradise of Eden,
A house of beauty or an altar of love?
No, not entirely so—
A bewildered palace haunted by deathly ghosts.

The Desk

At once all the inanimate things burst out singing:
Complaints from every part of the desk.
The ink case groans: "I am thirsty to death!"
The dictionary cries that the rain water is soaking its back.

The writing pad says its waist is aching with bending,
The fountain pen says the tobacco ash has clogged its mouth,
The ink brush says the match has burned its beard,
And the pencil says the toothbrush is weighing on its leg.

The incense pot grumbles: "The books are unreasonable—
Sooner or later they will throw me down!"
The steel-cased watch says its bones will rust with sleep.
"The wind is coming!" the writing paper fearfully laments
    aloud.

The inkstone claims it is meant to hold water:
"Why do I have to suffer cigar ash and stinking dirt?"
The desk says it is never cleaned more than once a year.
The inkpot proclaims: "I swilled you on a rainy day."

"Who the devil is the master of all of us?"
So all these inanimate objects burst out singing.
"If really we have to continue in this disorder,
It would be better if there were no existence at all."

The master bites his pipe and smiles blandly:
"The best thing to do is for all of you to remain where you are.
It is not my fault that you are all distressed.
The order of the universe is beyond my power."

Early Summer Night

The setting sun leaves the poet to the dreary night,
And he reminds her: "Reveal all your secret treasuries."
The violet sky spills broken pearls,
He believes they should be strung together
As adornments upon the breasts of death.

Claws of cold undertow comb the withered hair of starved
    willows,
Wringing out their reflections from the pond in slivers of gold.
Halfway up the hill there is a fallen cypress, hunchbacked.
Her dark bony fists shake defiance at the sun.
The sleepless toads are overcome with weariness,
The village dogs bark in mournful, inquiring tones.
How can the nerves of thieves stand up to the strain?
A fire-swallowing, mist-spitting dragon climbs the iron stair-
    way
With "War" engraved on the gray uniform, hoarsely shouting,
    sobbing.
The clapper of a great bell comforts the world,
Saying, "Sleep in peace," but who believes in the bell?
O God, knowing the pass the world has come to,
Are you not shuddering, O most benevolent God in the skies?

Translated by Ho Yung.

FENG CHIH

Feng Chih was born in 1905 in the province of Hopei. After graduating from Peking University, he studied German literature and philosophy at Heidelberg, and fell under the influence of Goethe, Hölderlin, and Rilke, who have been his gods ever since. Nearly all his poetry has been in sonnet form, which he uses with a peculiarly Chinese grace. He published *Songs of Yesterday* in 1927 and *Northern Wanderings* in 1930. More recently he published the considerably more famous *Twenty-seven Sonnets,* from which the present selection has been made.

Sonnets

I

Behold the vast cavalcades of horses,
Bringing merchandise from faraway regions,
And the rivers washing up mud and sand
From some unknown place beyond the frontiers.

The wind whistling across the deserts
Bears with it an immense sighing.
We, who have crossed so many mountains and rivers,
No longer possess them once we have gone on our way.

We are like birds circling in the air,
Seeming always to hold the sky in our power,
Yet unable ever to call anything our own.

Where, then, lies the truth in ourselves?
We can take nothing from the far regions,
And nothing from here may we carry away.

II

Standing together side by side on high mountains,
Projecting ourselves into the far distant plains
And into the broad landscape at our feet,
And the paths crisscrossing one another—

All these, roads, streams, are within us,
These winds, these clouds, all enter into us;
The mountains and cities and rivers we have passed through
Are all summoned up in our lives.

301

Our growing and our grief
Is a pine on a hill over there,
A mist in a town over here.

We follow the wind, flow in water.
We also are the paths crisscrossing on the plain,
And we are the people who travel on the plains.

III

For years you lived between life and death,
And now to this degenerate town you return,
Listening to the idiot singing in the streets.
You feel yourself an ancient hero,

Returning after centuries to his native place,
Seeing his changed, degenerate descendants,
Discovering nothing that sings of health and youth,
Crestfallen, stunned, dizzy with failure.

For on the battlefields you were a great hero.
In another world you lifted your face to the sky,
Who now resembles a stringless kite.

Wherefore blame fortune?
You have outstripped them all, for none can follow
Your upward eternal flight into the skies.

IV

Listening to the storm, the wind and the rain,
In this utter solitude of lamplight—
Yet though the cottage is so small,
Between us and the objects around us,

Thousands of miles extend into the distance.
The brass ewer yearns for the mountain ore,
The porcelain cup yearns for the riverine clay.
All, all are like birds in a storm,

Scattered east and west. So we hold ourselves tight,
As though afraid that our bodies would escape from us,
The strong gale lifting everything into the deep sky,

While the threshing rain beats all things into dust.
There is left now only the small trembling flame
To prove to us now that life still remains.

V

Here in the warm sunshine,
Once again we come out into the country.
We are like waters of many rivers
Coming together in a single sea.

There is the same warning call
Filling our hearts.
There is the same fate
Falling on our shoulders.

There is the same heaven
That guards us and saves us;
But when dusk falls

The roads leading in different directions
Call us back to ourselves,
And once again the sea becomes rivers.

VI

You say, The things I like best to gaze on
Are the country pathways quick with life,
For many are the feet of the nameless wanderers
Whose footsteps left imprints on these living roads.

So too in the fields of our mind,
There also are winding footpaths,
The paths of those who once traveled this way
And disappeared, no one knows whither.

There were children alone, and old couples;
Youths and maidens in their first rejoicing,
Old friends now dead. Then join

In treading for us those ancient pathways.
Therefore, in memory of their fading footsteps,
Let us prevent the paths from being choked by weeds.

VII

*For Tsai Yuan-pei, a great educator and
leader of the people, and president of
Peking University*

Many, without discrimination, mention your name
And place you together with others.
Yet do you keep perpetually
A steadfast, peculiar brilliance.

Only in the frail dawn light of evening and morning
Do people recognize you—morning and evening star.
At midnight you are indistinguishable
From other stars. Many were the young

Who through your quiet revelation were enabled
To seek a full life and a fuller death.
Now you also are dead, and deeply we regret

That never again will you help us along our tasks,
When once again the world is newborn
And all that is broken is mended and restored.

VIII

For Tu Fu

You suffered starvation in deserted villages,
Always you saw ahead of you a gutter death,
And yet you were incessantly singing
Of the glorious events that occurred each day.

Soldiers died, lay wounded on battlefields;
Stars fell down the sky,
A thousand horses vanished in scudding clouds.
To all these your life was a sacrifice.

Your poverty still glitters and shines
Like the rags of a deceased saint,
And the least tatter that remains

Is endowed with magic powers.
Their crowns and purples in this light
Are shoddy when compared with yours.

Translated by Chu K'an.

PIEN CHIH-LIN

Born in 1910 near the estuary of the Yangtze River, a fact to which he attaches considerable significance, Pien Chih-lin seems always to be gazing across a Pacific of the imagination. His roots are in China, but his branches are somewhere in New England with Henry James and in the France of Baudelaire. He has translated nearly all the modern French poets voluminously, accurately, and with an unexpected tenderness; and his reputation as a translator is only equaled by his reputation as a poet. He no longer writes poetry, but his collected poems composed of four parts, *Resounding Dust, Outside the Resounding Dust, Ornaments for Chang Hsuan,* and *Twenty Letters,* are already classics. He has spent years with the guerrillas and still more years in the exiled university of Lienta in Kunming. The poems are translations by himself.

————————❧————————

Peking

Peking city: flying kites on a rubbish mound,
here a butterfly, there an eagle
painted on the blue canvas over Madrid.
Across the sea of sky, what a pity that no one can see you,
Kyoto—

Oh, trailing a trail of dust
and leaving all the passers-by in a shower bath,
flying wheels, you swim in so shallow water,
yet in such high spirits?
Not so dusty indeed: even they are running away
from something hot at their heels, howling over their heads,
over everyone's head. Here it is again:
The yellow-haired wind makes a mess of the immense incense
    pot,
stirring up the ashes of many centuries,
sending them flying, flying, flying,
driving them into frightened horses, fierce wolves, furious
    tigers,
rushing, rolling, roaring along the streets,
swooping over your windowpane, giving you a puff,
swooping upon your ears' eaves, striking off an ear,
or a glazed tile?

"Dear me! Simply frightened me! Lucky it isn't
a bomb! Ha, ha, ha, ha!"
"Sweet, is it? Enough of your fragrant dream?

No rider in your ricksha, yourself lying there as on a sofa,
Luck indeed the tile has eyes!"
"The bird's dropping has also eyes—ha, ha, ha, ha!"

Ha, ha, ha, ha, what's the fun of it?
Hysteria, you understand, hysteria!
Sad, sad,
really sad to see the child imitating the old man,
young as he is, flying kites on a rubbish mound,
he also hums the threadbare tune "On recalling the past . . ."
Sad, sad to hear a city of hoary trees
crying vainly,
crying, crying, crying.
Homeward? Where? Homeward? Where?
Ancient capital, ancient capital, what can I do for you?
I am a kite already severed from the string,
having stumbled on you, how could I not cling
on your dear willow branches? You'll be my home, you'll be
        my tomb:
just send your catkins on every bower, every tower,
never mind if my looks are day by day withering away.
That's rotten, pardon. Look here,
Peking city: flying kites on a rubbish mound.
Yesterday the weather was really in a nice mess, wasn't it?
Old Fang complains against heaven every spring; cursed it
        yesterday,
because it crowned the city like an immense yellow tomb.
Old Wang said it looked ominous. If you once dropped asleep,
maybe you would never see daylight any more
until the excavations of the descendants many years later.
Today the weather is really splendid, isn't it?
See the flowering trees posed on barrows for a spring prome-
        nade,
and we'll enjoy lanterns of vermilion silk over peonies.
(Over there, are they now enjoying their cherry blossom?)
It's the doves' flutes that whistle in the sky,
blue sky with white doves, no airplanes—
Even the airplanes, appreciating the view, I assure you,
would not be so hardhearted as to lay eggs on these glazed
        tiles.
Peking city: flying kites on a rubbish mound.

The First Lamp

Birds engulf hard pebbles to grind the grain in their crops.
Beasts fear fire. Men keep fire, and so arises civilization.
Blessed are those who arise at sunrise and sleep at sunset.
Yet I praise the first lamp that opens on a new world.

YU MIN-CHUAN

Yu Min-chuan was born in 1915 in the province of Anhui and therefore belongs to the youngest generation of Chinese poets. Influenced largely by the West, and more particularly by Keats and Milton, he has also studied the ancient Taoist texts. In his poetry there seems to be a fusion of these two alien cultures more complete than in any other poet of his time. He writes little, but always carefully, and there is some significance in the fact that his complete works, published under the title *Thirty Poems* in 1946, should characteristically have included nearly forty poems. He is now a professor at Peking University.

Lady Macbeth

Eleven, twelve, one . . .
black strokes of the clock fluttering and dancing,
fluttering and dancing, then falling . . .
swarming wings of dying moths.

The cloud-eclipsed moonlight night
erects on the window
a tombstone a hundred years old.
Then I came across a revelation—
to be buried in a fish's belly.
Is this the dead solitude of high noon?

A piece of diamond cutting apart an ice field,
the neighboring baby crying out in nightmare.
So mamma is honey, is wine, is opium.

To look for the affection lost
or to dispatch the bewitching image?
Now Lady Macbeth stalks out of her chamber,
moves on tiptoe,
and with sleeves rolled up
displays her heroism.

AI CHING

He claims that he was chiefly influenced by Verhaeren, Mayakovsky, and Van Gogh, but no one has ever believed such nonsense. He comes from Kwangtung, in the deep south, and after studying painting in the south of France, he has made his home in the north. He is an expatriate, often looking away from the loess and the sands of the north to the green luxuriance of the south; and yet he belongs completely to the place where he lives. With the possible exception of Tien Ch'ien, he is the greatest poet produced by the war. He is simple, never relinquishing his vision of the sandy plains. "The Man Who Died a Second Time" gave him his greatest fame, but I have chosen "The Trumpeter" because it shows, I think, a greater mastery of form and imagery.

For some time after the Chinese Communist revolution, Ai Ching was regarded as the leading revolutionary poet. More recently there have been rumors that he has fallen in disfavor and is now exiled in a remote town on the borders of Mongolia.

The Trumpeter

They say the fate of the trumpeter is misery and sorrow.
He breathes on the delicate brass skin of the trumpet and cleans it,
And then again when he pours his blood through the hollow trumpet and sings,
His face is pale yellow. . . .

I

There are those who sleep miserably among spread paddy stalks,
There are those who are utterly exhausted and covered with grime,
There are those who wear gray clothes.
Among them he is the first to awake.
Strange in his waking;
As though shocked by the sudden return of the sun.
He wakes astonished.
Why is this?
The wheels of the dawn chariot are riding past him,
Rumbling into the distance.

He opens his eyes.
By the weak lamplight that is never put out at night,
He sees the trumpet hanging by his side.
Puzzled, then delighted,
Waking from sleep,
He sees his darling.
On such days
He is wholly in love with the trumpet.

So beautiful—
The slender body of it shining
With rude health,
And the red silk ribbons
Flowing down from it.

He rises among the paddy stalks,
Not complaining of having slept on moist earth.
He binds up his puttees;
Dashes cold water on his face,
Looks at the softly snoring companions,
Stretches his hands toward the trumpet.

And outside in the darkness
The dawn has not yet come.
He was awakened by
His eager longing for the dawn.
He walks up the slope of the hill
And stands there for a long while,
Watching the recurring miracle of the day.
Dark night has removed her mysterious curtains,
Thousands of weary stars are disappearing. . . .
Dawn! Thou art Time's bride!
Thou comest riding on a golden-wheeled chariot,
From afar, from the other side of the world.
Our world welcomes her
And hangs her banners in the East.
Behold!
Between heaven and earth the solemn bridals are consummated!

II

Now he lifts
Under the blue transparent firmament
The trumpet to his lips,
And blows.
The trumpet is filled with fresh air from the plains.
So in gratitude
He blows his refreshing songs across the plains.
In love for the tumultuous dawn
He sounds the reveille—
The song flows out into the distance.

All things in the world
In their glory and happiness
Accept his call. . . .

The forests awake,
The birds twitter,
The rivers call
The horses to drink.
The villages awake,
Peasant women pass along the banks of streams,
The gray-clothed people
Come from their rugged homes wearing a dress of light,
Going hither and thither. . . .

He climbs down the hill
And vanishes among these streams of people.
He has blown the reveille
And summoned them to their food.
The sun in thundering splendor
Rises in the firmament
And summons them all. . . .

III

The road goes on
Toward the never-ending peaks of heaven.
The road goes on
Trodden by a million footprints,
Wheel marks, layers of thick mud.
The road goes on,
Bringing the villages together.
The road goes on,
Climbing up one slope and down another,
And now
She is gilded with sunlight.
Then the trumpeter
Marches out into the glory of sun,
And sounds the advance.
A ceaseless ring of flowing sound
Comes from the gold trumpet.

IV

The gray flocks of the people
Disperse and spread over the wide plains,
Where in the fields
Endless green grass
Serves as an altar.
Listen, the deafening roar
Of thunder on the edge of heaven.
We breathe the mingled perfumes of earth and grass;

From the distance comes the odor of smoke.
In trenches we spend our winters,
Silently, waiting for orders
Like a woman giving birth
Who waits patiently for her child.
Our hearts, our breasts
Flow with new abundant love.
Now in these days approaching the end of life
Which Time has arranged for us,
We prepare ourselves,
Each one possessing a pure and holy will,
That he may deserve death in the glory of the battlefield!

v

The war began cruelly:
Multitudes of soldiers,
Astonished light gleaming from bayonets,
Leap from the trenches,
Running exquisitely,
Advancing toward the threatening enemy.
Thunder and lightning of death cries!
They will never march again—
Never again the impetuous running of feet.
And the trumpeter,
Inspired by the lips of life,
Violently, unassumingly
Blows the trumpet at the moment of his death.
His voice covering all,
His voice more beautiful than all,
Inspired by life, completing his prayer of victory
At the moment when a bullet pierced his heart and breast,
Falling silently—
No one saw him fall
Down to the earth he loved above all things,
In his hand
Still grasping the trumpet.

The smooth skin of the trumpet
Reflected this boy's blood
And his white face.
It reflects also
The advance of the soldiers,
Their continued striving,
Their horses neighing,
Their thundering chariots.
The sun, the sun
Glitters on the trumpet's smooth surface.

Listen,
The trumpet is still singing . . .

Snow Falls on China

Snow falls on the Chinese land;
Cold blockades China. . . .

The wind like an old woman with many grievances
Closely follows behind
And stretches out her claws,
Tugs at clothes.
Her words are as old as the earth,
Complaining, never ceasing.

From the forests
Driving their carts
Come the farmers of China,
Wearing their fur caps—
Where do they want to go?

I tell you, I too
Am a descendant of farmers;
Like you, my face
Is etched with pain,
So deeply do I know
Those months, those years of labor,
Knowing how people live in the plains,
Passing hard days.
No, I am not happier than you.
—Lying in the river of time,
Often the tides of distress
Have entirely overwhelmed me.
In exile and in prison cells
I spent my most precious youth.
My life
Like yours
Is haggard.

Snow falls on the Chinese land;
Cold blockades China. . . .

Along the rivers of a snowy night
A small oil flame drifts slowly
In a ragged boat with a black sail.
Facing the lamp and hanging her head,
Who sits there?

O you
Snot-haired and dirty-faced young woman,
Is this your warm house,
A warm and happy nest and cave,

Burned out by the invader?
On such a night as this
You lost your husband's protection.
In terror of death you were teased
Utterly
By the enemy's bayonets.

Aiee, on so cold a night
Numerous old mothers
Crouch in homes not theirs,
Like strangers
Not knowing
Where tomorrow's wheels will take them.
The roads of China
Are as rugged as theirs.

Snow falls on the Chinese land;
Cold blockades China. . . .

Throughout the snowy pasture in the long night
Are lands bitten by the beacons of war.
Numerous men of tillage
Live in the village of Absolute Despair.
The cattle they fed are robbed,
The fat rice fields plundered.
Over the hungry earth,
Facing the dark sky,
They hold out shivering hands
Asking for succor.

Oh, pain and distress of China,
Endless like the snowy night.

Snow falls on the Chinese land;
Cold blockades China. . . .

O China
On this lampless night,
Can my weak lines
Give you a little warmth?

The Highway

From this small humble village hidden in a valley,
From the powerful mountains have I come,
From the dim smoky tile-roofed house,
With a farmer's candor and with a farmer's troubles I come;
I run up the slopes of the mountain—
Now let wild air and sunlight

And the ocean-like wilderness stretching out from the foot of
    the mountain
Utterly destroy my troubles,
And let the endless area of blue skies,
So wide, so wide,
Loosen my heartstrings.
Let us walk in this enclosure of air,
And when we grow tired,
Let us rest among the roots of old trees,
Listening to the little streams among rock cliffs,
Watching the eagles, looking on rock doves.
And the mule trains carrying coal sacks,
And the men in rags,
And the weak whips and the weary voices
As they turn
Into a strange, dark ravine.
And we follow them,
Thinking of the ravine and the old temple,
And the row of small huts and co-operatives.

Then the lorries pass!
Oh, roar of thunder!
Everywhere merchandise flowing,
Young people in lorries waving their hands at me,
Their presence
Making my heart beat wildly.

And the sedan chairs passing,
The gleam of wet metal,
White wings of the sunlight,
Blood on the mountain veins,
And myself watching them
Intoxicated,
Racing after them with my heart's blood.

Oh, my soul reaches to freedom,
My lungs expand in the freshness of air,
My eyes penetrate all distance,
My legs stumble because I am happy.

Strong hands, strong hammers split the rock:
Explosions of dynamite,
There where the ten-thousand-foot precipice cuts across the
    road:
Stones, earth, cement,
Perspiration of a thousand workmen,
Sun shining above them,
Oceans of amusing blue;
And down below lies the broad river

Full of black-wood boats and ragged sailcloth
Motionlessly floating on the surface.
Oh, from here
They are like little pepper grains!
O pitiable heart, O simple heart,
Seeing again the broad white plains,
You awaken
Into deep pride of life.

Even though I were an ant or grasshopper
Crawling or flying along this highway
I would be happy,
Wearing a pair of sandals
And a summer hat made of wheat stalks,
Walking the new highway,
Pursuing freedom
In love and gaiety.
O road laid before me, how broad you are!
How even you are!
How unrestrained your progress!
How freely
You reach into far places!
We can follow the road you travel
As snakelike you climb to heaven,
Or as a string tying up the earth—
Looking around me I see
Rivers, mountains, roads, villages,
Clusters of beautiful forest,
Harmony everywhere,
And it seems to me now
That I stand on the heights of the world!

TIEN CH'IEN

Tien Ch'ien is the *enfant terrible* of modern Chinese poetry, a man who has attempted to create an entirely new style. Wen Yi-tuo has called him "the drummer of a new age," and "the apostle of a new kind of poetry that is intimately related to our primitive and more enduring emotions." He began by writing simply, almost childishly, in a way that suggested that there was no difference between the thing seen and the thing recorded; later he experimented with a drumlike rhythm. Both manners are represented here. He published two collections of poetry in 1936 called *It Is Not Yet Dawn* and *Chinese Ballads,* but it is for the poems he wrote during the war in Yenan that he will be remembered.

Children's Festival

O my young brothers,
You,
In the morning,
What roads did you come through?

Do you see
The soldiers walking in the streets,
Machine guns
Piled on their shoulders?

Help them,
Bring comfort to them;
They will fight,
They will die,
They will bleed. . . .

O my younger brothers,
Do not fear them;
Forbear,
For a little while.

Stretch hands to them.
Say:
Long live China!

More Than a Hundred

More than a hundred
Farmers are coming,
Full of wrath,
Full of melancholy—

The enemy
May seize
More than a hundred guns;
They will not fall.

The hearts of farmers
Marching . . .

Grief
Ceases . . .

They shout:
    There on the sands where the blood is not yet dry.
The hearts of the farmers
Marching.
A star on fire!

Their lances
Are raised at the front.
In the van
Lies the flag.

Children, women, everyone,
Marching, marching . . .

"Do not fear burning,
Do not fear killing,
We are on the road to search
A new way . . ."

More than a hundred farmers
Marching, marching
Packed close like iron . . .

Snow ceases,
All hands,
All faces
Stretch to the earth.

The children
Sit in the snow,
Scrabbling snow,
Putting snow in their mouths.

Even tears
Are changed
To weapons. . . .

The more tears shed,
The more enemies die.
They wipe away their tears,
They cry out:

DOWN WITH THE ENEMY!

The snow stops:
More than a hundred
Push away the new flakes of snow,
New stains of blood.

Grief ceases;
They begin
To sing.

Translated by Chu Chun-i.

MAO TSE-TUNG

He was born in 1893 in Hsiangtan, Hunan. He enlisted in the revolutionary army in 1911, but later resigned to work in peasant movements in his native province. In 1919 he was an assistant librarian in Peking University. Since 1937 he has been chairman of the military council of the Eighth Route Army. Recently he edited a collection of his poems under the title of *Feng Chien Tze* (Wind Sand Poems). The poem "The Snow," written in Chungking in November 1945, has been deliberately included here because it seems to sum up more perfectly than anything else that could be found the peculiarly visual quality of the Chinese mind attempting to embrace the whole of the Chinese scene. The poem was deservedly popular on both sides of the battle lines during the civil war.

Until recently few of Mao Tse-tung's poems have been published. In 1957 a small selection of his poems was published in the magazine *Poetry*, with an introduction in which Mao complained that his poems were hardly worthy of publication because they were written in the old-fashioned scholarly style derived from Han dynasty models. "Poetry should be written in the new forms," he wrote, "but it does no harm to write a little in the old style, so long as it does not set an example for the young." In spite of this disclaimer Mao is still highly regarded as a poet even by those who have no sympathy for his political beliefs.

Since 1950 he has been Chairman of the People's Republic of China.

The Snow

All the scenery in the north
Is enclosed in a thousand li of ice,
And ten thousand li of whirling snow.
Behold both sides of the Great Wall—
There is only a vast confusion left.
On the upper and lower reaches of the Yellow River
You can no longer see the flowing water.
The mountains are dancing silver serpents,
The hills on the plains are shining elephants.
I desire to compare our height with the skies.

In clear weather
The earth is so charming,
Like a red-faced girl clothed in white.
Such is the charm of these rivers and mountains,
Calling innumerable heroes to vie with each other in pursuing
   her.
The emperors Shih Huang and Wu Ti were barely cultured,
The emperors Tai Tsung and Tai Tsu were lacking in feeling,
Genghis Khan knew only how to bend his bow at the eagles.
These all belong to the past—only today are there men of
   feeling!